ROUTLEDGE LIBRARY EDITIONS: 18TH CENTURY LITERATURE

Volume 4

THE THIRD EARL OF SHAFTESBURY

THE THIRD EARL OF SHAFTESBURY
A Study in Eighteenth-Century Literary Theory

R. L. BRETT

LONDON AND NEW YORK

First published in 1951 by Hutchinson's University Library

This edition first published in 2020
by Routledge
2 Park Square, Milton Park, Abingdon, Oxon OX14 4RN

and by Routledge
52 Vanderbilt Avenue, New York, NY 10017

Routledge is an imprint of the Taylor & Francis Group, an informa business

© 1951 R. L. Brett

All rights reserved. No part of this book may be reprinted or reproduced or utilised in any form or by any electronic, mechanical, or other means, now known or hereafter invented, including photocopying and recording, or in any information storage or retrieval system, without permission in writing from the publishers.

Trademark notice: Product or corporate names may be trademarks or registered trademarks, and are used only for identification and explanation without intent to infringe.

British Library Cataloguing in Publication Data
A catalogue record for this book is available from the British Library

ISBN: 978-0-367-44270-5 (Set)
ISBN: 978-1-00-302027-1 (Set) (ebk)
ISBN: 978-0-367-82012-1 (Volume 4) (hbk)
ISBN: 978-0-367-82017-6 (Volume 4) (pbk)
ISBN: 978-1-00-301145-3 (Volume 4) (ebk)

Publisher's Note
The publisher has gone to great lengths to ensure the quality of this reprint but points out that some imperfections in the original copies may be apparent.

Disclaimer
The publisher has made every effort to trace copyright holders and would welcome correspondence from those they have been unable to trace.

The Right Honorable Anthony Ashley Cooper Earl of Shaftesbury, Baron Ashley of Winbourn St Giles, & Lord Cooper of Panlett

J. Closterman Pinx.   Sim Gribelin Sculp.

THE THIRD EARL OF SHAFTESBURY

A STUDY IN EIGHTEENTH-CENTURY
LITERARY THEORY

by

R. L. BRETT

Lecturer in English in the University of Bristol

HUTCHINSON'S UNIVERSITY LIBRARY
Hutchinson House, London, W.1

New York   Melbourne   Sydney   Cape Town

First Published - 1951

*Printed in Great Britain by
William Brendon and Son, Ltd.
The Mayflower Press (late of Plymouth)
at Bushey Mill Lane
Watford, Herts.*

To
My Father and Mother

CONTENTS

		Page
	Preface	xi
Chapter I.	The Cambridge Platonists	13
II.	The Life and Writings of Shaftesbury	33
III.	Shaftesbury's Philosophy	59
IV.	The Ancients and Moderns	86
V.	The Creative Imagination	100
VI.	The Aesthetic Judgment	123
VII.	The Sublime	145
VIII.	The Doctrine of Ridicule	165
IX.	The Influence of Shaftesbury's Thought	186
X.	The Crisis of Reason	208
	Appendix	224
	Index	225

NOTE

All references to Shaftesbury's *Characteristics* are to the modern edition by J. M. Robertson, London, 1900.

References to Shaftesbury's *Second Characters or the Language of Forms* are to the edition by Benjamin Rand, Cambridge University Press, 1914. References to *Rand*, when unaccompanied by a title, are to *The Life, Unpublished Letters and Philosophical Regimen of Anthony, Earl of Shaftesbury*, edited by Benjamin Rand, Swan, Sonnenschein & Co. Ltd., London, 1900.

PREFACE

IN the essay which follows I have tried to do three things, though these are not entirely distinct from each other: to give an account of Shaftesbury's aesthetic and literary theory; to discuss the part he played in furnishing the minds of the Augustan writers with some of their guiding ideas; and to estimate the success of his attempt to keep alive a philosophy that he considered more sympathetic to the arts than the new philosophy of empiricism.

The third Earl of Shaftesbury is generally known as the founder of the "moral sense" school of philosophy; a school which made an important contribution to ethics in the eighteenth century. Although in recent years there has been a steadily increasing recognition of his importance to literature and literary criticism, no full-length study has yet been devoted to this. Indeed, no extensive modern study of his thought exists, apart from Fowler's *Shaftesbury and Hutcheson*, published in 1882. I am concerned primarily with those aspects of Shaftesbury's writings which merit the attention of the student of literature, but this concern has led me in places to discuss questions of a philosophical importance. Though I apologize to those of my readers who happen to be philosophers for any philosophical ineptitude I may have shown, I hope I need not apologize to those whose interests are mainly literary; for an understanding of Shaftesbury's place in literature such philosophical excursions are necessary and he himself would have considered the modern fashion of rigid specialization merely vulgar.

This book has grown out of research which I carried out at Oxford under the supervision of Professor D. Nichol Smith. It gives me great pleasure to acknowledge the help he gave and the kindness he has always shown me. I should like also to thank the following of my friends: Dr. Stephan Körner, who discussed much of the book with me during its writing, but who does not necessarily agree with all I have said; Professor D. G. James and Mr. M. H. Carré, both of whom read the typescript and made many valuable suggestions; and Mr. Basil Cottle, who very kindly read the proofs with scholarly care and exactness. I have also to thank the Earl of Shaftesbury for courteously answering certain questions I asked him concerning his family's history; and Miss K. Hek, who typed the whole of the MS.

I wish to acknowledge permission granted by the following for the use of copyright material: Messrs. John Murray and the English Association, for allowing me to reproduce part of the substance of my essay, 'Coleridge's Theory of the Imagination', which was published in *English Studies* 1949; Messrs. Allen and Unwin Ltd., for permission to quote from *The Life, Letters and Philosophical Regimen of Anthony, Earl of Shaftesbury*, ed. Benjamin Rand; the Cambridge University Press, for the quotations from *Shaftesbury's Second Characters*, ed. Benjamin Rand; Mr. T. S. Eliot and Messrs. Faber and Faber Ltd., for allowing me to quote a short excerpt from *East Coker*; and Mrs. W. B. Yeats, Messrs. Macmillan and Co., and A. P. Watt and Son, for permission to reprint some lines from 'The Tower' from the *Collected Poems of W. B. Yeats*.

Finally, I express my indebtedness to my wife; her preparation of the index was a small part of the help she gave me in so many ways.

R. L. BRETT.

CHAPTER I

THE CAMBRIDGE PLATONISTS

"All things are artificial, for nature is the art of God."
(Sir Thomas Browne: *Religio Medici*.)

I

BEFORE we approach Shaftesbury directly it is necessary in this first chapter to say something of the history of ideas in the seventeenth century and particularly of the disputes that centred in the figure of Hobbes. With few exceptions everything that has been written about Shaftesbury sees him as a thinker of the Enlightenment. He was this, of course, but his writings are an endeavour to answer questions which had been posed in the latter half of the seventeenth century. To fail to understand this is to fail to understand Shaftesbury. Nor is this a consideration that applies only to Shaftesbury. The habit of dividing literature into periods leads us to think of the Age of Anne as quite separate from the preceding century, and little attention has been paid to the transition between the two and the sources from which the Age of Anne drew its inspiration. This is particularly so with literary criticism, where the early part of the eighteenth century is seen as the beginning of a modern period and judged merely from that viewpoint. Though there is much to support this view, such a habit of mind leads us to overlook features that do not fit into this pattern. The general idea of the reign of Anne is that it was an age of reason, with critics such as Addison unaccountable exceptions to the general neo-classical rule, but to regard it in this way is to miss much of the complexity of the age. Its chief characteristic was an appeal, not to pure reason, but to common sense and experience. It was an age above all of empiricism, but an empiricism that was sometimes modified by an idealism deriving from quite a different philosophical tradition. This tradition was the Platonic one and its importance to literature and criticism at the end of the seventeenth century and during the reign of Anne has too frequently been overlooked. It was from this tradition that Shaftesbury sprang, and with it most of this chapter will be concerned.

A good deal of attention has been paid in recent years to the effect of philosophy on literature, and especially on poetry, in the seventeenth century. The whole movement of philosophy which started with Descartes and which was accompanied by the vast expansion of scientific inquiry and achievement, has been seen, and no doubt rightly, as producing an atmosphere inimical to poetry. The view of the universe its influence had made the generally accepted one, was that of a mechanism run on mathematical principles and devoid of colour, scent, taste and sound. Science had enlarged the size of the universe, but had turned it into a lifeless machine, which worked by forces that could be expressed in mathematical formulae, but not in poetry. What was real was what could be measured, weighed and expressed in numbers, not what could be made the subject of poetry. Such writers as A. N. Whitehead, Basil Willey and Douglas Bush have all made the point that the mechanical view of the world is one that does not commend itself to the poet. Its declaration that what is "really real," is a world of atoms in motion, devoid of all secondary sense qualities, such as colour, scent, taste and sound, ordered by causal laws and explicable only in terms of mathematics, is one that gives little status to the poet. It is one, indeed, that gives little status to man himself, since, once the process of scientific explanation had started, it was soon seen that man himself, as part of the natural order, could be explained in similar terms. Poetry was not alone in suffering the effects of the new movement; religion itself was its companion.

The main stream of thought in the seventeenth century developed in such a way that poetry found it increasingly difficult to justify its own existence. The influence of Descartes had been harsh enough. As Jean-Baptiste Rousseau said in an often-quoted letter, "la philosophie de Descartes avait coupé la gorge à la poésie." But the philosophy of Hobbes was even worse. For both men the task of philosophy was to bring as many phenomena as possible within a system of explanation based on the laws of motion. The Cartesian philosophy, however, did at least leave an independent place in the universe to both God and mind. For Hobbes, on the other hand, God was only the 'prime-mover', the first link in a causal chain which, once started, required no further help. Mind was explained in terms of motion. Once given the Cartesian dualism, it is easy to see that subsequent thinking would be tempted into trying to resolve one side of the dualism into the other; to explain everything either in terms of mind, or in terms of matter. It is equally obvious, so impressive were the results of the physical sciences, that the likelier choice in the seventeenth century should be matter and not mind.

Neither the theories of Descartes nor of Hobbes could justify the claim of poetry to be dealing with the truth. Poetry is concerned with the sort of experience that their philosophies could not account for. In particular, religious poetry, which attempts to reach out from the finite to the infinite, was robbed of its meaning. Poetry could take over the truths worked out by rational processes in philosophy and science, but it could not adumbrate its own truths. The relationship between the finite and infinite, in any case, was merely a simple one of causation; the relation between the clockmaker and the clock which he winds. Poetry, in attempting to find another or more profound relationship, was doing something that could not be justified on rational grounds and the attempt was either stupid or presumptuous.

This summarizes what is by now a well-known account of the relationship between philosophy and poetry in the seventeenth century. Less has been written about what might be called the counter-movement to what has been described; yet if we are to understand Shaftesbury properly we must consider this opposition in some detail. The impact of the mechanical philosophy on poetry was so great that perhaps attention has been paid to this at the expense of recognizing how strong was the fight put up against a mechanical view of the universe. Some, at least, both philosophers and poets, in the seventeenth century, realized the implications of the scientific movement and saw that it led to a view of reality which cut across the truths of both religion and poetry. For, as Ralph Cudworth said, the writings of Hobbes and Descartes

> "make God to be nothing else in the world, but an idle spectator of the various results of the fortuitous and necessary motions of bodies; . . . They made a kind of dead and wooden world, as it were a carved statue, that hath nothing neither vital nor magical at all in it." (*True Intellectual System*, ed. Harrison, I, 220–221.)

The opponents of Hobbes were, in the main, theologians and philosophers, who saw the problem intellectually, though there were poets, too, who felt the new philosophy to be uncongenial to their work and welcomed an alternative more sympathetic to a poetic view of things. The answer in general terms that they made to mechanism was based upon a spiritual interpretation of reality derived from Christianity and Platonism, though their

Platonism was often combined with neo-Platonic elements that were a later gloss on the philosopher's work.

At Cambridge, especially, there had been a revival of Platonic studies in the sixteenth and seventeenth centuries. From the time when Roger Ascham became the first Regius Professor of Greek in 1540, there had been a steady increase in Greek studies, accompanied by a new interest in Platonism. In particular, in the latter half of the seventeenth century, there was a group of theologians in the University, who have come to be known as the Cambridge Platonists. These men were distinguished both for their intellectual ability and the spiritual quality of their lives. Bishop Burnet, describing the Church in the reign of Charles II, pays great tribute to them. The good divines, he tells us, were

"so few, that, if a new sect of men had not appeared of another stamp, the Church had quite lost her esteem over the Nation. These were generally of Cambridge, formed under some divines, the chief of whom were Drs. Whitchcot, Cudworth, Wilkins, More and Worthington." (Burnet's *History of His Own Time*, pubd. posthumously, 1724–1734, Vol. I, 186.)

Burnet describes each of the men in turn and refers to their fight against Hobbes. He sees very clearly that Hobbes for them was the most formidable opponent and that their chief work, spread over nearly half a century, was in combating his influence. His account of Hobbes, though too long to quote in full, is shrewd as well as quaint.

"Hobbes, who had long followed the Court, and passed there for a mathematical man, tho' he really knew little that way, being disgusted by the Court, came into England in Cromwell's time, and published a very wicked work, with a very strange title, *The Leviathan*. His main principles were, that all men acted under an absolute necessity, in which he seemed protected by the then received doctrine of absolute decrees. He seemed to think that the universe was God, and that souls were material, Thought being only subtil and unperceptible motion. He thought interest and fear were the chief principles of society; And he put all morality in the following that which was our own private will or advantage. He thought religion had no other foundation than the laws of the land. . . . So this set of men at Cambridge studied to assert, and examine the principles of religion and morality on clear grounds, and in a philosophical method." (*ibid*, pp. 187-8.)

The Cambridge Platonists, or 'Latitude-men' as they were sometimes called, were liberal theologians who wished to reconcile the claims of Christianity with the findings of science. While remaining orthodox in religion, they wished to give due place to scientific discovery and some of them, indeed, were well abreast of the scientific developments of their day. At first some had been attracted by the Cartesian philosophy and it was only later, when they realized its implications, that they disowned it. What they disliked was the view of the universe that was being built up on the foundation of scientific achievement. They felt that the philosophy of thinkers like Hobbes denied the possibility of certain sorts of experience which to them were real and important. They were sufficiently impressed by the methods and achievements of science, however, to feel that the old Christian cosmology could not be accepted literally, and yet they were passionately intent on retaining the truths of the Christian faith, which they felt gave the only satisfactory explanation of the whole of man's moral, spiritual and intellectual experience.

The work of the Cambridge Platonists consisted, therefore, in building up a new world-picture which would reconcile religion and science. There were those who claimed that not only the mythology,[1] but the truths behind the mythology of the Christian faith, had been invalidated by the new science. It was here that the Cambridge Platonists joined issue with the mechanistic philosophers and defended their religious beliefs against the writings of men like Hobbes and other "professed theists of later times, who might notwithstanding have an undiscerned tang of the mechanic atheism, hanging about them" and who admitted

> "no other causes of things as philosophical, save the material and mechanical only; this being really to banish all mental, and consequently divine causality, quite out of the world; and to make the whole world to be nothing else but a mere heap of dust, fortuitously agitated." (*True Intellectual System*, I, p. 217.)

As might be expected, any conflict between Christianity and science came to a head on the question of how far the Scriptures

[1] By mythology I do not, of course, mean something that is untrue. I mean the presentation of facts in allegorical or symbolic forms.

B

could be accepted as true. Can we believe both the Bible and the findings of modern science? The answer in the seventeenth century, as in the nineteenth century, was that we cannot, if the Old Testament is accepted as a literal and historical account. On the other hand, if such narratives as Genesis are regarded as allegory or myth, the conflict can be resolved. The Cambridge Platonists, by giving the Scriptures an allegorical interpretation, were able to avoid difficulties at certain points where modern science appeared to conflict with the literal narrative. Thus Henry More, in his *Conjectura Cabbalistica* (1653), argued that the Bible is not always to be regarded as a literal and historical record, but can be viewed on different levels of explanation of a symbolic and mythical kind.

This sort of explanation is very old in the history of scriptural exegesis. It seems to have become prominent in the Alexandria of the first century B.C., where Greek culture met the Hebrew religion. Philo and other Alexandrian Hellenists were faced, as were the Cambridge Platonists later, with the problem how to reconcile a religious mythology with a philosophical tradition that worked in logical and conceptual language. It was not that the philosophical tradition invalidated or superseded the religious mythology, but that the religious mythology had to be translated into terms acceptable to the philosophical understanding.

Such a method of interpreting sacred writings so that the products of the religious imagination could be seen as myths embodying general truths, was not new even to Philo and his school. It had been used by the Greeks in interpreting the Homeric writings and it is something, although not without its dangers, which must commend itself to the poetic imagination, which expresses its meaning in symbols and myth. It is something, in fact, which commends itself to everyone, for everyone is to some extent an artist. When we read how Christ talked with Moses and Elias, in a cloud on the Mount of Transfiguration, and again, at His Ascension, was taken up into a cloud, we easily comprehend that the cloud represents the presence of God, and scarcely need to be told that the New Testament writers were using an example of imaginative expression well known in the Old Testament. This kind of interpretation is not limited to sacred writings; all poetry uses the language of imagery rather than that of systematic thought. This was one of the reasons, as we shall see, why the philosophy of the Cambridge Platonists was welcomed by many contemporary poets. The scientific way of thinking regarded language as meaningful only in so far as it dealt in straightforward statements of fact. The philosophy of the Cambridge men, on the other hand, took seriously the work of the artistic imagination.

Like the Alexandrian Hellenists, the Cambridge Platonists were faced with the task of relating an old religion to a new sort of knowledge. There have been those in the Christian tradition who have felt that such an effort is misplaced and that the attempt to work out a natural theology is not only doomed to failure, but is a sinful presumption on the part of human reason. The Cambridge Platonists were convinced that the attempt should be made and that the natural world could be related to the supernatural by reason as well as by special revelation. They felt that the natural world was God's world and that He could be discerned therein, not in a manner that rendered the Incarnation superfluous, but in a way that was congruous with it. Their favourite image for describing God was that of Light. God is Light. This world, they claimed, is only a shadow of the real world which lies behind it; a shadow cast by the radiance of God Himself.

What is most real is not this present world of physical objects, or even material substance stripped of the qualities given it by sense experience, but the world of spirit of which this is a counterpart. The natural world, according to this account, is symbolical of the real which stands behind it. We can apprehend the nature of the infinite by analogies drawn from the finite, just as the example of light, quoted above, for instance, is an analogy taken from finite experience to describe something of God's nature. Such a doctrine can easily be debased, of course, and lead to a conception of this world as merely a reflection (even if an imperfect one) of heaven; a sort of mirror-image of reality. It can lead to a crude anthropomorphism, which makes God in the image of man. But this is to miss the point the Cambridge Platonists were making. On their view, man tends to think of God in terms of his own experience, not because of wishful thinking but because God is really in human nature. Not only does man make God in his own image, but God makes man in His image.

II

Such a view of reality was congenial to the poetic mind. Instead of the natural world's being a collocation of atoms in motion, governed by inexorable laws and understandable only in mathematical terms, it could be seen as a copy of a spiritual world. Natural objects could have a meaning and reference beyond themselves.

Professor Willey, in his *The Seventeenth Century Background*, feels that the influence of the Cambridge Platonists was of no help to the "dwindling forces of poetry." On their view, he says, only what is abstract and conceptual is real; the rest is only "shadow, image or at least 'type' or symbol." It is true that a large part of the Platonic tradition tells us to mistrust sensory knowledge and declares that truth is apprehended only by the reason. It has been suggested that for Plato the Ideas were of the nature of mathematical truths, and certainly not archetypes of which physical objects are the copies. Yet even this doctrine, paradoxical as it may seem, has inspired some of our best poetry; in the *Hymn of Heavenly Beautie*, Spenser, after declaring that God can be seen in His handiwork, nevertheless bids us leave behind the world of sense.

> "And looke at last up to that soveraine light,
> From whose pure beams all perfect beauty springs;
> That kindleth love in every godly spright,
> Even the love of God; which loathing brings
> Of this vile world and these gay-seeming things;
> With whose sweete pleasures being so possest,
> Thy straying thoughts henceforth for ever rest."

There is, however, another part (even if less authentic) of the Platonic tradition, which sees the natural world as a copy of a world beyond. This present world may be only a world of symbols, but it is precisely this characteristic which gives it importance for poetry. Nature becomes a second book of Scriptures, as hinted by Spenser in the same poem,

> "The meanes, therefore, which unto us is lent
> Him to behold, is on His workes to looke,
> Which He hath made in beauty excellent."

The danger of such a belief is that it may easily degenerate into a cabbalistic magic that sees the natural world as a kind of cryptogram or series of symbols, having a too literal relation to the spiritual world. Perversions of Platonism of this sort were not unknown in the seventeenth century and were often accompanied by the theory that the Scriptures, too, were a collection of anagrams and cyphers from which hidden meanings had to be wrung.

The Cambridge Platonists avoided such dangers. In their interpretation of the Bible they disowned both an extreme literalism and a crude symbolism. The view of nature which they gave to contemporary poetry was neither that of a world so fallen that God could not be discerned in it, nor that of a literal copy or exact reflection of heaven. For them the natural world and the poetic imagery of the Bible were symbolical in the same way. The natural world was, indeed, like a vast poem in which the symbols, as in poetry itself, had a significance beyond themselves, but natural objects were not to be taken as mere copies of the thing beyond. When Herbert talks about "church bells beyond the starres heard", he is saying something about his spiritual experience which is not just a fanciful notion, or yet something to be analysed in a logical manner. He is not saying that there are counterparts in heaven to the church bells we hear on earth, though perhaps Milton comes near this belief when he writes:

". . . . . what if Earth
Be but the shadow of Heaven, and things therein
Each to other like, more than on Earth is thought?"
(*Paradise Lost*, V, 574–6.)

Natural objects are not symbols of a literal kind, but neither are they arbitrary symbols devised by man's own mind. The supernatural is seen in and through the natural world; in the words of Henry Vaughan, we can see, "through all this fleshly dresse, Bright shootes of everlastingnesse."

This conception of nature is essentially a poetic one. Nature, in fact, is seen as a divine poem. Just as poetic imagery expresses truths which cannot be expressed in prose or mathematical formulae, so nature can be seen as the expression of a reality which cannot be measured, weighed, or comprehended in mathematical terms or the language of factual statement. God is a poet as well as a mathematician and philosopher and the world must be seen as the expression of God's thought in artistic as well as other forms.

Some of the Cambridge circle were themselves poets. John Norris, who, although an Oxford man, belonged to the group and who was at one time rector of George Herbert's parish of Bemerton, wrote poetry such as his *Hymns to Love and Beauty*, and his *Divine Hymn on the Creation*, which are clearly a product of Platonism. Henry More's *Psychozoia, or, the Life of the Soul* is also the explicit expression of Platonic doctrines. But Platonism is encountered not only in the poetry of the group itself; it is an important force in the poetry of Herbert, Vaughan, Crashaw and Traherne. The labelling of these poets as 'metaphysicals' has tended to obscure the element of Christian Platonism in their poetry. It is not suggested that the controversy which came to a head in the debate between Hobbes and the 'latitude-men' can be seen directly in their writings; all that I would wish to establish is that poets of the time found inspiration in Platonism.

The beliefs of Milton also were evidently influenced by the same current of thought. As Coleridge wrote in a letter to his friend Sotheby in September 1802,

> "How little the commentators of Milton have availed themselves of the writings of Plato, Milton's darling!"

Like the Cambridge group, Milton was endeavouring to advance the truths of Christianity in an age which was becoming increasingly sceptical. Even more than they, he was confronted as an epic poet with the task of using a mythology not favourably regarded by the scientific understanding. The writing of a great religious epic in an age impatient of the traditional religious mythology was no easy one. The failure of Cowley's *Davideis* is some indication of this. As one of the first members of the Royal Society, Cowley was an enthusiastic supporter of science; indeed, his *Ode to the Royal Society* suggests that his attitude to the physical world was more that of the scientist than the poet. Dr. Johnson was right when, in his *Life* of the poet, he wrote, "Cowley gives inferences instead of images:" the central fault of the *Davideis* is that it never achieves the level of myth, but always remains on the level of literal narrative and argument.

The attempt of Milton, too, to write a great religious epic was viewed with apprehension by Marvell, at least, amongst his contemporaries.

> "When I beheld the Poet blind, yet bold,
> In slender Book his vast Design unfold,
> *Messiah* Crown'd, *Gods* Reconcil'd Decree,
> Rebelling *Angels*, the Forbidden Tree,
> Heav'n, Hell, Earth, Chaos, All; the Argument
> Held me a while misdoubting his Intent,
> That he would ruine (for I saw him strong)
> The sacred Truths to Fable and Old Song."
> (*On Mr. Milton's Paradise Lost.*)

There were two ways in which Milton was helped to surmount the difficulty. Firstly, his interpretation of the Biblical story was to a certain degree allegorical. This gave the poem conviction; the truth could be presented by 'imagery' instead of 'inference' and the poem could avoid the abstract and conceptual. The story of the Fall could be at once an eternal and universal truth as well as the study of individuals, God and Satan, and Adam and Eve. Secondly, in *Paradise Lost* he drew upon the philosophical principles of the Cambridge Platonists to a greater extent than has always been recognized and so invested the poem with a certain contemporary idiom and reference which made it more acceptable.

In Raphael's speech to Adam, describing the revolt of Satan, Milton might almost be describing his own task as a Christian poet.

> "High matter thou enjoin'st me, O prime of Men,
> Sad task and hard; for how shall I relate
> To human sense the invisible exploits
> Of warring Spirits? how, without remorse,
> The ruin of so many, glorious once
> And perfect while they stood? how, last, unfold
> The secrets of another world, perhaps
> Not lawful to reveal? Yet for thy good
> This is dispensed; and what surmounts the reach
> Of human sense I shall delineate so,
> By likening spiritual to corporal forms,
> As may express them best—though what if Earth
> Be but the shadow of Heaven, and things therein
> Each to other like, more than on Earth is thought?"
> (*Paradise Lost*, V, 563–76.)

Milton's interpretation of the Fall seems to be much the same as Henry More's. Adam represents the reason and Eve the passions. The Fall is not (or not only) an historical event so much as an eternal truth about the nature of man. Reason in man partakes of the divine nature and man is nearest to God and unfallen when his reason governs his passions and actions. The Fall is the overthrowing of the reason by the passions; an interpretation which bears the stamp of Platonism. The passions should be in subjection to the reason and ordered by it. The first effect of the Fall is to set Adam and Eve quarrelling:

> "Nor only tears
> Rained at their eyes, but high winds worse within
> Began to rise, high passions, anger, hate,
> Mistrust, suspicion, discord, and shook sore

> Their inward state of mind, calm region once
> And full of peace, now tost and turbulent:
> For Understanding ruled not, and the Will
> Heard not her lore, both in subjection now
> To sensual Appetite, who, from beneath
> Usurping over Sovran Reason, claimed
> Superior sway."
>
> (*ibid.*, IX, 1121-31.)

Once man ceases to be ruled by the reason he ceases to be free, for man is free when he is most like his own true nature, which is rational. Freedom is self-determination, as Michael points out to Adam in Book XII of the poem.

This view of the Fall in *Paradise Lost* has its parallel in Milton's treatment of the subject of *Paradise Regained*. One would have thought that a poem on the regaining of paradise would concern itself with the Redemption and Atonement and that its climax would be the Crucifixion, but the poem is concerned entirely with Christ's temptation in the wilderness and the Crucifixion is barely mentioned. Paradise is regained not by any transcendental act of Atonement, but by the victory of the reason over the passions.[1]

The interpretation of the Fall as the overthrow of the reason by the passions, is not the only point where Milton shares the same ideas with the Cambridge Platonists. Both Mr. C. S. Lewis[2] and Miss Marjorie Hope Nicolson[3] have demonstrated Milton's debt to Henry More's philosophy. In particular, they have shown that by giving his angels bodies and allowing them to be fired upon by very material artillery, he was drawing upon More's doctrine of the corporeality of spirits. Such a doctrine was very useful, of course, in enabling Milton to construct a celestial geography and give heaven a 'local habitation' as well as a name; but it was much more than just a useful device taken by Milton from contemporary controversy. Miss Nicolson is very convincing in the parallel she draws between Milton and the Cambridge Platonists. Both of them were fighting against the mechanism, first of Descartes and then of Hobbes. Milton, although unlike the Cambridge men in attempting

---

[1] This theme of temptation as the struggle between the reason and passions— "To triumph in victorious dance, O'er sensual Folly, and Intemperance"—is, of course, central in *Comus* and *Samson Agonistes* as well as in *Paradise Lost* and *Paradise Regained*.

[2] *Preface to Paradise Lost*, Oxford, Chap. XV.

[3] *The Spirit World of Milton and More* (*Studies in Philology*, 1925); *Milton and Hobbes*, (Ibid., 1926).

the task in poetry, was at one with them in justifying God's ways to men against the arguments of contemporary agnosticism and atheism. Against the view that pictured nature as a machine the Cambridge Platonists advanced the belief that physical objects are not final reality, but the manifestation of a world beyond themselves. It is thus that Henry More argues against the mechanism of Descartes, whose clear rationalism had attracted him at an earlier date.

"It is as confessed a Principle with him, that matter alone with such a degree of motion as is supposed now in the Universe will produce all the phenomena of the World, Sun, Moon, and Stars, Air, Water, Earth, Plants, Animals, and the Bodies of Men, in such order and organization as they are found. Which Principle in his Philosophy certainly must prove a very inept Interpreter of Rom. i. 19, 20, where the externall Power and Godhead is said clearly to be seen by the things that are made." (*Preface to Divine Dialogues*, 1668.)

Not only are the invisible things of reality made visibly manifest in God's creation, but within the natural world there is an organic principle, which, though not God Himself, is a secondary and subordinate spirit which animates matter. This principle was a development by the Cambridge Platonists of the neo-Platonic doctrine of the *anima mundi*. Only by such a principle, they contended, could an account be given of those phenomena which were inexplicable in terms of mechanism. Such a theory was needed to explain features of growth and purposive behaviour which had been neglected by the thorough-going mechanical philosophers. The doctrine was held in some form or other by most of the group, but it received its most detailed and profound treatment from Cudworth, who developed from it a theory not unlike that of nineteenth-century emergent evolution. The principle of growth which, according to him, animates the natural world, he called a "plastic nature." This "one plastic inconscious nature," rather similar to Bergson's *Élan Vital*, is the principle

"by which vegetables may be severally organized and framed, and all things performed which transcend the power of fortuitous mechanism." (*op. cit.*, I, 283.)

As an important part of a spiritual interpretation of the universe, the doctrine was welcomed by those who were sensitive to the implications of mechanism. It was even given poetical expression;

John Norris's *Divine Hymn on the Creation* describes how God created first "a formless mass":

> "First matter came undress'd.
> She made such haste t'obey."

Then, by the operation of the plastic power at work in matter, the creative process begins;

> "But soon a plastick spirit did ferment
> The liquid dusky element.
> The mass harmoniously begins to move,
> 'Let there be light,' said God! 'twas said and done,
> The mass dipt through with brightness, shone."

This belief in the natural world as 'vital' and 'magical' rather than 'dead and wooden' was welcome to the poets of the time and provided them with a more congenial philosophy than the other prevailing systems. Such a philosophy could give their work a sense of worthwhileness which had been denied it by mechanism. The current of scientific thought was running too strong for poetry, but though the forces of poetry were dwindling, the Cambridge men enabled them to put up a stubborn fight.

The Platonic tradition, as we have seen, had always held that natural phenomena are symbolic of an ideal world behind the flux of space and time. Christian Platonism had taught that the natural order was created by the impress of the Divine mind on unformed matter. Natural objects are not simply copies of the Divine Ideas, for these Ideas have a perfection which is beyond being, but they are a representation of the mind of God. They are a sort of alphabet by which God expresses His thought: Nature, as Sir Thomas Browne wrote in *Religio Medici*, is the "art of God." Now such a picture of nature had been discredited by the rise of science; natural objects, according to science, were simply and irremediably natural objects, nothing more and nothing less. They were not symbolic of a world beyond themselves. What Cudworth's theory of a "plastic nature" did was to rehabilitate the Christian Platonic view in such a way that it could face the challenge of science. It substituted for the cruder view that the Divine Ideas were stamped on matter in one determinate act, the more sophisticated theory that God works in nature by a plastic power which produces new forms by a process of growth. The theory carried the war into the enemy's own camp by showing that it could explain certain natural phenomena that mechanism could not. But the Cambridge Platonists attempted more than this. Their philosophy was an attempt to preserve an attitude of mind, a manner of looking at things, different from the scientific one.

It is always difficult to put ourselves imaginatively into the thinking of another period. This is particularly so when the period was early enough not to have been under the domination of modern categories of thought. Our own thinking is done so much within a framework erected for us by modern thought that it is hardly possible to imagine ourselves thinking within any other framework. The modern mind feels at home with scientific categories and it is difficult for us to imagine how a seventeenth-century mind that had not embraced the new science would organize and carry out its thinking. Thinking before the rise of science had often proceeded by analogy and symbol. In the Middle Ages the family, the guild, the State and every other institution were supposed by analogy to manifest the same hierarchical structure as was believed to exist in the universe. Neo-Platonism, which had encouraged this habit of mind from the beginning, reinforced Thomism in this respect. To the medieval thinker it was natural to assume that the human body was composed of the four elements which constituted the physical universe and that a person's temperature was dependent upon their balance. It was equally natural to argue that the authority of the Papacy was greater than that of the empire, just as the moon (which symbolized the empire) shines only by light reflected from the sun (which symbolized the Papacy).

This habit of thinking by analogy and symbol did not die with the Middle Ages; if anything, it was strengthened by the revival of Platonism which occurred at the Renaissance. Miss Rosemary Freeman's recent *English Emblem Books* has thrown new light on the Elizabethan and Jacobean taste for allegory and shown it to have been rooted in analogical thinking. Miss Freeman contends that the last coherent formulation of this way of thinking was Bunyan's *Pilgrim's Progress*. In this, of course, she is right: the rising tide of scientific thought swept away symbol and analogy. The scientific habit of thinking in terms of cause and effect became stronger than the habit of perceiving symbolical relationships.

The Cambridge circle did not wish to construct a system of analogical thinking; such, indeed, would no longer have been a practical possibility. Their endeavour, though it, too, was doomed to failure, was rather to maintain a habit of mind, a habit of looking at this world as a counterpart of the one beyond it; and to provide such an attitude with a philosophical justification. Shaftesbury's philosophy, as we shall see, owed much to seventeenth-century Platonism and the above account has been necessary for an understanding of his philosophical purpose. What Shaftesbury sought to establish was the position that the symbolism of the poetic imagination can be as true as conceptual statement. His aim was to provide the arts with a philosophy that would answer the attacks of scientific thought.

III

The quarrel between Platonism and mechanism is important not only for an understanding of seventeenth-century poetry; it had important repercussions on literary criticism. In particular it raised two questions: (1) What is the nature of poetic composition? or, How does poetry come to be written? (2) What is the nature of the aesthetic judgment? or, What do we mean by calling a thing beautiful? It is to these two questions that we must now turn.

Any account of reality as physical bodies in motion must give some explanation of mental activity and provide an answer to John Norris's question of "whether Matter can think". Hobbes, who, whatever his physical courage, was never afraid of going where the argument might lead, faced this question quite boldly. He categorically says that perception is nothing but external objects working upon the senses. All thought is based on sensation:

"For there is no conception in a man's mind, which hath not at first, totally, or by parts, been begotten upon the organs of sense." (*Leviathan*, I, i.)

Cudworth rejected the radical empiricism of Hobbes, insisting that the mind is active in perception and has a creative function in knowledge. He did not base his argument upon the usual appeal to innate ideas, but elaborated the kind of theory that was to be used by later forms of idealism. The senses can give us data such as colour, shape and texture, but for such qualities to cohere and produce the perception of an actual object, he saw that a creative activity of the mind is needed. Hobbes had scornfully dismissed the consideration of universals by saying that there is

"nothing in the world Universall but Names; for the things named, are everyone of them Individuall and Singular." (*ibid.*, I, iv.)

Cudworth countered this nominalism by taking the example of a white triangle and arguing that the sense-data which are included in our perception of it, do not constitute the perception itself. We do not build up a picture of the triangle by putting together such qualities as its whiteness and triangularity; for these qualities are universals and our recognition of them involves an act of judgment. He does not go into the question of whether such universals have an existence of their own, but uses his argument to show that the mind is active in perception. For knowledge to be possible the mind must possess a power which forms concepts and anticipates and orders sense experience.

Hobbes's account of mental activity when applied to literary composition led to his famous Judgment-Fancy theory of the imagination. His belief that consciousness merely supervenes upon physical changes in our sense organs led him to declare that imagination is "nothing but decaying sense." "Imagination and memory are but one thing," he declares. The poetic imagination is subordinate to the inferential processes of the mind; merely decorating the artistic structure designed and erected by the judgment.

> "Time and Education begets experience; Experience begets memory; Memory begets Judgement and Fancy; Judgement begets the strength and structure, and Fancy begets the Ornaments of a Poem." (*Answer to Davenant*, Spingarn, *Critical Essays of the Seventeenth Century*, II, 59.)

This associationist psychology was echoed in contemporary criticism. Dryden, for instance, keeps very close to Hobbes's account of the imagination, when he writes:

> "So then, the first happiness of the Poet's imagination is properly Invention, or finding of the thought; the second is Fancy, or the variation, driving, or moulding, of that thought as the judgment represents it proper to the subject; the third is Elocution, or the Art of clothing and adorning that thought so found and varied, in apt, significant, and sounding words." (*Preface to Annus Mirabilis*.)

The Hobbesian tradition had no conception of the imagination as creative.[1] The human mind for Hobbes is like the universe,

---

[1] Mr. Thorpe in his *The Aesthetic Theory of Thomas Hobbes*, Oxford, 1940, argues that Hobbes's "imagination" is a creative power which anticipates Coleridge's theory. There must be, of course, even on Hobbes's view, some power of the mind, which orders in artistic form the material supplied by the senses. There is nothing, however, to suggest that the mind is the architect of its own knowledge, and this power is an associative not a creative one.

simply a machine, and one does not expect a machine to be creative. It is a pity that Cudworth never concerned himself directly with the subject of the artistic imagination. In describing the 'plastic nature', Cudworth did, indeed, refer to art, but simply to contrast the 'plastic nature', working *within* the material order of the world, with the artist working *outside* his medium. Unfortunately his argument led him to deal here with the difference, rather than the similarity, between artistic activity and the 'plastic nature'. A comparison of the two would have been of great interest and might have led to a theory of the imagination far profounder than that of his contemporaries, but for that we have to wait for Shaftesbury.

The other question raised by the dispute between Hobbes and the Platonists, the question concerning the nature of the aesthetic judgment, was an outcome of their quarrel over morality. It was in morals that Hobbes's influence was felt to be most pernicious. Here the Platonists had as their allies those who could not understand metaphysical subtleties and who were not abreast of scientific discovery, but thought they recognized a rascal when they saw one. But, though the fight was conducted on a popular level, it raised questions of fundamental importance for literary criticism.

Hobbes's theory of society led him to view the will and the reason merely as means of achieving those ends which men desire. On his view we call a thing good because we desire it.

> "But whatsoever is the object of any man's Appetite or Desire; that is it, which he for his part calleth *Good*: And the object of his Hate, and Aversion, *Evill*; ... For these words of Good, Evill, and Contemptible, are ever used with relation to the person that useth them: There being nothing simply and absolutely so; nor any common Rule of Good and Evill, to be taken from the nature of the objects themselves; but from the Person of the man (where there is no Common-wealth;) or, (in a Common-wealth,) from the Person that representeth it." (*Leviathan*, I, 6.)

The reason, for Hobbes, is not the faculty which makes judgments of value; it is merely the servant of the desires, being concerned with means and not ends.

> "For the thoughts are to the desires, as scouts, and spies, to range abroad, and find the way to the things desired." (*ibid*, I, 8.)

This relativity of judgments of value was, of course, anathema to orthodox Christians, who held that a thing is good whether we think it so or not, and that the reason, not desire or self-satisfaction, is the judge of what is good. For them the end of man was conformity to the divine nature, which, as Milton argued, meant conformity to reason.

> "Judge not what is best
> By pleasure, though to nature seeming meet;
> Created, as thou art, to nobler end
> Holy and pure, conformity divine."
> *(Paradise Lost*, XI, 603–6.)

Now this distinction between an absolute standard and personal liking applies to aesthetic as well as moral judgments. When we say that a work of art is good, either we can mean that we like it, or we can mean that it is good in an absolute sense and that other people ought to like it as well. The difficulty arising from this ambiguity was felt quite acutely at the end of the seventeenth century. Those who upheld personal taste in literary matters pointed out that aesthetic pleasure is a feeling, while the supporters of reason claimed that if the aesthetic judgment were to be universally valid, it must be made at the bar of reason. The latter, too, were able to point out that when a critic declares a poem a good one, he generally implies that other people should consider it a good one as well. He is not concerned merely with his own reactions. Similarly, when two people disagree about a poem, one of them saying it is good and the other taking the opposite view, it is felt that one of the parties must be right and the other wrong. In other words, the supporters of reason maintained that we believe aesthetic judgments to have a universal application and validity. This conflict between the claims of reason and taste can be clearly seen in the literary criticism of the late seventeenth century. So far was it from being an age of reason that there was at this time a considerable body of critics who made their cardinal article of faith a belief in taste, in the sense of individual sensibility and personal preference.

Such writers as Dennis, Temple, Gildon and Farquhar all reflect in their criticism the importance of 'taste', and all of them try to answer this problem of how to reconcile the conflicting claims of the reason and the feelings. A belief in the relativity of moral judgments quickly brought about a similar belief with respect to aesthetic judgments, and it was not easy to see where the truth of the matter lay. What such critics were doing, without really knowing it, was raising the large question of the nature of aesthetic judgments.

Once the prestige of the Ancients had passed and criticism, along with other matters, had ceased to be based on authority, it became necessary to examine the presuppositions on which it should rest. In the work of Hobbes, Davenant and Dryden, an attempt had been made to deal with literature as the product of the writer's mind, and in them we meet the first real discussions in English criticism of the mental processes which give rise to literature. Such terms as 'wit', 'fancy', 'invention', 'imagination', were given new and more precise shades of meaning. But this was not enough. Literary criticism had arrived at a stage when it was necessary to subject its methods to a more philosophical inquiry. Criticism, in fact, had given rise to aesthetics. It was to this task of formulating an aesthetic theory that Shaftesbury addressed himself.

Shaftesbury was a disciple of the Cambridge Platonists and, like them, detested the doctrines propounded by Hobbes. Although Hobbes belonged to an earlier generation, his influence still persisted in Shaftesbury's day. Shaftesbury saw, as the Cambridge Platonists had done, that Hobbes's doctrines undermined any spiritual interpretation of the universe and turned morality into mere expediency. He also saw that these doctrines, and others like them, destroyed the artistic impulses and achievements of mankind. The Cambridge Platonists had fought the Hobbesian tradition over the questions of religion and morality and were not concerned with literature and the arts. Shaftesbury, on the other hand, was passionately concerned for the arts and realized that a mechanical view of the universe not only opposed religion, but was uncongenial to the artist and did not take artistic endeavour seriously. He realized that the associationist psychology robbed the artistic imagination of any importance and made the poet a mere trifler. He saw that a relativity of morality would be paralleled by a relativity of aesthetics; that, if we decide what is good by our likes and dislikes, we shall also decide what is beautiful in the same way, and any standard of taste would disappear. Shaftesbury's philosophy, in fact, had the same starting point as that of the Cambridge Platonists. It was designed to counter the mechanical interpretation of reality, but it went further than theirs in its endeavour to safeguard the arts from the effects of such thinking; it sought to provide a basis not only for truth and goodness, but also for beauty.

CHAPTER II

THE LIFE AND WRITINGS OF SHAFTESBURY[1]

"The generous Ashley thine, the friend of man;
Who scann'd his nature with a brother's eye,
His weakness prompt to shade, to raise his aim,
To touch the finer movements of the mind,
And with the moral beauty charm the heart."
(Thomson: *The Seasons*.)

I

For an understanding of Shaftesbury's life and character it is necessary to see them against the background of the age in which he lived. Born in the reign of Charles II and a youth of eighteen at the Glorious Revolution of 1688, he spent his adult life in the reigns of William III and Queen Anne. It was the period which saw the emergence of 'Whiggism', of a more tolerant and stable political order following upon the violence of the Civil War. It is true that the Whig leaders of Charles II's time, Shaftesbury's own grandfather among them, have themselves been regarded as turbulent spirits; Dryden was not the only one to see them as headstrong and self-willed. Yet it would be wrong not to recognize in the spirit that animated those who engineered the removal of James II an element of restraint and a belief in moderation, that argue great political maturity. So contends Professor Butterfield in *The Englishman and his History*, where he contests the view that what happened from 1688 onwards was a matter of good fortune rather than judgment.

"Sometimes it has been assumed," he writes, "that the politic nature of the Englishman is innate—a product of climate or character perhaps; as though in the seventeenth century we had never run to wildness and shocked the world by beheading a king. Sometimes our good fortune has been ascribed to insularity—to the fact that we have escaped that intensity of conflict which has so often afflicted the nations of continental Europe; as though our

[1] A list of the materials available for a Life of Shaftesbury is given in a note at the end of this chapter. This account, unless otherwise stated, is based on the sketch of his father's life, written by the fourth Earl, which is referred to there. Quotations, when not otherwise indicated, are taken from this sketch.

freedom from fanatical cleavages were in no part due to any exercise of moderation; as though our own seventeenth century itself had not shown what intensities of passion could be evoked if Englishmen neglected to be politic."[1]

We have only to reflect that Locke himself, who was almost the personification of tolerance, was adviser to the first Earl of Shaftesbury and the architect of the political theory on which the settlement of 1688 was based, to realize that the Whig Party was not a mere collection of irresponsible self-seekers. We have only to be aware of the third Earl's intimate connection with the new flow of ideas, his family relationships and his education at the hands of Locke, to understand the qualities of fairmindedness and love of freedom which characterize his life and writings.

The end of the seventeenth century was remarkable not only for the change it brought about in English politics, but also for its intellectual vigour. In many ways it was an age of genius. It saw the establishment of the Royal Society, the publication of Newton's *Principia*, and a revival in scholarship that was unprecedented since the Renaissance. It was a period in which new ideas manifested themselves in lively debate between men disciplined in scholarship, yet possessing freedom of thought. Accompanying these political and intellectual changes was the social development which they made almost inevitable. The Great Fire of London had been followed by a period of rapid rebuilding, made all the more possible by the rise of a great and wealthy merchant class. A greater proportion of the population now lived in the capital, which had become the busy centre of the world's commerce and the European terminus of most of the important shipping routes. The continual appearance of new Wren spires above the city sky-line witnessed to both the wealth and energy of the London populace, and the new mansions that were springing up in the country betokened a general prosperity in England. It is true that not everything was fine and splendid: the dark shadows of war with France were thrown across a long period of Shaftesbury's life; politics were not always conducted as a matter of high principle, but could descend to intrigue and shifty expedients; the plays produced in the Restoration theatre often fell sadly below the standard of Dryden's; and the new urban population were not always satisfied with diversions as innocent as those provided by the coffee-houses. Yet, all things considered, it was an age of considerable distinction and achievement.

[1] *The Englishman and His History*, C.U.P., 1944, p. 84.

A Whig by temperament, family ties and education, Shaftesbury was very much a child of his age; conscious both of its fresh opportunities and its responsibilities. Forced by health and encouraged by inclination and circumstance to take a fairly detached interest in current affairs, he was able to combine a respect for tradition with a progressive outlook. His Whig sympathies provided him with a source of political inspiration and an attitude of mind rather than a clear-cut programme and he was able to judge contemporary events from the light thrown on them by ancient philosophy and history, as well as from the doctrines of the Revolution. He was a liberal in the fullest sense of the word, taking the best of the age in which he lived, and tempering it with the wisdom which can come only from a knowledge and appreciation of what was best in the past.

Anthony Ashley Cooper, the third Earl of Shaftesbury, was born on 26th February, 1671, at Exeter House, the London home of his grandfather, the famous Lord High Chancellor of Charles II. His father, also named Anthony, according to all accounts, was robust neither in body nor mind; Dryden, whose verdict, it is true, cannot altogether be trusted, calls this son of his Achitophel

". . . . that unfeathered two-legged thing . . .
Born a shapeless lump, like anarchy."
(*Absalom and Achitophel*, 169–172.)

Whatever the facts, from the very beginning the child who was to become the third Earl was handed over to the care of his grandfather and it thus came about that his education and upbringing were supervised by the philosopher Locke. Locke, besides being the confidential secretary, was medical attendant to the first Earl and had also assisted at the birth of the grandson. Indeed, it was his skill as a doctor that brought about Locke's long connection with the Shaftesbury family. In a letter of February 1705, to Jean le Clerc, a professor of the College of Remonstrants at Amsterdam, the third Earl later gave an account of Locke's introduction to his family.

"Mr. Locke came into my grandfather's family in the summer of the year 1666. . . . The occasion of it was thus: My grandfather had been ill for a great while, after a fall, by which his breast was so bruised that in time it came to an imposthumation within and appeared by a swelling under his stomach. Mr. Locke was at that time a student in physic at Oxford, and my grandfather taking a journey that way to drink the waters . . . he had this young physician presented to him, who, though he had never practised physic, yet appeared to my grandfather to be such a genius that he valued him above all his other physicians, the great men in practise of those times. Accordingly by his direction my grandfather underwent an operation which saved his life, and was the most wonderful of the kind that had been heard of till that time. His breast was laid open and the matter discharged, and an orifice ever afterwards kept open by a silver pipe, an instrument, famous upon record in the writings of our Popish and Jacobite authors who never failed to reproach him with this 'infirmity'."

The truth of the third Earl's last statement is amply borne out. In days when manners were less sensitive and kindly, the political enemies of a public man were not slow to use even a physical disability of this sort as a peg on which to hang their vituperation. Dryden caricatured his opponent's infirmity in one of the scenes of his *Albion and Albanius*, while Richard Duke, in *The Review*, described the first Earl thus,

"The working ferment of his active mind,
In his weak body's cask with pain confined,
Would burst the rotten vessel where 'tis pent,
But that 'tis tapt to give the treason vent."

Shaftesbury proceeds with his letter to le Clerc (who later published the material in an *Eloge Historique de feu M. Locke* in the *Bibliothèque Choisie*):

"After this cure, Mr. Locke grew so much in esteem with my grandfather, that as great a man as he had experienced him in physic, he looked upon this but as his least part; he encouraged him to turn his thoughts another way: nor would he suffer him to practise at all in physic, except in his own family, and as a kindness to some particular friends. He put him upon the study of the religious and civil affairs of the nation, with whatsoever related to the business of a Minister of State, in which he was so successful, that my grandfather began soon to use him as a friend, and consult with him on all occasions of that kind. He was not only with him in his library and closet, but in company with the great men of those times...."[1]

---

[1] Rand, *The Life, Unpublished Letters and Philosophical Regimen of Anthony, Earl of Shaftesbury*, London and New York, 1900, 329-30. For information on this and the other collections of Shaftesbury's letters, see the note at the end of this chapter.

It was natural that the grandfather should make Locke responsible for the education of the grandson, since years before the philosopher had been responsible for the later stages of the education of the boy's father. Locke had joined the Shaftesbury family when the third Earl's father was fifteen or sixteen years old, and not only completed the youth's education but undertook the negotiations for choosing him a wife. On the instructions of his master, he accompanied his pupil to the seat of the Earl of Rutland at Belvoir Castle and successfully arranged the marriage of his charge to the daughter of the house. In the same letter to le Clerc, Shaftesbury tells the story of his father's match in characteristic style.

"The affair was nice, for though my grandfather required not a great fortune, he insisted on good blood, good person and constitution, and above all good education and a character as remote as possible from that of a court or town-bred lady. All this was thrown upon Mr. Locke, who being already so good a judge of men, my grandfather doubted not of his equal judgment in women. He departed from him entrusted and sworn as Abraham's head servant *that ruled over all that he had*, and went into a far country (the north of England) to seek for his son a wife, whom he as successfully found."

The education of Shaftesbury, together with that of his six brothers and sisters, was supervised by Locke and was based on those principles which were later to be expounded in *Thoughts concerning Education*. Locke's charge included the children's physical as well as mental well-being and was so successful that Shaftesbury tells le Clerc,

"we all of us came to full years with strong and healthy constitutions."

In his own case, however, his good health did not continue long into manhood. Shaftesbury disagreed very profoundly with Locke in philosophical matters, as we shall see later, but his personal regard for his tutor was very high and he always speaks most affectionately of him as a man and a friend. The manner in which he concludes the letter gives us some indication of his feeling.

"I was his more peculiar charge, being as eldest son taken by my grandfather and bred under his immediate care, Mr. Locke having the absolute direction of my education, and to whom next my immediate parents, as I must own the greatest obligation, so I have ever preserved the highest gratitude and duty. I could wish that my time and health would permit me to be longer in the account of my friend and foster-father Mr. Locke."

While Locke supervised the young Shaftesbury's education, the day-to-day teaching was given by a Mrs. Birch, the daughter of a schoolmaster. This lady could herself speak Greek and Latin fluently and at Locke's suggestion taught her pupil these languages by the conversational method. The method was a success, for his son tells us that Shaftesbury could read Greek and Latin quite easily when eleven years old. At this age he was sent to a private school where he stayed till his grandfather's death and then, in 1683, his father entered him at Winchester. His time here was an unhappy one. His schoolfellows taunted him because of his grandfather's Whiggery and, as with many other schools of the time, the life seems to have been rough and brutal. From a letter Shaftesbury wrote to his father, in July 1689, after he had left Winchester, we learn that drunkenness was a common vice there and that the habit was shared by masters and boys alike.

Shaftesbury's stay at Winchester was comparatively short, for in 1686 he left and went on a tour of the Continent which lasted three years. Shaftesbury's tutor on this tour was a Scotsman by the name of Daniel Denoue[1] and he was accompanied by two friends of about his own age, Sir John Cropley and Mr. Thomas Sclater Bacon. A considerable part of the tour was spent in Italy and Shaftesbury's son tells us that he here "acquired a great knowledge in the polite arts," including painting, sculpture and the rudiments of music. A letter to his father speaks of his visiting Vienna and coming home by way of Germany and Holland. He acquired not only an acquaintance with the arts, but seems to have perfected his command of Italian and French; his French was so good, indeed, that in France he was taken for a native of the country.

On his return to England Shaftesbury spent nearly five years in private study. There are no details of what this study consisted of, or where he carried it out, but we can be sure that it was directed to a study of the classics and, in particular, of Greek philosophy. This period of his life was brought to an end in 1695, by his entering Parliament as the member for Poole, on the death of Sir John Trenchard, who had represented that borough. His maiden speech

[1] Or Denoune

in the House of Commons was in support of a famous Bill, the purpose of which was to allow the assistance of a counsel to those on trial for treason. Shaftesbury had written a carefully prepared speech, but on facing a full House of Commons, he was so intimidated that he could remember none of it. He quickly turned the occasion to use, however, by saying:

"If I, sir, who rise only to speak my opinion on the Bill now depending, am so confounded that I am unable to express the least of what I proposed to say, what must the condition of that man be who is pleading for his life without any assistance and under apprehensions of being deprived of it?"[1]

The Bill was passed, Shaftesbury's brilliant improvisation playing an important part in winning the support of the House.

II

Shaftesbury maintained an interest in politics throughout his life. The letters to his friend Mr. Furley,[2] an English Quaker merchant settled in Rotterdam, provide a most interesting account of the political events of the Age of Anne as seen through Shaftesbury's eyes. He had met Furley when returning through Holland from his continental tour and his correspondence with this friend lasted from then until the end of his life. Shaftesbury, though a confirmed Whig, was no mere party-man and at this time of shifting factions and tactical groupings he retained an independence based on principles rather than party. One of his political convictions was that England should remain friendly with Holland. His love for Holland was strengthened by the many friendships he had made there, but he also saw in Holland a toleration and freedom which he believed were lacking in England. He suspected, with good reason, the Tories' profession of friendship with Holland. He knew that their desire was for an alliance with France and, in common with the other Whigs, opposed a policy which he considered might put another Stuart on the throne.

[1] The story has been told of Charles Montagu, later Earl of Halifax, but it is given by Shaftesbury's son with such a wealth of detail, that there is little doubt of its authenticity. Birch, in the *General Dictionary*, says that it has wrongly been attributed to Halifax; and Horace Walpole, in his *Catalogue of Royal and Noble Authors*, also refers the story to Shaftesbury.

[2] These are contained in the *Original Letters of Locke, Algernon Sidney and Shaftesbury*, edited by T. Forster, London, 1830.

"What they might have done farther as to our succession here at home," he writes to Furley, "so as to have wholly brought us back again to where we were before the Revolution, this I must leave to you to guess, but will not venture to mention in a letter."

An alliance with France was anathema to Shaftesbury, who disliked that country and hated the possibility of a Catholic, or near Catholic, monarch. During the elections of January 1701, Shaftesbury wrote to his friend in Rotterdam, expressing his fears of what might happen if there were a Tory majority.

"The only thing to be hoped and pray'd for, is, that the Tory party may not be superior: for, if but ever so little inferior, their numbers will be of service rather than of injury: for, as it is said of water or fire, so it may be said of them, that they are good servants, but ill masters; and, as by principles they are slaves, so they are only serviceable when they are kept so, and their slavery and subjection is the only pledge of our freedom, or of the freedom of the world, as far as we in England are contributors to it, and let our friends in Holland know their friends here, and take notice that it is that party that hate the Dutch and love France, and the Whiggs the only contrary party that can now save them and England: Farewell."

With such views, it can be understood that when peace was finally made with France, Shaftesbury was a bitter man. The peace was made in 1713 and though Shaftesbury died a few weeks before the Treaty of Utrecht, it was obvious from the preliminary negotiations that, contrary to the provisions of the Grand Alliance, England was seeking for separate and advantageous terms for herself and leaving Holland to fare as best she could. In the last letter he wrote to Furley, in July 1712, Shaftesbury expresses the shame he feels for his country's behaviour and his own gloom at the prospect facing those who love freedom. Even such Tories as Marlborough and Godolphin, who had wished to carry on the war against France and who had received Shaftesbury's support against the advice of some of his friends, "now can only keep their heads by our endeavours and support." No wonder that Shaftesbury in his last fatal sickness writes to his friend on "the most sad shame and reproach of our nation",

"which I never thought to have liv'd to see, and which makes my sad health and little prospect of recovery the less grievous to me, as a means to end that sense of shame, which I shall ever retain for my country ... never was I dejected till this turn."

Though Shaftesbury remained interested in politics and played an influential part in the councils of the Whigs, he relinquished his seat in the House of Commons after only three years as a member. The reason for this was ill health. Like Locke, Shaftesbury was afflicted with asthma and the smoke and fog of the capital made life in London intolerable for him. From this time, whenever he had to be in London, he stayed in lodgings in Chelsea, but even here he found the air unhealthy, and at one period he stayed in Hampstead, at that time a pleasant country village some way out of London. The asthma either produced, or was accompanied by, a general weakening of his constitution and henceforward he was obliged to nurse his strength and safeguard his health. His son attributes his father's breakdown to the pressure of parliamentary work.

"The fatigues of attending regularly upon the service of the House (which in those active times generally sat long) as well as upon committees at night, in a few years so impaired my father's health, who was not of a robust constitution, that he was obliged to decline coming again into Parliament after the dissolution in 1698."

On giving up his seat in the House, Shaftesbury went to Holland for a year and, as Locke had done before him, found the air of Rotterdam beneficial to his asthma. At Rotterdam he joined the literary and philosophical circle which ten years previously had entertained his old tutor and which included Jean le Clerc; Pierre Bayle, the author of the *Dictionnaire Universelle*, who was then a professor at Rotterdam; Benjamin Furley, the Quaker merchant; and Phillipe van Limborch, the Dutch theologian. Holland at this time was the centre of liberal thought in Europe and many an English exile in the latter half of the seventeenth century had found Holland a safe refuge, to which to take theological, political, or philosophical opinions that were less welcome at home. Here there flourished a freedom of speech and thought and a spirit of intellectual inquiry that had disappeared from strife-ridden England. There is no doubt that Shaftesbury enjoyed the company as well as the air during his stay.

During this visit there occurred the surreptitious publication of

Shaftesbury's *Inquiry Concerning Virtue*.[1] The person responsible for this was John Toland, who used a rough draft which the author had made when only twenty years old. Shaftesbury, not unnaturally, was annoyed by such treatment from one who had received much kindness at his hand. He bought up as many copies of the book as possible and set about preparing a final and authentic version of his own work. The incident has interest also for the light it throws on Shaftesbury's generosity to men of letters. He had allowed Toland an annual stipend and, according to his son, this was but one instance of the way in which he bestowed pensions on young men who were struggling for recognition. Shaftesbury returned to England in November 1699, and shortly afterwards, on his father's death, inherited the title.[2] During the first parliamentary session after he succeeded to the peerage, Shaftesbury was fully occupied with family business and took little part in national affairs. The next session, however, was concerned with the famous second Partition Treaty, by which in March 1700 England, France and Holland had agreed to the partition of the Spanish possessions on the death of Charles II of Spain. A Tory House of Commons was so incensed at the terms of the treaty that they impeached the Whig leaders who had agreed to them. As a counter-measure the Whig peers managed to persuade the Upper House to address a prayer to the Throne asking for an annulment of the impeachments.

In the event, the Commons did not appear to support their charges and the whole thing fell through, but it was an anxious moment for the Whigs. Shaftesbury's advice and influence must have been considered very highly by his party, for an urgent appeal for his presence from Lord Somers, the Whig leader, brought him to the House of Lords. Not only did he speak against the Commons' proposal, but he was one of those who drafted the address to the King.

The tide of Tory success was now already on the turn. Charles II of Spain died in November 1700, and Louis XIV at once went back on his treaty-promise when he learnt that his own grandson, Philip, Duke of Anjou, had been named as heir in Charles's will. As France became increasingly hostile, it became quite clear that England would

---

[1] In the MS. *Life* written by the fourth Earl this incident is assigned to the visit Shaftesbury made to Holland in 1703-4. In the account by Birch in the *General Dictionary*, which was seen and corrected by the fourth Earl, it is given the earlier date. There is no doubt that this is correct and I have followed Fowler and Rand (see the note at the end of the chapter) in placing it here.

[2] For the sake of clarity I have referred to him throughout as Shaftesbury, but until this time he was, of course, Lord Ashley.

have to look elsewhere for friends. Other nations, too, were suspicious of French intentions and the growing fear at the turn of events led to the formation of the Grand Alliance.

As the prospects of war with France became more certain so Tory influence waned. Shaftesbury's son tells of the part his father played in all this. After relating the story of Somers's appeal, he continues:

> "He attended the House the remainder of the session as much as his health would permit, being earnest to support King William's measures, who was at that time projecting the Grand Alliance. In my father's judgment nothing could assist that glorious undertaking more effectually than the choice of a good Parliament."

In spite of poor health, Shaftesbury threw himself into the task of achieving a Whig majority in Parliament at the next election and was so successful that the King himself told him that his efforts had turned the scale, and offered him the post of Secretary of State in the new Government.

> "This, however, his declining constitution would not allow him to accept. But, although he was disabled from engaging in such a course of business, he was not prevented from giving the King his advice, who frequently consulted him on matters of the highest importance; and it is pretty well known that he had the greatest share in composing that celebrated last speech of King William, 31st December, 1701."

Unfortunately for Shaftesbury, William was not to reign for long. Perhaps, on the other hand, it was to his advantage, for the accession of Anne removed the conflict between his political duty and the growing need to safeguard his health. It is true that at first there was no great change in foreign policy and Marlborough, the Queen's favourite, was given every opportunity of exercising his military genius against the French. But the Whigs were out of favour. Anne supported the High-Church party and disliked the Whigs with their questionable orthodoxy and radical views. Shaftesbury, least of all, was a Queen's-man. He was even deprived of the only small public office he had, the Vice-Admiralty of Dorset. "Mightily impaired by fatigues in the public affairs", he retired to a life of privacy and once again, in an attempt to regain health and in search of a freedom he felt lacking at home, he made another visit to Holland. This visit was again for the duration of a year, during which Shaftesbury lived in quiet seclusion. The letters asking Furley to make arrangements for his lodgings in Rotterdam all insist on the need for privacy and a desire to avoid all visitors, except his most intimate friends. So resolute was he in this respect that even the whereabouts of his lodgings were kept secret. Shaftesbury returned in August 1704, much recovered, yet still obliged to lead a fairly retired life.

III

It is likely that during the next few years Shaftesbury occupied himself with writing. The letters to Furley testify that he never lost an interest in public affairs and was well acquainted with each new development in politics, but he never again played the active part he had done. The business of his estate, too, must have occupied a large part of his time; even when absent in Holland, Shaftesbury maintained a close watch over his domestic affairs. His letters to Wheelock, the steward at the family seat at Wimborne St. Giles in Dorset, show the grasp which he kept on points of even minute detail in such business. His instructions[1] to Mrs. Cooper, the housekeeper at St. Giles, are further evidence of the concern he felt not only for the administration of his estate, but for the welfare of his servants and tenants. She is instructed to show hospitality to all strangers, and especially foreigners, who may call at St. Giles, and to report to him all cases of need in the neighbourhood, so that he may know how best to distribute assistance. No ostentation is to be displayed in all this and she is told not to distribute food at the gates of the house as this penalizes "the modest poor" and merely encourages vagabonds. In particular, she is to find out which of the children on the estate need encouragement and help. She is to report "of their schooling (which my Lord allows them)" and let him know which of them are worth further education and suitable for taking into his service.

One can have no doubt in reading the letters of Shaftesbury that he was a man of toleration, kindliness and integrity, whose philosophy regulated his life and inspired a most serious sense of public duties and personal responsibilities. That his kindness was not always paid in kind did not cause him to swerve from his course; his benevolence was not sentimentalism, but the outcome of a judicious and well-tempered attitude towards his fellows. A similar

[1] These instructions are contained in the Shaftesbury Papers at the Public Record Office.

example to John Toland's ingratitude is seen in the case of Henry Wilkinson. Wilkinson had been educated at Shaftesbury's expense and had been received into Furley's counting-house at Rotterdam as a clerk. His correspondence with Furley and with the boy himself shows the real concern that Shaftesbury had for him. Wilkinson was a very ambitious and self-seeking young man. When Lord Peterborough, just made Governor of the West Indies, was looking for a young man to take with him as a member of his staff, Wilkinson put himself forward, though the prior claim undoubtedly belonged to Arent Furley, his employer's own son. Yet Shaftesbury's kindness to him remained unchanged. The details of the story are not known to us, but evidently Wilkinson broke faith with his master and, one can guess, left his employment for what he thought better opportunities. But even here, Shaftesbury reserves his judgment in writing to Furley.

"I cannot as yet understand a tittle of that affaire of H. Wilkinson's, and the letters and correspondences hinted. I am wholly a stranger to all; and if said to be otherwise it is imposture and juggle. I hope he is not so false as to pretend he or any other has made me acquainted with what I know nothing off. He is indeed but too vain, and talkative, and pragmaticall; tho' with abilityes and talents sufficient, if he would well employ them. I have been at great trouble, and know not how to dispose of him, having been fouly disappointed by some who kept off of other advantages by false expectations for him. I have now left him to the wide world with a small sum and cloaths fitted out to take his fortune."

Soon after Shaftesbury's return from his second stay in Holland, the public interest was aroused by the arrival in England of the Protestant peasants from the Cévennes, who had been driven from their homes by the Revocation of the Edict of Nantes. These peasants were known as the "French Prophets" and the emotional extravagances and the excesses of evangelical fervour which marked their religion soon brought them into disfavour with the English people, who had had a surfeit of religious extremes and strife. Some even advocated persecution of these sincere fanatics. It was as a contribution to this controversy that Shaftesbury composed his *Letter concerning Enthusiasm*; this was written as a private letter to Lord Somers, then President of the Council, but was published, though anonymously, in the next year, 1708.

The burden of Shaftesbury's *Letter* was that the most effective way to treat fanaticism was by ridicule and that the test of truth was whether a belief or principle could stand up to such treatment. The *Letter* was greeted with a storm of abuse and its opponents rushed into print against what they considered an attack on religion itself. One can understand the suspicion which met the view that religious truths should be tested by 'good humour' and 'raillery', and the belief that Shaftesbury was a Deist was given an early start by this *Letter*. The later essay *Sensus Communis: An Essay on the Freedom of Wit and Humour* (1709), where he elaborated his views, did nothing to remove that impression. By many people in the eighteenth century Shaftesbury was regarded as a sceptic and the downfall of Miss Williams in *Roderick Random*, for instance, was attributed in the first place to her reading of "Shaftesbury, Tindal and Hobbes."

Shaftesbury's son was anxious to vindicate his father from such a charge and, indeed, the evidence which he assembled in his biography cannot be explained merely as an attempt to hallow his father's memory. To any reader of his letters it is apparent that Shaftesbury was a sincere Christian. He obviously had no love for the High-Church party and his religion was one that demanded rational grounds, but there can be no doubt that he sincerely believed in a liberal or 'latitudinarian' theology. The letter to his brother Maurice, in which he gives his views on religious enthusiasm and which the fourth Earl quotes in the biographical sketch, shows something of Shaftesbury's religious temper.

"Being risen both of us pretty late in the morning which was Sunday, we went (you know) to church for the first time this New Year. Thither I never went with truer zeal, in a better disposition or with wholesomer reflections. And what satisfied me still the more, it was by appointment that we were that day to receive the Sacrament together, having had no opportunity of a long time. Here we both joined in blessing that good Providence which had by reason and education separated us from the impure and horrid superstitions, monstrous enthusiasms, and wild fanaticisms of those blasphemous visionaries we saw abounding in the world, and which had given us on the contrary side such established rites of worship as were so decent, chaste, innocent, pure; and had placed us in a religion and church where in respect of the moderate party and far greater part the principle of charity was really more extensive than in any Christian or Protestant church besides in the world; ... where a good and virtuous life, with a hearty endeavour of service to one's country and mankind, joined with a religious performance of all sacred duties and a conformity with the established rites, was enough to answer the highest character of religion, and where all other pretences to gifts or supernatural endowments beyond these moral and Christian perfections were justly suspected and treated as villainy, cheat, imposture, and madness."

It is true that the tone is rather Erastian, but this was a time when the Church of England itself put little emphasis upon the supernatural and found it easy to come to terms with secular power. There is no reason to doubt that Shaftesbury was a conforming member of the church and we have his son's statement that he "was very constant in his attendance at church and in receiving the Communion when his asthma would permit." He also had a high regard for Burnet, the Bishop of Salisbury, in whose diocese his family estate was situated. Burnet, of course, was a Whig and spent much of his time in political controversy, but he was also a most conscientious Bishop and devout churchman; and it is clear that Shaftesbury's admiration of him sprang from more than political sympathy.

In reading Burnet's life and writings, one is impressed with the zeal and thoroughness with which he carried out his charge. The Bishop took a close and personal interest in the training of candidates for the ministry, a rare thing in the early eighteenth century. One such candidate for ordination by Burnet was a young protégé of Shaftesbury, Michael Ainsworth, who had been one of the village children at Wimborne St. Giles and whose ability at an early age had led Shaftesbury to arrange for his schooling. Ainsworth had profited so well by this that Shaftesbury then sent him to University College, Oxford. While 'the good Michael' was an undergraduate at Oxford, Shaftesbury wrote to him a series of letters which were published in 1716. In these he advises the young man to read the dialogues of 'the divine Plato' and Henry More's *Enchiridion Ethicum*, which he calls "a right good piece of sound morals". He encourages him to take Holy Orders and, when the time comes recommends him to Burnet as a suitable person for ordination. In the same series of letters he calls the Bishop, "the truest example of *laborious, primitive, pious,* and *learned Episcopacy*", and in a later letter, writes:

"he has done more than any man living for the good and honour of the church of England and the reform'd religion; so he now suffers more than any man from the tongues and slanders of those ungrateful *church-men*; who may well call themselves by that single term of distinction, having no claim to that of *Christianity* or *Protestant*."

In none of this is there any indication that Shaftesbury was a sceptic. Private letters such as these are a sure guide to his beliefs, and it is most unlikely, had he been a sceptic, that he would have forwarded Ainsworth's project to become ordained and expressed the wish to Burnet of making the young man his domestic chaplain. The picture we get of Shaftesbury in this matter, as in his friendships with Locke, Limborch, the Quaker Furley, and others, is that of a convinced but latitudinarian churchman, whose life as well as principles were in accordance with a sincere and rationalistic piety. Shaftesbury, in fact, stood in the tradition of the Cambridge Platonists. His writings are less concerned with theology than theirs and it is difficult to determine accurately his doctrinal position, but his whole philosophy is greatly indebted to the Cambridge men. His references to them were always very cordial and, in 1698, he had written a *Preface* to a selection of Whichcote's *Sermons* which he had gathered together for publication. In this he speaks highly of Whichcote, whom he calls "our excellent divine, and truly Christian philosopher".

In 1709, Shaftesbury married Miss Jane Ewer, a distant relative and the youngest daughter of Thomas Ewer, Esquire, of Lea in Hertfordshire. Shaftesbury was now almost forty years of age and the marriage was occasioned, in the first place, more by the desire for an heir than any stirring of the heart. Indeed, after the match had already been arranged, Shaftesbury had yet to see his future wife. There was, perhaps, something of pique in his action, since he had only recently been unsuccessful in his addresses to another lady and only at the conclusion of this unfortunate affair resolved to take a wife whom he had never seen and who had no fortune.

What details we have of this earlier and unsuccessful love-affair come from the letters Shaftesbury wrote to his friend Robert (afterwards Viscount) Molesworth. These letters were published with an Introduction by John Toland, in 1721. They contain the story of Shaftesbury's earlier and fruitless courtship, and his subsequent marriage to Jane Ewer; and Toland, by publishing them in the life-time of the two ladies concerned, must have given considerable annoyance and pain to both of them. When we remember this and the earlier injury Toland had done the family in publishing an unauthorized version of Shaftesbury's *Inquiry*, we can appreciate why the fourth Earl is so bitter in his references to him.

Shaftesbury's health seemed to get no better. This, with the fact that his brother Maurice appeared likely to remain a bachelor, raised the question of who would succeed to the family title and property. In September 1708, in a letter to his friend Molesworth, he refers to his desire to get married. In October, this is followed by two more letters in which he writes that the young lady he has in mind is a friend of one of Molesworth's female relations. Will Molesworth use this connection in his behalf? No mention is made of the name of Shaftesbury's choice, but her virtues are great and many. There is no doubt of his real esteem and affection for the lady.

> "She is in every respect that very person I had ever framed a picture of from my imagination, when I wished the best for my own happiness in such a circumstance."

The lady's father was a peer and she herself possessed a great fortune. This, however, added to Shaftesbury's uneasiness: apart from its making the match more difficult to negotiate with the lady's father, his motives in the case might be misconstrued and his friends think him in love with her wealth. To add to his difficulties he suspected the existence of a rival who was favoured by the lady's father. He tells Molesworth that this rival is one of the leaders of the Junta who had sat with them in the House of Commons, but has recently been elevated to the peerage. He is a man noted for his wit, gallantry, magnificence, and eloquence. Now the Junta, the small party caucus of the Whigs, was composed of the Lords Orford, Somers, Wharton, Halifax and Sunderland, and the rival Shaftesbury refers to has generally been thought to be Charles Montagu, first Lord Halifax. The above description fits him exactly and Halifax was, indeed, a widower at this time, but since he did not remarry, we get no clue to the lady's identity from this quarter.

In the end Shaftesbury was defeated not by Halifax, but by his asthma. Molesworth made every effort on his friend's behalf, but as winter drew on, the weather and atmosphere sent Shaftesbury out of London. Instead of returning to Dorset, he stayed with another old friend, Sir John Cropley, at Beachworth in Surrey, so as to be near London if his health improved. The odds were too much for him, however, and he wrote to Molesworth telling him that he must retreat to St. Giles:

"Cou'd I make a show of health with safety, and pursue the lady, when I might have opportunity to win her liking by this means, and appearing better without doors than I am within at ordinary hours; I wou'd not do this, whatever depended on it. But as the season is, and the severe North-east winds, and town-smoke, I am driven from my quarters at *Chelsey*; and think not that I shall be able to return there, till the strength of the winter is over: so will take the first fair weather, to go to my winter quarters at *St. Giles's*."

There is something very pathetic in the picture of Shaftesbury having to spend the winter in Dorset, struggling against his asthma and watching his hopes recede. With the spring he returned to London, but again was laid low with asthma. Once more he retired to the house of Sir John Cropley, in Surrey, and by June 1709, was well enough to seek an interview with his prospective father-in-law in London. This interview convinced him that his case was hopeless. It is fairly obvious that "the old lord" was not at all happy about having a son-in-law in Shaftesbury's state of health, and Shaftesbury himself would be too honest to dissemble on such a matter. It was after this interview that he determined, as he wrote to his old friend, Lady Russell, to look for a bride without fortune and chosen by the dictates of prudence rather than by the heart.

"It was my misfortune (your ladyship knows) to be detained this last year or two in the prosecution of an affair in which I have had no success; though I would gladly have taken the lady without anything, and upon whatever terms her father would have thought fit. When I had the honour to mention these particulars to your ladyship, I assured you at the same time that since I despaired of success in this place I would pursue my intentions for my family's sake without further delay, being resolved in my circumstances of health (which kept me from living in or near the town) to have no other regard in the choice I made, than merely that of a good family, a good character, and such an education as might best suit a lady's temper to my circumstance and way of life." (*Rand*, p. 408.)

His match with Jane Ewer was successful beyond what might have been hoped for. He had already assured himself of her "temper, person and health," but on meeting the lady he was surprised and delighted to find that, though in popular esteem she had no reputation that way, she was, in his opinion, quite beautiful. Certainly she was a devoted wife. When one reflects on Shaftesbury's age, temperament, interests and health and the manner in which the match was contracted, one realizes that he is in fact giving his wife high praise when he writes to Molesworth shortly after his marriage,

"Were I to talk of marriage and forced to speak my mind plainly, and without the help of humour and raillery, I should doubtless offend the most part of sober married people, and the ladies chiefly; for I shou'd in reality think I did wonders in extolling the happiness of my new state, and the merit of my wife in particular; by saying, *that I verily thought myself as happy a man now as ever.*"

Shaftesbury was married to Jane Ewer in 1709 and their only child was born on the 9th February, 1710. It was as well from the point of view of begetting an heir that the marriage took place when it did. Shaftesbury's health continued to grow worse, and in July 1711 he set out for Naples, hoping that the warm air of Italy might do something to cure, or at least arrest, his bad health. The war with France was still in progress at this time and Shaftesbury had to pass through the army of the Duke of Berwick (a natural son of James II), which was encamped on the borders of Piedmont. The Duke, with a courtesy foreign to modern warfare, entertained Shaftesbury (who had nothing but loathing for his cause) most politely, and conducted him safely to the domain of the Duke of Savoy, one of the English allies.

IV

Shaftesbury lived in Italy for nearly two years, which, as his son says, "was a long time considering the severe illness he was afflicted with and which nothing but the excellence of the air in Italy and the uncommon care of my mother in attending him could have achieved." He spent this time in revising his *Characteristics of Men, Manners, Opinions, Times*, which had first appeared in 1711, and in writing the short treatises on aesthetics called *A Notion of the Historical Draught or Tablature of the Judgment of Hercules*, and the *Letter concerning Design*. He also made notes and formed a scheme, shortly before his death, for writing a *Discourse on the Arts of Painting*,

Sculpture, etc. From the letters he wrote home from Italy we know that during this period Shaftesbury devoted a considerable time to a study of the fine arts, or what he called 'virtuosoship'. Shaftesbury at this time acted as an agent for his friend Cropley in buying Italian paintings and the letters occasioned by this duty are interesting for the light they throw both on his own and the contemporary taste in painting. Like many other writers of this time, he admired greatly the Carracci and Guido Reni, who were emotional and sentimental painters of the late Italian school, and his letters reveal that the wild and romantic landscapes of Poussin and Salvator Rosa were already beginning to be popular in England at this date. In fact there is some reason for thinking that Shaftesbury himself had some responsibility for the vogue these painters were to enjoy and for the new cult of landscape painting in England. Mrs. Manwaring in her *Italian Landscape in Eighteenth Century England* declares that he is the first in whom she has discovered anything like a modern taste in painting. In a letter to Cropley he writes:

"And as a hundred pound or two will go but a little way in the great pieces of humanity or history of the Carachs, the Guidos, and such great masters as those; the next degree of painting (which is that of nature in perspective or landskip) will be that which best suits you, and which, I think, you have the most taken to of late. For, as I remember, you have, besides the copies of Poussin, a copy of Salvator Rosa, also by Mr. Closterman. ... Now I could at this instant, for little more than double what you paid for such poor 'prentice-copying, procure an original piece or two of the same Salvator Rosa (a townsman of this very place), equal and even beyond those very fine originals which Mr. Closterman, by the help of his journeymen, took copies of, and sold to you." (*Rand*, pp. 469–470.)

The John Closterman mentioned in this letter was a German-born portrait painter who had settled in England. He had gained some reputation, having painted Queen Anne in her coronation robes and a family group of the Duke and Duchess of Marlborough with their children, but today his work is considered no more than competent. It says something for Shaftesbury's critical acumen that his letters refer not only to the painter's assistants, but to Closterman himself as simply as a 'journeyman', and he would have had good reason for making such a criticism, for in 1699 he had commissioned Closterman to visit Italy and no doubt it was on this visit, and at

Shaftesbury's order, that Closterman made his copies of Salvator Rosa. This is only one instance of the interest Shaftesbury had taken throughout his life in painting, sculpture and architecture.

Now at the end of his days and with death ever present to his mind, he devoted his stay in Naples to a study of how his philosophical ideas might be expressed through the medium of art. His *Judgment of Hercules*, a series of instructions to the Neapolitan painter, Paolo de Mattheis, for a painting of the incident in Xenophon's *Memorabilia*, where Hercules has to choose between the two goddesses Virtue and Pleasure, is really a discussion of the way in which painting can be an expression of thought. In his scrupulous preparation of a second edition of the *Characteristics* for the press, Shaftesbury now designed emblems, which were drawn for him by a young artist named French, who happened to be in Naples. These he sent home with his instructions to Simon Gribelin, the most famous of contemporary engravers, who made the plates for the new edition. Like the painting of the Choice of Hercules, the emblems were an attempt to convey his teaching pictorially. The possibility of doing this had occupied Shaftesbury's mind for some time and, as we shall see later, had a profound effect upon his aesthetic theory.

Besides his wife, there had accompanied Shaftesbury to Italy Bryan Wheelock, the nephew of the steward of St. Giles, and a young Pole named Crelle, who acted as his secretary. Crelle had been educated at Leyden and Cambridge at Shaftesbury's expense and at the very end, when his patron was too ill to write, acted as an amanuensis; and he tells us that Shaftesbury died on 15th February, 1713, after much pain, "in resignation to the will of God . . . with perfect cheerfulness and the same sweetness of temper he always enjoyed in the most perfect health." Shaftesbury was only forty-one years of age at his death. Probably, in the words of his son, his life would have been longer,

"if he had not worn it out by great fatigues of body and mind, which was owing to his eager desire after knowledge, as well as to his zeal to serve his country . . . which confirmed the truth of Mr. Locke's observation on him that the sword was too sharp for the scabbard."

Something which helped to relieve the pain of Shaftesbury's last years was the welcome given by the world of letters to the first edition of his *Characteristics*. Many of his last letters to his two friends,

Sir John Cropley and Thomas Micklethwayte, are concerned with this and with the preparation of the second edition. Micklethwayte, a young man on whose behalf Shaftesbury had used his influence in public affairs, repaid this kindness by supervising, at the author's direction, the publication of this second edition, and both he and Cropley sent Shaftesbury encouraging accounts of the reception given to the *Characteristics*. Another frequent correspondent of these last two years was Pierre Coste, a young French Protestant who would have accompanied Shaftesbury to Italy but for the Revocation of the Edict of Nantes which had prohibited his entry into France. Coste had already been chosen by Shaftesbury to become in due course the tutor of the little Lord Ashley. He was a young writer acquainted with Shaftesbury's friends, the philosophers Jean le Clerc and Des Maizeaux, and from him Shaftesbury had news of the reputation the *Characteristics* was achieving on the Continent. He it was who arranged for a copy of Shaftesbury's works to be sent to Leibnitz and who subsequently sent their author a copy of Leibnitz's very favourable review.

The tribute Shaftesbury valued most, however, was from General Stanhope. Stanhope, afterwards first Earl Stanhope and Chancellor of the Exchequer in the time of George I, was a brilliant army commander, and had served with distinction in Spain until his capture there in December 1710. Shaftesbury was delighted to receive the news from Sir John Cropley that Stanhope had been spending his time in captivity in reading the *Characteristics*, and had expressed a desire to journey to Italy on his release, in order to visit their author. Stanhope's letter to Cropley would have delighted him even more, for it recognized in the *Characteristics* that combination of instruction and pleasure which had been Shaftesbury's aim.

"I cease not to study *Characteristics*," wrote Stanhope, "and find my value and admiration for the author increase daily, nor do I believe anything hath been writ these many ages so likely to be of use to mankind, by improving men's morals as well as their understandings. I can at least affirm of myself that I am the better man for the study I have bestowed on them, and if I mistake not very much they will occasion a new turn of thinking as well as writing, whereby our English authors may become hereafter more instructive and delighting."[1]

[1]Letter to Sir J. Cropley, 26th April, 1712; Rand, *op. cit.*, 500.

Shaftesbury in all his writings wished to bring philosophy out of the study and into the conversation of polite society. In the preceding century philosophy had generally been written in technical language and in the large treatises favoured only by scholars. The success of writers like Hobbes and Locke was due partly to the fact that they wrote in a language understood by the ordinary educated reader, the man of affairs and business. Shaftesbury went even further and endeavoured to write philosophy so that the fashionable world, the readers of the *Spectator* and *Tatler*, would understand it and come to regard it as their concern.

Shaftesbury's first publication, as we have seen, was in 1698 and consisted of a collection of Whichcote's sermons to which he contributed a preface.[1] It is significant that this should have been his first published work, for in these *Sermons* we find the basis of much of his own philosophy. The view of man and society put forward by Whichcote was in opposition to that of Hobbes, whom Shaftesbury also regarded as *advocatus diaboli*. The Cambridge men had written in a style that soon made their work neglected and were concerned with the theological implications of Hobbes's theories rather than their effect on society and the arts. The purpose underlying Shaftesbury's writings was to argue the case against Hobbes and all that he stood for, in a polished style suited to the *salon* rather than the pulpit, and showing the controversy to be one not only of theological debate, but concerned with life and society, manners and the arts.

In 1699, there had appeared the unauthorized publication by Toland of Shaftesbury's youthful *Inquiry Concerning Virtue or Merit*. In 1708, the *Letter Concerning Enthusiasm*, which Shaftesbury addressed to Lord Somers, was published anonymously. These were followed by the *Essay on the Freedom of Wit and Humour* and *The Moralists*, both published in 1709, and the *Advice to an Author*, 1710. All these formed the first two volumes of the first edition of the *Characteristics*, which appeared in 1711, while a third volume contained *Miscellaneous Reflections on the preceding Treatises, and other Critical Subjects*. Shaftesbury's other works were written in Italy and were the two essays already noted, a *Letter on Design*, and *The Judgment of Hercules*. These were part of a larger work which he intended as a companion volume to the *Characteristics* and which was never completed. Besides these two essays, there were to have been *An Appendix concerning the Emblem of Cebes* and *Plastics or the Original Progress and Power of Designatory Art*. The *Emblem of Cebes*

[1] A detailed list of the publications of Shaftesbury is given in an appendix.

was never written, while *Plastics* was left only in the form of notes. The *Letter concerning Design* was published for the first time in the fifth edition of the *Characteristics* (1732). The *Judgment of Hercules* appeared first of all in a French version in the *Journal des Sçavans* for November 1712; an English translation which appeared separately in 1713 was then incorporated in the second edition of the *Characteristics* (1714). Only in our own day have these aesthetic writings of Shaftesbury's last years been brought together and published as a single work.[1]

Shaftesbury's intention of making philosophy interesting to the man of taste and culture was certainly effective. The *Characteristics* went into eleven editions by 1790, a sufficient indication of their popularity, and had an influence which the writings of such men as the Cambridge Platonists never achieved. Some have accused Shaftesbury of being too concerned to avoid high seriousness and sober language, too much at pains to bring politeness and polish to his work. His desire to be, at all costs, the man of breeding and culture, certainly gives him at times the appearance of a *dilettante*. There is a quality about his prose which is best described by Charles Lamb as 'genteel', and frequently it exhibits an elegance which led De Quincey, in irritation, to call him "the most absolute and undistinguishing pedant that perhaps literature has to show," and which caused Gray to accuse him of "writing with the coronet on his head." Nevertheless, on the whole Shaftesbury was successful in his purpose. If his style lacks Addison's lightness, we should remember that he was handling at much greater length and with far greater profundity, topics with which the *Spectator* only occasionally dealt. One can read his work with pleasure and can grasp his ideas without difficulty. There is sometimes an ambiguity of language which is perplexing, but this is a matter of thought rather than of style and is because he sometimes uses, without exact definition, words and phrases which have since become more precise. It would be unfair, however, to blame Shaftesbury for lacking our knowledge of the subsequent development of issues which were new in his day. To combine clarity with literary style is always a most difficult task and, though Shaftesbury may not equal the greatest writers of philosophical prose, his writings will always command interest. Besides urbanity there is intellectual vigour, besides elegance there is penetration and wit, and the *Characteristic* will bear comparison with any other work of literary criticism published in the first half of the eighteenth century.

[1] *Shaftesbury's Second Characters*, edited Rand, Cambridge, 1914.

Note on the Materials for a Life of Shaftesbury

The two main sources of information about the life of Shaftesbury are the *Life Sketch* by his only son, the fourth Earl, and his own letters.

The sketch by his son was printed, without much alteration, by Thomas Birch in the *General Dictionary* (1734-41), one of the early biographical dictionaries. Although no mention is made of the fourth Earl in this account in the *General Dictionary*, we know he approved and revised it.[1] Apart from this finished *Life Sketch* there is also a MS. rough draft by his son which includes several paragraphs and sentences left out of the printed version. Both of these *Lives* are amongst the Shaftesbury Papers in the Public Record Office. The finished *Life Sketch* has been reprinted, together with some of the additional paragraphs and phrases from the MS. *Life* as footnotes, in Benjamin Rand's *The Life, Unpublished Letters and Philosophical Regimen of the Earl of Shaftesbury* (London: Swan, Sonnenschein & Co., 1900). I have followed this *Life Sketch* in the account I have given of Shaftesbury's life.

The letters of Shaftesbury may be found in four different published works. The earliest published collection of letters were those addressed by Shaftesbury to his young friend and protégé, Michael Ainsworth, a commoner at University College, Oxford. It is not known by whom they were published, but they appeared, in 1716, under the title, *Several Letters written by a Noble Lord to a Young Man at the University*. In 1721, a second collection of letters was published by John Toland. This collection contains fourteen letters of Shaftesbury to his friend Robert (afterwards Viscount) Molesworth, together with two letters from Sir John Cropley, Shaftesbury's lifelong friend, to Molesworth. These letters are chiefly about Shaftesbury's first and unsuccessful courtship and his subsequent marriage to Jane Ewer. Toland had been given these letters by Molesworth, but without permission for publication, and their appearance in the lifetime of Shaftesbury's widow was a poor return for the kindness Shaftesbury had shown Toland. Such an action on Toland's part only increased the bitterness Shaftesbury's family already felt for him since the time of his unauthorized publication of the *Inquiry* in 1699. For this reason it is as well to regard with caution Toland's *Preface* to these letters, as a source of biographical information.

The *Original Letters of Locke, Sidney and Shaftesbury* was published by T. Forster in 1830. Most of the letters of Shaftesbury in this volume are addressed to Benjamin Furley (or Furly), a Quaker

---
[1] See the Birch MSS. in the British Museum: Addit. 4318 and Addit. 4254.

merchant and friend of Shaftesbury, who lived in Rotterdam. The remainder are to Furley's sons and to Henry Wilkinson, a poor boy, whom Shaftesbury had placed in Furley's counting-house. The contents of most of the letters to Furley are concerned with politics and especially Anglo-Dutch relations. The originals are with the Shaftesbury Papers in the Public Record Office.

The fourth collection of letters is contained in Rand's *The Life, Unpublished Letters, and Philosophical Regimen*. This is by far the most comprehensive and varied collection. It contains some of the letters in the other three collections, but consists chiefly of the large number of hitherto unpublished letters in the Shaftesbury Papers in the Public Record Office. There are also included some letters of Shaftesbury to Locke, which are part of the Lovelace collection.

The most detailed and scholarly account of Shaftesbury's life in modern times is that by Thomas Fowler, *Shaftesbury and Hutcheson*, London, 1882. This is fuller, in some details, than the account given here. My main purpose has been to throw such light on the life and character of Shaftesbury as may be useful to an understanding of his thought.

CHAPTER III

SHAFTESBURY'S PHILOSOPHY

> Order without us, what imports it seen,
> If all is restless anarchy within?
> Fired with this thought great Ashley, gen'rous sage,
> Plann'd in sweet leisure his instructive page.
> (Wm. Melmoth: *Of Active and Retired Life*, 1735.)

I

IN speaking of Shaftesbury's philosophy, one must recognize at the start that there is no coherent or comprehensive system in his writings. He himself said that "the most ingenious way of becoming foolish" is by a love of systems,[1] and one of the difficulties in estimating his importance as a thinker is that his work lacks systematization. This is not entirely a disadvantage, however, for it frees Shaftesbury from having to fit all his observations into a neat and self-contained pattern which neglects awkward features. It is not that Shaftesbury is inconsistent, but rather that he drops hints without bothering to press them home, or to make them sufficiently precise. He has defied all attempts to label him as a member of this or that school and perhaps this is one of his great merits. He has been called in turn a Stoic, a Deist, a sceptic, a Platonist and a disciple of Spinoza. He has been assigned to both of the opposed schools of eighteenth-century moral philosophy; those who made reason and those who made feeling the faculty of moral judgment.

There can be no doubt, however, that Shaftesbury was steeped in ancient philosophy. A note appended to the life-sketch by his son in the *General Dictionary* tells us that he read constantly and

> "carried always with him . . . the moral works of Xenophon, Horace, the *Commentaries* and *Enchiridion* of Epictetus as published by Arrian, and Marcus Antoninus. These authors are now extant in his library, filled throughout with marginal notes, references, and explanations, all written with his own hand."

Dr. Kippis in his account of Shaftesbury in the *Biographia Britannica*, referring to this passage, very rightly says,

[1]*Characteristics*, I, 189.

"To this catalogue Plato should undoubtedly have been added, of whom it is evident that the Earl of Shaftesbury was a diligent reader, an ardent admirer, a zealous imitator."

The full-length portrait of Shaftesbury by John Closterman, an engraving of which by Gribelin was included in the second edition of the *Characteristics* and is reproduced as a frontispiece to the present volume, shows the philosopher in classical robes; on one side are displayed two volumes bearing the names of Plato and Xenophon. In view of the importance that Shaftesbury attached to such pictorial representation, one must consider this piece of symbolism to be of particular significance. We can regard his philosophy, in fact, as deriving its inspiration from the teaching of Socrates, not only as expressed in what might be called its more orthodox form by Plato, but also as interpreted by Xenophon in a more popular way.

Though the inspiration of Shaftesbury's philosophy was Greek thought, its main purpose was practical and related to contemporary needs. He was interested not so much in discursive reasoning as in reforming the manners and taste of his own day. For, he writes,

"To philosophise, in a just signification, is but to carry good-breeding a step higher. For the accomplishment of breeding is, to learn whatever is decent in company or beautiful in arts; and the sum of philosophy is, to learn what is just in society, and beautiful in Nature and the order of the world . . . the taste of beauty and the relish of what is decent, just and amiable perfects the character of the gentleman and the philosopher." (*Characteristics*, II, 255–6.)

Certainly he thought he was breaking away from contemporary philosophy and he tells us that his

"design is to advance something new, or at least something different from what is commonly current in philosophy and morals." (*ibid.*, II, 251–2.)

It was the same practical purpose that made Shaftesbury employ a style which would be understood by readers unversed in the technical terminology of philosophy. Hobbes and Locke, it is true, had already written in plain language and had enormously strengthened their influence by doing so, but those outside the empirical tradition had prejudiced their cause by writing in an outmoded manner. Shaftesbury's endeavour was to rescue the philosophical tradition of the Cambridge Platonists from the dull and pedantic folio volumes in which it had been presented and to make it available to the man of culture and sensibility. For, he wrote of philosophy,

> "we have immured her, poor lady, in colleges and cells, and have set her servilely to such works as those in the mines. Empirics and pedantic sophists are her chief pupils." (*ibid.*, II, 4–5.)

He seems to have persuaded his contemporaries of the value of such a purpose, for Addison, always a close reader of the *Characteristics*, informed the subscribers to the *Spectator* that the paper's policy would be to bring "philosophy out of closets and libraries, schools and colleges, to dwell in clubs and assemblies, at tea-tables and in coffee-houses."

The *Characteristics* were called into existence by their author's conviction that his age was dominated by a narrow and unsatisfactory philosophy. On the one hand, he had to counter an empirical and mechanistic system of thought, which had been strengthened by the writings of Hobbes and Locke and which was unsympathetic to the imaginative endeavours of the arts. On the other, he had to meet the Puritanical distrust of beauty, which, though not so powerful a factor as the other, had never been given a final answer. His writings are a reassertion of man's feeling for natural beauty and an attempt to free the human spirit from both the asceticism of the Puritans and the crippling influence of the mechanical philosophy. He disliked Hobbes and the extreme Puritans for the same reasons; the views of nature and man held by both parties were repellent and, at bottom, remarkably alike. Hobbes had advanced a theory which banished God from the universe and left it a mere movement of atoms, and the Puritans had separated the world of grace and the world of nature so irrevocably that they, too, were left in a universe without any evidences of its Maker. Moreover, both had debased man to a level of total depravity: for Hobbes the life of the natural man was "nasty, brutish and short", and for the Puritans the *imago Dei* in man was so defaced that he was hopelessly corrupt. On both accounts man's only motive was self-interest and morality merely a matter of expediency. In the one case, man looked for his reward on earth, in the other, in heaven; but either way, duty was submerged in hedonism.

Shaftesbury's answer to Hobbes and the Puritans must be seen against the background of the controversies we glanced at in the first chapter. The questions he attempted to answer and the form in which they presented themselves were the result of discussions started in the previous century. The dispute between Hobbes and the Platonists may be formulated, in fact, in the following three questions. (1) Is the physical world around us related to another order of reality, and if so, what is the nature of this relation? (2) Are moral judgments the product of the reason or the feelings? (3) Is the human mind active or passive in perception, in morality and in artistic creation? Shaftesbury's answer to the second of these questions is the best known part of his philosophy, though its bearing on aesthetics has not been fully recognized. Of equal, or greater importance to aesthetics, however, are his views on the nature of the universe and his discussion of the mental processes involved in moral and aesthetic experience. We shall discuss in turn, then, his cosmology, his theory of morals and his psychology.

II

Shaftesbury's Cosmology

The view of nature which had become the generally accepted one by the end of the seventeenth century was based on the analogy of the machine. Mechanism as an interpretation of reality was undoubtedly the result of the development of scientific thinking. As the late R. G. Collingwood wrote in his book *The Idea of Nature*, in contrasting this view with the Greek one,

"The printing-press and the windmill, the lever, the pump, and the pulley, the clock and the wheelbarrow, and a host of machines in use among miners and engineers were established features of daily life. Everyone understood the nature of a machine, and the experience of making and using such things had become part of the general consciousness of European man. It was an easy step to the proposition: as a clockmaker or millwright is to a clock or mill, so is God to Nature."[1]

We have seen in the first chapter how such a view reacted on literature and theology and how both poets and theologians were reluctant to adopt it. But the issue was one they could hardly avoid.

[1] *The Idea of Nature*, O.U.P., 1945, pp. 8-9.

The Cartesian dualism had separated mind and matter in such a way that some account had to be given of the relation between them. The problem was met with not only in the question of how God is related to this world, but also in terms of the individual, in the question of how body and mind could be connected.

Shaftesbury was not directly interested in the metaphysical question, but he realized that the account of nature which had been based on the machine analogy was disastrous to morals and art, and so he attempted to elaborate his own theory of nature. The work in which he did this was *The Moralists*. *The Moralists, A philosophical Rhapsody*, is a dialogue in the Platonic manner, where truth is pursued in a series of discussions between Philocles, Theocles and one or two minor characters. Broadly speaking, it is an essay expounding the philosophy of Optimism, and Leibnitz, whose own *Theodicée* appeared in the following year, 1710, declared that it anticipated most of his own theories.

The style in which Shaftesbury wrote *The Moralists*, as the title would suggest, is a rhapsodical one. In prose which comes near to being poetry, Theocles (who represents Shaftesbury) apostrophizes nature in a series of hymns of a most romantic sort. In visionary terms and in an almost Wordsworthian way, he addresses nature as the dwelling place of a spiritual power and the language in the third part of the dialogue becomes so lyrical that it offended Horace Walpole's sensibilities.

"He delivers his doctrines," wrote Walpole in *Royal and Noble Authors*, "in ecstatic diction, like one of the Magi inculcating philosophic visions to an eastern auditory!"

Pope, too, who was not above adopting Shaftesbury's philosophy in other places, wrote scathingly of the picture of nature,

"Which Theocles in raptur'd vision saw,
While thro' poetic scenes the Genius roves,
Or wanders wild in Academic Groves."
(*Dunciad*, IV, 488–90.)

Briefly, the story of *The Moralists* is the conversion of Philocles (the sceptic) to theism by Theocles (the philosopher). The whole dialogue is related by Philocles in a letter to his friend, Palemon, who had learned of his conversion with some surprise. The setting is Theocles' country seat. On the first day Philocles and Theocles are joined by two other visitors; one an old gentleman who is a narrowly religious bigot, and the other a younger man of more moderate opinions. The conversation turns to a discussion of atheism and the old gentleman works himself into a passion of hatred against all atheists. Philocles and Theocles are agreed, however, that a fair and rational hearing must be given to those who advance atheism. They refer to Cudworth and the author of the *Inquiry Concerning Virtue* (Shaftesbury himself), who had been branded as atheists themselves simply because they had been fair-minded. Theocles declares himself a friend of the author of the *Inquiry* and asserts that its principles are thoroughly in accordance with religion. The *Inquiry*, however, had been confined to morality in its narrow sense and had not concerned itself with any religious sanctions. Theocles now proposes to advance a system of natural theology which he knows will be agreeable to the author of the *Inquiry*.

The conversations that follow this are of the kind familiar to readers acquainted with the deistical writings of the time. The old religious gentleman seems to think that miracles, ghosts, apparitions and anything which appears to contravene the law of causation are a proof of the existence of God, but Philocles bases his argument for the existence of God on the order and regularity of the laws of nature. Without such laws the universe would be a chaos of atoms showing no purpose, whereas it is in the design of the universe that we see evidence for the Supreme Mind at work. There is nothing unusual about any of this and the discussion is meant chiefly to clear the ground of what are considered to be the false arguments which had been advanced for the reasonableness of Christianity. Theocles, in the course of it, attempts also to vindicate the *Inquiry Concerning Virtue*, by declaring that morality needs no recourse to a theory of rewards and punishments in an after life.

> "But as many as are the difficulties which Virtue has to encounter in this world, her force is yet superior. Exposed as she is here, she is not however abandoned or left miserable. She has enough to raise her above pity, though not above our wishes, and as happy as we see her here, we have room for further hopes in her behalf. Her present portion is sufficient to show Providence already engaged on her side." (*Characteristics*, II, 58.)

Theocles advances his positive beliefs about religion at the end of the day, when he answers some of the objections put forward by

Philocles, and even more at the beginning of the next day, when the other guests have departed. Philocles follows his host out of the house; it is just dawn and Theocles has walked into the surrounding fields for his morning meditations. There then follows the remarkable passage in which Theocles gives Philocles some account of his faith. The discussion between them oscillates between philosophical argument and poetic rhapsody and it is clear that Theocles bases his final convictions on presuppositions which he does not argue. This is not to say that his position is unreasonable, but that reason, having taken him so far, must give place to belief. This is necessary if all his other logically demonstrated opinions are to fit together into one system. He avoids the metaphysical controversy of the relation between mind and matter, but echoing the Cartesian element he found in the Cambridge Platonists, asserts his belief in the primacy of thought. He pins his faith to the intuitive apprehension of the universal mind by the individual mind; an experience which cannot be explained away by Hobbesian argument.

"In vain we try to fathom the abyss of space, the seat of thy extensive being, of which no place is empty, no void which is not full.

In vain we labour to understand that principle of sense and thought, which seeming in us to depend so much on motion, yet differs so much from it and from matter itself as not to suffer us to conceive how thought can more result from this than this arise from thought. But thought we own pre-eminent, and confess the realest of beings, the only existence of which we are made sure by being conscious. All else may be only dream and shadow. All which even sense suggests may be deceitful. The sense itself remains still; reason subsists, and thought maintains its eldership of being. Thus are we in a manner conscious of that original and eternally existent thought whence we derive our own. And thus the assurance we have of the existence of beings above our sense and of thee (the great exemplar of thy works) comes from thee, the all true and perfect, who hast thus communicated thyself more immediately to us, so as in some manner to inhabit within our souls, thou who are art original soul, diffusive, vital in all, inspiriting the whole.

All Nature's wonders serve to excite and perfect this idea of their author. 'Tis here he suffers us to see and even converse with him in a manner suitable to our frailty. How glorious is it to contemplate him in this noblest of his works apparent to us, the system of the bigger world!" (*ibid.*, II, 111–112.)

Even this amount of philosophizing, however, is distasteful to the sceptical Philocles and he welcomes the transition Theocles makes to a consideration of the works of nature.

> "Here I must own, 'twas no small comfort to me to find that, as our meditation turned, we were likely to get clear of an entangling abstruse philosophy. I was in hope Theocles, as he proceeded, might stick close to Nature, since he was now come upon the borders of our world." (*ibid.*, II, 112.)

Shaftesbury's problem in dealing with nature was to find some alternative to the mechanistic account which had become so dominant in the previous century and which, he considered, made nonsense of morality and the arts. As mechanism was based on an analogy between nature and the machine, so his own account is an analogical one. In the first place, he goes back to the analogy which he found in Greek thought (and in particular in Xenophon's *Memorabilia*) and compares nature with the human body. As in the human organism the mind animates the body, so in nature there is a spirit diffused through all things which governs natural phenomena. It is mind which governs the body, not body which governs or gives rise to mind. This is true both of the individual organism and of the whole of nature for Shaftesbury; the human organism is a reflection of the larger, outside world.

> "For my own share," says Theocles, "(thank Providence), I have a mind in my possession which serves, such as it is, to keep my body and its affections, my passions, appetites, imaginations, fancies, and the rest in tolerable harmony and order. But the order of the universe, I am persuaded still, is much the better of the two. Let Epicurus, if he please, think his the better and, believing no genius or wisdom above his own, inform us by what chance 'twas dealt him, and how atoms came to be so wise." (*ibid.*, II, 105.)

It is partly this doctrine which has led to Shaftesbury's being called a pantheist. He is not a pantheist in the strict sense, for he never identifies God and nature, but if this mind of the universe is the same as God, then certainly he would seem to stress the immanence rather than the transcendence of God. It is doubtful, however, whether Shaftesbury believes that this mind in nature is identical with God. It often seems as though he regarded it as a subordinate principle working at God's command. That the analogy of the human body-mind relationship is not to be pressed too far is seen from the other element in his theory of nature. This is derived from yet another analogy which is implicit in his whole philosophy; the time-honoured analogy in Christian thought of God as the supreme artist. He sees the relationship between God and His world as the sort of relationship which obtains between the artist and a work of art; this is what Shaftesbury substitutes for the mechanical explanation of nature.

The success of the mechanical account of nature lay in the fact that scientists and philosophers used it as a framework within which they could elaborate theories that led to a mastery of nature. The analogy of the machine formed the basis of a system of thought which brought immediate and, indeed, tremendous practical achievements. The analogy of the world as a work of art could claim no such success, and perhaps for this reason we have overlooked the importance which it once had for aesthetics and literary criticism. Mechanism could give the arts no justification and could provide the artist with little satisfaction in what he was doing, but here in Shaftesbury's writings was an alternative which at once gave significance to art and, indeed, raised it to the level of divine activity itself. As an alternative it may have had no widespread popularity and was perhaps unable to put up more than a losing fight against the influence of mechanism, but at any rate it provided art with a philosophical basis and, as we shall see, in due course gave birth to forces that were to deliver criticism from the bondage of eighteenth-century empiricism.

The first and obvious result of Shaftesbury's view of nature, so far as aesthetics is concerned, is that nature was no longer regarded as something to be exploited and utilized; not something merely to be manipulated for man's benefit, but an object to be contemplated for its own sake. Beauty, in fact, was seen to be distinct from utility; something in its own right, which gives pleasure of a special and aesthetic kind. The artist was felt to be akin to God, working in the same way, even if on a lower plane; and nature was to be regarded as a work of art, giving us on a larger scale the kind of aesthetic pleasure we get in contemplating a human work of art. Furthermore, if art were to be an imitation of nature, it could not just be the mechanical copying of natural phenomena, but had to be an imitation of the whole creative process going on in nature. Art, in other words, was rightly comprehended as creation, not mechanical construction. In this underlying analogy between nature and art are to be found many of the main elements of Shaftesbury's contribution to aesthetics and literary criticism, which form the subject of later chapters.

Having rescued nature from the mechanists, Shaftesbury developed his theory along neo-Platonic lines. The natural world, if, indeed, it were a work of art, could now be viewed as symbolical of a world lying behind sense appearances, just as a poem expresses imperfectly the incommunicable conception which exists in the poet's mind. God is the great artist and this world is the imperfect manifestation of what exists in a perfect form only in His mind. Shaftesbury comes very near at this point to the doctrine that matter itself is the source of evil or imperfection, which limits even God's will. This is not his intention, however, for early in *The Moralists* Theocles argues against such a theory. To ascribe evil to the operation of a subordinate yet rebellious principle in nature, says Theocles, is only to push the argument one stage back, as the ancients did in the myth of Prometheus.

"For the Gods . . . either could have hindered Prometheus's creation or they could not. If they could, they were answerable for the consequences; if they could not, they were no longer Gods, being thus limited and controlled. And whether Prometheus were a name for chance, destiny, a plastic nature, or an evil daemon, whatever was designed by it, 'twas still the same breach of omnipotence." (*ibid.*, II, 16.)

The world is not an imperfect expression of the ideas in God's mind, in the sense that it is a thwarted expression of these ideas, but rather consists of a particularized and symbolical manifestation of a reality which transcends being.

"No wonder, replied he [Theocles], if we are at a loss when we pursue the shadow for the substance. For if we may trust to what our reasoning has taught us, whatever in Nature is beautiful or charming is only the faint shadow of that first beauty. So that every real love depending on the mind, and being only the contemplation of beauty either as it really is in itself or as it appears imperfectly in the objects which strike the sense, how can the rational mind rest here, or be satisfied with the absurd enjoyment which reaches the sense alone?" (*ibid.*, II, 126.)

The same holds good of the work of art created by the human artist; for though the sensible expression of the poet's conception may be beautiful, it loses something of that original beauty which can never pass beyond the bounds of the mind that created it. Real and intrinsic beauty lies in the forming power of the mind itself and all that we can apprehend in a work of art comes from the imprint of the creative mind on the raw material. As Coleridge expressed it in his *Dejection, An Ode*:

> "And would we aught behold of higher Worth,
> Than that inanimate cold world allow'd
> To the poor, loveless, ever-anxious crowd;
> Ah! from the soul itself must issue forth
> A light, a glory, a fair luminous cloud,
>   Enveloping the earth!
> And from the soul itself must there be sent
> A sweet and powerful voice, of its own birth,
> Of all sweet sounds the life and element!"

Mind can communicate certain aspects of its own experience to other minds only by the sensible objects of artistic creation. Not only is this so, but there is a sense in which mind apprehends itself in contemplating beauty. For all minds are related to the one supreme and universal Mind and the finite mind, in contemplating beauty, becomes aware of the Mind of God, the author and ground of its own being, just as all rivers finally return to the sea whence they came. This is the culmination of Theocles's argument with Philocles.

> "... it should appear from our strict search that there is nothing so divine as beauty, which belonging not to body, nor having any principle or existence except in mind and reason, is alone discovered and acquired by this diviner part, when it inspects itself, the only object worthy of itself. For whatever is void of mind, is void and darkness to the mind's eye. This languishes and grows dim whenever detained on foreign subjects, but thrives and attains its natural vigour when employed in contemplation of what is like itself." (*ibid.*, II, 144.)

Shaftesbury distinguishes three orders in a hierarchy of beauty. In the first place, there are inanimate forms, which receive their beauty from the creative power, either of the minds of men, or the supreme Mind operating in nature: these consist of works of art and natural objects. In the second place, there are animate creatures, who can not only propagate their own species, but fashion these inanimate forms. But these animate forms receive their creative power from a forming power above them, which is the third and highest order, the source of all beauty, which is the Mind of God.

"Do you not see then, replied Theocles, that you have established three degrees or orders of beauty? As how? Why first, the dead forms, as you properly have called them, which bear a fashion, and are formed, whether by man or Nature, but have no forming power, no action, or intelligence. Right. Next, and as the second kind, the forms which form, that is, which have intelligence, action, and operation. Right still. . . . And here you have unawares discovered that third order of beauty, which forms not only such as we call mere forms but even the forms which form. For we ourselves are notable architects in matter, and can show lifeless bodies brought into form, and fashioned by our own hands, but that which fashions even minds themselves, contains in itself all the beauties fashioned by those minds, and is consequently the principle, source and fountain of all beauty." (*ibid.*, II, 132–3.)

Shaftesbury's explanation of evil is also bound up with his analogy between the world and a work of art. Shaftesbury's philosophy is an optimistic one which denies the ultimate and independent existence of evil. For him the universe is a harmony in which all the parts subserve a totality which is good. God is characterized by a universal benevolence, which can be seen in the order and government of the world; for this world is not a conglomeration of meaningless elements; it is a planned unity.

"All things in this world are united. For as the branch is united with the tree, so is the tree as immediately with the earth, air, and water, which feed it. As much as the fertile mould is fitted to the tree, as much as the strong and upright trunk of the oak or elm is fitted to the twining branches of the vine or ivy; so much are the very leaves, the seeds, and fruits of these trees fitted to the various animals; those again to one another, and to the elements where they live, and to which they are, as appendices, in a manner fitted and joined, as either by wings for the air, fins for the water, feet for the earth, and by other correspondent inward parts of a more curious frame and texture. Thus in contemplating all on earth, we must of necessity view all in one, as holding to one common stock. Thus too in the system of the bigger world. See there the mutual dependency of things! the relation of one to another, of the sun to this inhabited earth, and of the earth and other planets to the sun! the order, union, and coherence of the whole! and know, my ingenious friend, that by this survey you will be obliged to own the universal system and coherent scheme of things to be established on abundant proof, capable of convincing any fair and just contemplator of the works of Nature." (*ibid.*, II, 64-5.)

The "fair and just contemplator", in answer to such an assertion, might, of course, put forward the fact of evil. If the world is such a harmoniously arranged system based on universal good, how is it that righteous men suffer and wickedness is seen everywhere? Shaftesbury's answer to this is that evil is only apparent: what appears to be evil is something which subserves a more ultimate good. Man's suffering and the power of acting wickedly, which is given by his freedom of will, are only evils which form part of a more comprehensive good. Evil, in the final account of reality, is merely negative; it has no ultimate existence and seems real only because it appears as a feature of experience at lower levels of existence. Shaftesbury is not saying that the experience of evil is itself something illusory, a figment of the imagination; his concern for the improvement of men's morals is sufficient indication of this. What he is saying is that ultimately it has no place in the structure of reality; that the things we call evil appear to be so only because of our partial and limited view of things. Evil can be predicated of part of the universe but not of the whole.

"Therefore if any being be wholly and really ill, it must be ill with respect to the universal system, and then the system of the universe is ill or imperfect. ... So that we cannot say of any being that it is wholly and absolutely ill, unless we can positively show and ascertain that what we call ill is nowhere good besides, in any other system, or with respect to any other order or economy whatsoever." (*ibid.*, I, 246.)

He makes use here again of the analogy with the work of art, for, says Shaftesbury, the partial evils we see by our limited apprehension are like the darkness in a painting, or the dissonances in a piece of music. They provide an element which in a final reckoning brings about a greater and less superficial harmony. Virtue would never develop and have a testing ground without the conflict with evil.

"Where," we are asked, without this, "had the virtues had their theatre or whence their names?"

Similarly, in our apprehension of the world, it is

"from this order of inferior and superior things that we admire the world's beauty, founded thus on contrarieties, whilst from such various and disagreeing principles a universal concord is established." (*ibid.*, II, 22.)

What we think are evils, or flaws, are a necessary part of a more comprehensive pattern which embraces everything, just as

"in painting there are shades and masterly strokes which the vulgar understand not, but find fault with; in architecture there is the rustic; in music the chromatic kind, and skilful mixture of dissonances." (*ibid.*, II, 130.)

Pope summed up the doctrine admirably in the *Essay on Man*:

"All nature is but art, unknown to thee;
All chance, direction which thou canst not see;
All discord, harmony not understood;
All partial evil, universal good." (*Epistle I*, 289-92.)

The whole argument is an interesting example of the way in which literature and philosophy were related at this time. It had always been a principle in literary criticism from Aristotle onwards, that flaws in a work of art could be forgiven for the sake of the excellence of the whole. Horace made the same point and it was a cardinal element in the criticism of Longinus. Boileau's translation of the treatise *On the Sublime*, in 1674, may have helped to popularize this principle again at the end of the seventeenth century, for it is to be found in Rapin's *Réflexions sur la Poétique*, in Dryden's *Essay of Dramatic Poesy* and in most of the writers of the School of Taste in England; but it was the optimistic philosophy of the period which gave it a new sanction, a metaphysical status that secured its place in critical theory.

Instead of faults being forgiven for the sake of the whole, the theory now became a belief that what at first sight may appear faults may be a *necessary* part of a total harmony. Instead of being a matter of mere critical practice it was transformed into a principle of aesthetics and provided with a metaphysical backing. Not that the application of an optimistic world-view to aesthetics was entirely novel. Bosanquet in his *History of Aesthetic* attributes something of the kind to St. Augustine and a hint of the same thing is to be found in the *Meditations* of Marcus Aurelius, which Shaftesbury knew so intimately. But it was undoubtedly given a new life at the beginning of the eighteenth century and was henceforward to prove a great liberalizing factor in criticism. Dennis, in his *Epistle Dedicatory to the Advancement and Reformation of Modern Poetry* (1701), was one of the critics who saw that their critical instincts had been confirmed by contemporary philosophy.

"But as in some of the numerous parts that constitute this beauteous all," he writes, "there are some appearing irregularities, which parts notwithstanding contribute with the rest to complete the Harmony of universal Nature; and as there are some seeming irregularities even . . . purposely appointed by Divine Foreknowledge for the carrying on the Profound Design of Providence; so if we may compare great things with small, in the creation of the accomplish'd Poem, some things at first sight may be seemingly against Reason, which yet at the bottom are perfectly regular, because they are indispensably necessary to the admirable conduct of a great and just Design."

Pope, as we saw, regarded nature as a work of art and he is another to make the same parallel.

"In prospects thus, some objects please our eyes,
Which out of nature's common order rise,
The shapeless rock, or hanging precipice.
Great wits sometimes may gloriously offend,
And rise to faults true Critics dare not mend."
(*Essay on Criticism*, 156–160).

The optimistic view of nature was of importance to the poet as well as the critic, for if all parts of nature are equally parts of the total harmony, then surely we are wrong to select particular features only for our admiration. All nature should be an object of contemplation and all its features a source of aesthetic delight. Here we see the beginnings of an attitude that could appreciate the awful, the rugged and the horrible aspects of nature as well as the more gentle and traditionally admired ones. It is no accident that historically there now began that rehabilitation of nature which brought with it the admiration of mountain scenery and the sterner aspects of the earth's surface. We can see here the opening out of that pathway which was to lead public taste away from the formal delights of Vauxhall and bring it to the romantic appeal of Lakeland. There were those in the late seventeenth century who may have thought of nature as a machine, but a century later their descendants were to see it as the abode of a spirit

> "Whose dwelling is the light of setting suns,
> And the round ocean and the living air,
> And the blue sky, and in the mind of man."

The doctrine of Optimism gives a clue to why the change came about, but this is a story which must be left to later chapters.

III

Shaftesbury's Theory of Morals

Shaftesbury's theory of morals is given fullest expression in his *Inquiry Concerning Virtue and Merit*, which was published first in 1699, but later as part of the *Characteristics*. His whole philosophy is concerned very closely with ethics, but it is in the *Inquiry* that we have his most systematic account of the subject. Here again it is not always easy to obtain a consistent and comprehensive view of his beliefs, but the following is a summary of what would appear to be his theory of morals, especially as it is related to aesthetics.

Virtue, for Shaftesbury, consists in the well-balanced personality which reflects inwardly the harmony and order of the outside world. The virtuous character is one in which all the elements are in accord with each other. Harmony is the key idea of his moral theory. Even benevolence can become a vice if it is out of proportion to our other motives.

> "But it may be necessary to remark, that even as to kindness and love of the most natural sort (such as that of any creature for its offspring) if it be immoderate and beyond a certain degree it is undoubtedly vicious. For thus over-great tenderness destroys the effect of love, and excessive pity renders us incapable of giving succour." (*Characteristics*, I, 250.)

This internal order is a part of the larger order which, according to Shaftesbury, constitutes the universe. By regulating his passions the virtuous man attunes himself to the harmony of the larger system; becomes part of the scheme of things instead of setting himself at odds against it.

Good, in fact, can be referred only to the whole scheme of things. We cannot say of anything that it is good or bad in itself, without knowing whether it is part of a larger whole which may transcend its goodness or badness and, on a final assessment, alter its nature.

> "Therefore if any being be wholly and really ill, it must be ill with respect to the universal system; and then the system of the universe is ill or imperfect. But if the ill of one private system be the good of others; if it makes still to the good of the general system (as when one creature lives by the destruction of another; one thing is generated from the corruption of another; or one planetary system or vortex may swallow up another), then is the ill of that private system no real ill in itself, any more than the pain of breeding teeth is ill in a system or body which is so constituted that, without this occasion of pain, it would suffer worse by being defective." (*ibid.*, I, 246.)

Everything, as we saw when considering *The Moralists*, has its own particular place in the universe and is organized in a great chain of being, which stretches from the meanest of creatures up to God. The cruelties of the animal creation may appear as evils, but are necessary if higher forms of life are to be preserved. The existence of the spider, for instance, is dependent upon the fly, whose "needless flight, weak frame, and tender," make him the natural prey of the spider. Shaftesbury concludes that

> "there is a system of all animals: an animal-order or economy, according to which the animal affairs are regulated and disposed." (*ibid.*, I, 245–6.)

But this 'animal-order' is only a part of the whole scheme; it forms merely the lower rungs of a ladder which stretches right up, through human kind, to the highest forms of existence.

The virtuous man, in being virtuous, is most really himself and acting in accordance with his own nature. He is a man in the fullest sense of the word and thereby plays his part in this all-embracing system of the universe. It follows that the individual's good is identical with the good of the whole. Such a belief can, of course, lead to the comfortable theory that the individual, in pursuing his own ends, is promoting the good of the community, but this is a superficial reading of Shaftesbury's theory. Shaftesbury would not say that to pursue one's own happiness is to be virtuous. Rather, he would say that to be virtuous is to bring happiness and that being virtuous is the only true and lasting kind of happiness. Even Pope, in his ready optimism at the conclusion of the *Essay on Man*, continues the phrase,

> SELF-LOVE and SOCIAL are the same,

with the couplet which declares,

> That VIRTUE only makes our Bliss below;
> And all our Knowledge is, OURSELVES TO KNOW.

Shaftesbury's position is best seen in the proposition he sets out to demonstrate:

> " 'That to have the natural, kindly, or generous affections strong and powerful towards the good of the public, is to have the chief means and power of self-enjoyment'; and 'that to want them, is certain misery and ill.' " (*ibid*, I, 292.)

And he sums up his argument in the final sentence of the *Inquiry*,

> "And thus virtue is the good, and vice the ill of every one."

Shaftesbury's picture of the virtuous personality, as one in which all the elements are balanced and harmonized, inevitably suggests an analogy with a work of art. His argument throughout is framed in language derived from music, but it would equally well suggest a parallel with painting or literature. This is no accident, for he quite explicitly identifies beauty with goodness: the virtuous character is also the beautiful character, and the good action is one which displays symmetry and form both intrinsically and in relation to the whole scheme of things. Shaftesbury's optimistic theory also implies degrees of beauty as well as of goodness. The perception of sensible objects may give us a feeling of beauty which is pleasurable and good in itself, but the beauty of sensible objects is not as great as that of actions, sentiments and characters.

"Nothing affects the heart like that which is purely from itself, and of its own nature; such as the beauty of sentiments, the grace of actions, the turn of characters, and the proportions and features of a human mind." (*ibid.*, I, 90.)

The human mind will tire of mere sensory beauty and, as it develops, will wish to pass to spiritual or mental beauty.

"Coming therefore to a capacity of seeing and admiring in this new way, it must needs find a beauty and a deformity as well in actions, minds and tempers, as in figures, sounds or colours. If there be no real amiableness or deformity in moral acts, there is at least an imaginary one of full force." (*ibid*, I, 260.)

So far we have been concerned with Shaftesbury's conception of the good character and have said nothing of his moral theory as it affects actions. Shaftesbury's argument so far has really been concerned with what he considers a matter of fact. For him, it is a fact that if we do good we shall achieve our own happiness and the happiness of our fellows. It would be wrong, however, to assume that he makes the production of happiness a definition, though it may be a criterion, of goodness. Happiness will result from, but must not be the motive of, our being virtuous. In the *Advice to An Author* he makes the very true psychological observation that if we consciously act from the motive of desiring pleasure, we shall rarely get it.

"I shall be weary of my pursuit, and, upon experience, find little pleasure in the main, if my choice and judgment in it be from no other rule than that single one, because I please." (*ibid*, I, 218.)

Shaftesbury regards the conception of obligation as an *a priori* one and he disagrees with those who would try to infer it from experience. Those he chiefly censures are the hedonists, who endeavour to resolve obligation into self-interest. He dislikes equally the disciples of Hobbes and the extreme Puritans and condemns them for the same reason: both transform morality into a 'calculating hedonism.' The Puritans assessed pleasure in terms of a heavenly reward, while Hobbes measured it in terms of a material one. In a passage in the *Freedom of Wit and Humour*, he argues against the assertion of Hobbes that obligation is the result of a contract which brought man out of a state of nature into society. Obligation, he contends, existed prior to any such contract and must, in fact, have been the basis of such a contract.

> " 'Tis ridiculous to say there is any obligation on man to act sociably or honestly in a formed government, and not in that which is commonly called the state of nature . . . that which could make a promise obligatory in the state of nature, must make all other acts of humanity as much our real duty and natural part. Thus faith, justice, honesty and virtue, must have been as early as the state of nature, or they could never have been at all." (*ibid.*, I, 73.)

Hobbes's account of morality was an elaborate attempt to explain it in terms of something else, whereas Shaftesbury was convinced that

> "If the love of doing good be not, of itself, a good and right inclination, I know not how there can possibly be such a thing as goodness or virtue." (*ibid.*, I, 66.)

Equally detestable to Shaftesbury was the belief of certain religious people that man acts virtuously only because he expects a reward in heaven and is afraid of punishment in an after life if he does wrong. This was just as much a perversion of morality and constituted a blasphemy against God.

> "If . . . there be a belief or conception of a Deity, who is considered only as powerful over his creature, and enforcing obedience to his absolute will by particular rewards and punishments; and if on this account, through hope merely of reward, or fear of punishment, the creature be incited to do the good he hates, or restrained from doing the ill to which he is not otherwise in the least degree averse. . . . There is no more of rectitude, piety, or sanctity in a creature thus reformed, than there is meekness or gentleness in a tiger strongly chained, or innocence and sobriety in a monkey under the discipline of the whip."   (*ibid.*, I, 267.)

With this idea of morality there was often coupled a definition of goodness in terms of the divine will; good, on this view, was what God ordained. Shaftesbury disagrees very profoundly with such a doctrine. For him moral obligation is as much prior to the will of God as it is to any social contract; it is not the case that what God ordains is good, but rather must we believe that God ordains what is good. There is a moral law which governs God's actions as much as men's; if it were not so, good would be merely arbitrary. It is on this point that Shaftesbury disagrees so radically with his own tutor, Locke.

His reverence for Locke was great and sincere and he always acknowledged quite frankly the debt he owed to Locke's instruction. In writing to Michael Ainsworth he freely admits that:

"No one has done more towards the recalling of philosophy from barbarity, into use and practice of the world, and into the company of the better and politer sort; who might well be ashamed of it in its other dress. No one has opened a better or clearer way to reasoning."[1]

He was well aware, however, that there were profound differences between his own and Locke's philosophy. Though these were rarely expressed in his published works, in his letters he describes the grounds of this disagreement. On the particular question of the basis of morality, he writes to Ainsworth in a later letter of 3rd June, 1709,

"Thus virtue, according to Mr. Locke, has no other measure, law or rule, than *fashion* and *custom*: morality, justice, equity, depend only on *law* and *will*: and God indeed is a perfect *free agent* in his sense; that is, *free to any thing, that is however ill*; for if he wills it, it will be made good; virtue may be vice, and vice virtue in its turn, if he pleases. And thus neither *right* nor *wrong*, *virtue* nor vice are anything in themselves; nor is there any trace or idea of them *naturally imprinted* on human minds." (*op. cit.*)

He is making the same point but is careful to avoid direct reference to Locke, when he writes in the *Inquiry*:

"If the mere will, decree, or law of God be said absolutely to constitute right and wrong, then are these latter words of no significancy at all." (*Characteristics*, I, 264.)

Shaftesbury does not wish to separate morals and religion entirely; he is aware that one's beliefs affect one's conduct and is convinced that morality must be rooted in religion. What he wishes to preserve is the idea that the sense of obligation is *sui generis* and cannot

[1] Letter of 24th February, 1706, *Letters by a Noble Lord to a Young Man at the University*, 1716.

be inferred from, or explained away in terms of, something else.

"Nor does the fear of hell or a thousand terrors of the Deity imply conscience, unless where there is an apprehension of what is wrong, odious, morally deformed, and ill-deserving. And where this is the case, there conscience must have effect, and punishment of necessity be apprehended, even though it be not expressly threatened.
And thus religious conscience supposes moral or natural conscience. And though the former be understood to carry with it the fear of divine punishment, it has its force however from the apprehended moral deformity and odiousness of any act with respect purely to the Divine Presence, and the natural veneration due to such a supposed being. For in such a presence the shame of villainy or vice must have its force, independently on that further apprehension of the magisterial capacity of such a being, and his dispensation of particular rewards or punishments in a future state." (*ibid.*, I, 305–6.)

It is such a view of the relation between religion and morality which causes him, when writing to a friend in December 1704, to speak so caustically of Locke's well-known farewell letter to Anthony Collins. Shortly before his death Locke had expressed to Collins his belief that "this life is a scene of vanity, that soon passes away, and affords no solid satisfaction but in the consciousness of doing well, and in hopes of another life." Shaftesbury's somewhat severe criticism of these sentiments when it later became known, was always used as an occasion of attack upon him. But the attacks were ill-merited, for Shaftesbury's comments spring from a philosophical disagreement and are in no way personal abuse. He tells his friend that he hopes he will meet his own death with greater philosophical detachment.

"Thank heaven I can do good and find heaven in it. I know nothing else that is heavenly. And if this disposition fits me not for heaven, I desire never to be fitted for it, nor come into the place. I ask no reward from heaven for that which is reward itself. Let my being be continued or discontinued, as in the main is best. The author of it best knows, and I trust Him with it." (Rand, *Life, Letters and Philosophical Regimen*, 347.)

There remains one further point in Shaftesbury's discussion of moral theory which has a direct importance for aesthetics; the question of which faculty makes moral judgments. Shaftesbury's answer to this question forms his most famous contribution to ethics. According to him, the judgment whether an action is right or wrong is made by the 'moral sense'. Shaftesbury uses this phrase in the *Inquiry* and since his time it has become a well-known and familiar term. His use of the phrase seems to spring from a desire to free the faculty of moral judgment from both the reason and the feelings. We have already seen that he will not accept mere liking or feeling as the arbiter of our actions, but he also wants to clear the faculty of moral judgment from any identification with reasoning. He believes it to be a faculty which apprehends the rightness or wrongness of actions immediately, without recourse to reasoning, and that this is as true of beauty as of goodness.

> "The case is the same in the mental or moral subjects as in the ordinary bodies or common subjects of sense. The shapes, motions, colours, and proportions of these latter being presented to our eye, there necessarily results a beauty or deformity, according to the different measure, arrangement, and disposition of their several parts. So in behaviour and actions, when presented to our understanding, there must be found, of necessity, an apparent difference, according to the regularity or irregularity of the subjects." (*Characteristics*, I, 251.)

To make his meaning clear Shaftesbury gives an actual example of how moral consciousness works.

> "A man who in a passion happens to kill his companion, relents immediately on the sight of what he has done, his revenge is changed into pity, and his hatred turned against himself. And this merely by the power of the object." (*ibid.*, I, 306–7.)

The use of the phrase 'moral sense' does not betoken a wish to set up a separate faculty, but simply a desire to describe accurately the nature of the moral judgment. His theory is a form of intuitionism that emphasizes the immediacy of such judgments. At times he seems to suggest that it is the reason which is the faculty and this is in keeping with the rest of his theory; for what he objects to is the idea that we make moral judgments by a process of *reasoning*. The term 'moral sense' gets rid of this suggestion, but if 'reason' could be freed of such an association then he would probably accept its use. 'Reasoning' implies a process by which we desire an object and then decide by ratiocination the best means of achieving it. Hobbes had identified 'reason' with 'reasoning' and perhaps because of this Shaftesbury chooses another term to avoid such ambiguity. On those occasions when he speaks of the faculty of moral judgment as reason, it is always in a way that shows he means by it an act of direct and intuitive apprehension.

> "Let us suppose a creature who, wanting reason and being unable to reflect, has notwithstanding many good qualities and affections, as love to his kind, courage, gratitude, or pity. 'Tis certain that if you give to this creature a reflecting faculty, it will at the same instant approve of gratitude, kindness, and pity; be taken with any show or representation of the social passion, and think nothing more amiable than this, or more odious than the contrary. And this is to be capable of virtue, and to have a sense of right and wrong." (*ibid.*, I, 266.)

The doctrine of a special sense which perceives the beautiful and the good, whether it be merely an attempt to emphasize the spontaneity and intuitive nature of such apprehension or not, is one that is particularly useful in aesthetics. In fact, its importance is probably greater in this field than in that of ethics, for it witnesses, as we shall see later, to features which are perhaps even more a part of aesthetic than moral experience.

IV

Shaftesbury's Psychology

Shaftesbury's psychological observations form part of his argument for an *a priori* theory of morals, but they are of equal importance to aesthetics. In psychology, as in morals, his chief antagonists were the Calvinists and Hobbists. Just as in dealing with nature they had driven God out of His universe, so in dealing with human nature they had driven Him out of His creation. The denigration of human personality by each party had been in different terms, but both were agreed that man's most fundamental motive was self-interest.

Shaftesbury's argument that there is an innate power of goodness as well as evil can be found in the Preface to his edition of Whichcote's *Sermons*, where he has in mind chiefly the Calvinists; but in the *Freedom of Wit and Humour* he turns to the Hobbesian account of human nature and writes ironically:

"The studiers of this mechanism must have a very partial eye to overlook all other motions besides those of the lowest and narrowest compass." (*ibid.*, I, 77.)

His quarrel with Hobbes was the more fundamental and protracted. Hobbes's doctrine had been bolstered up with a hedonistic empiricism which declared that morality can be deduced from experience. According to him we should recognize that to behave well is simply a matter of our own advantage and there is no such thing as an innate consciousness of obligation. To make matters worse, Locke himself had devoted a considerable part of his *Essay Concerning Human Understanding* to a denunciation of innate ideas. In his famous comparison of the human mind with a blank sheet of paper he had laid the foundations of his philosophy on the belief that the mind is passive in perception.

The problem of whether innate ideas exist or not is a vexed one in the history of philosophy and it is doubtful whether any one ever held a belief in innate ideas in the crude form that says we are born complete with ready-made ideas. This is not the real point. The question is whether the mind is only a passive recipient of sense knowledge, in which simple sense-data are combined by a process of association to provide us with our more complex ideas, or whether in some sense the mind is active in perception and an architect of its own knowledge. Shaftesbury's concern in this dispute was to rescue morality from a philosophy that reduced conduct to mere expediency. He never suggests that we are born with clear ideas of what actions are right or wrong, or that we are created with ready-made rules of behaviour clearly formulated within our minds as part of our mental heritage. He realizes that experience has to provide the materials and the occasions for moral judgments, but he is convinced that there exists a sense of obligation prior to and independent of experience.

This disagreement with Locke's "new way of ideas" constitutes the real ground of dissension between the two men. For Shaftesbury, Locke had played into the hands of the arch-enemy Hobbes. Certainly, Shaftesbury does not entertain the naive view that moral ideas exist complete at birth; this is a figure of straw which the empiricists had put up simply for the pleasure of knocking down again. In a letter to General Stanhope, dated 7th November, 1709, Shaftesbury explains his differences with Locke. He gives the reason, too, why these differences are never linked with Locke's name in his published writings.

"Thus have I ventured," he tells Stanhope, "to make you the greatest confidence in the world, which is that of my philosophy, even against my old tutor and governor, whose name is so established in the world, but with whom I ever concealed my differences as much as possible."

Most of the letter is taken up with this question of innate ideas which evidently had been raised by Stanhope. It is clear that his view is not the crude one attacked by Locke, but a more sophisticated theory that will stand up to the psychological probing of the empiricists.

"As for *innate principles* which you mention, it is, in my opinion, one of the childishest disputes that ever was. Well it is for our friend, Mr. Locke, and other modern philosophers of his sire, that they have so poor a spectre as the ghost of Aristotle to fight with. A ghost indeed! since it is not in reality the Stagyrite himself nor the original Peripatetic hypothesis, but the poor secondary tralatitious system of modern and barbarous schoolmen which is the subject of their continual triumph. Tom Hobbes, whom I must confess a genius, and even an original among these latter leaders in philosophy, had already gathered laurels enough, and at an easy rate, from this field." (*Rand*, 414).

In the letter to Michael Ainsworth which has already been quoted, he sets out his objection to Locke's theory of the mind at even greater length. The whole passage is of great interest for the light it throws on the relations between the two philosophers.

"Mr. Locke, as much as I honour him on account of other writings (viz. on government, policy, trade, coin, education, toleration, etc.) and as well as I knew him, and can answer for his sincerity as a most zealous *Christian* and believer, did however go in the self-same track [i.e. as Hobbes].... 'Twas Mr. Locke, that struck the home blow: for Mr. Hobbes's character and base slavish principles in government took off the poyson of his philosophy. 'Twas Mr. Locke that struck at all fundamentals, threw all *order* and *virtue* out of the world, and made the very *ideas* of these (which are the same as those of God) *unnatural*, and without foundation in our minds. *Innate* is a word he poorly plays upon: the right word, tho' less used, is *connatural*, for what has *birth* or *progress* of the *foetus* out of the womb to do in this case? the question is not about the *time* the ideas enter'd, or the moment that one body came out of the other: but whether the constitution of man be such, that sooner or later (no matter when) the idea and sense of *order, administration,* and a God will not infallibly, inevitably, necessarily spring up in him."

Shaftesbury was not alone in maintaining the creative nature of the mind in the face of the new empiricism. Cudworth and Norris, in particular, among the Cambridge Platonists had insisted that perception was a creative process which could not be explained in terms of simple sense-data combined by the laws of association. Shaftesbury is more concerned with morals than theory of knowledge and his chief purpose is to emphasize the *a priori* character of the sense of obligation. Perhaps respect for Locke forbade his dealing directly, and in his published work, with the question of how the human mind comes to have knowledge, for he never comes to issue with Locke on his own ground, or attempts to confute empiricism with a detailed account of precisely how the mind transforms sensation into perception. We should be mistaken, however, if we believed that he is content merely to uphold an *a priori* theory of morals. He believes the mind to be really creative and denies that knowledge can be derived only from sense experience. Moreover, in *The Moralists,* where he discusses the possibility of innate ideas at some length, he regards art as a creative process. Theocles introduces the discussion in these words:

". . . the mind conceiving of itself, can only be, as you say, assisted in the birth. Its pregnancy is from its nature. Nor could it ever have been thus impregnated by any other mind than that which formed it at the beginning; and which, as we have already proved, is original to all mental as well as other beauty." (*Characteristics,* II, 135.)

This picture of the mind is of the greatest importance to aesthetics and literary criticism and its implications for a theory of poetic imagination must be reserved for a later chapter.

CHAPTER IV

THE ANCIENTS AND MODERNS

> "As for any obligations they [i.e. the moderns] owed to the ancients, they renounced them all. It is true, said they, we are informed some few of our party have been so mean to borrow their subsistence from you; but the rest . . . our horses are of our own breeding, our arms of our forging, and our clothes of our own cutting and sewing. Plato was by chance up on the next shelf, and observing . . . their jades lean and foundered, their weapons of rotten wood, their armour rusty, and nothing but rags underneath; he laughed aloud, and in his pleasant way swore by ——, he believed them."
>
> (Swift: *The Battle of the Books*.)

I

BEFORE we consider Shaftesbury's contribution to critical theory it is necessary that something should be said, if only very briefly, of the state of literary criticism at the time when he started to write. Shaftesbury was born in 1671, three years before the death of Milton, and one year before the birth of Addison. His critical writings cover the all too short period from 1707 to 1713, the year of his death; in other words, they were roughly contemporaneous with the early poems of Pope and the publication of the *Spectator*. To be exact, Shaftesbury was the immediate predecessor of Addison and Pope, for his opinions were already decided by the time that their most important work appeared. His formative years, if we may so describe them, were the last decade of the seventeenth century; the period which saw the famous dispute that has come to be known as the Ancients and Moderns controversy.

The original quarrel, which has been deservedly forgotten, save in the account given in the lively but misleading pages of Swift's *Battle of the Books*, turned upon the authenticity of the so-called *Epistles of Phalaris* to which Swift's patron, Sir William Temple, had had recourse in an effort to demonstrate the superiority of ancient over modern learning. That great scholar, Richard Bentley, Royal Librarian and Master of Trinity College, Cambridge, had no difficulty in his *Dissertation upon the Epistles of Phalaris* (1699) in disposing of Temple's *Essay upon the Ancient and Modern Learning*, but that fact need not detain us, since the whole quarrel within this narrow compass is really completely irrelevant to the history of criticism. Bentley, though the fact does not detract from one's enjoyment of Swift's satire, was a man of vast erudition and profound classical scholarship, quite unlike the caricature in the *Battle of the Books*. His love of classical antiquity was as great as Temple's and his knowledge probably greater, while Temple, on the other hand, was a man with a cultured and liberal appreciation of modern literature, by no means a die-hard conservative in his judgments. It is an historical irony that these two men should thus have been thrust into rôles for which they were so little suited.

Why is it that this dispute over what was little more than a technical point of scholarship should have caused such a stir in the literary world? The answer is that it brought to a head a controversy that had been making itself more manifest as the century wore on. From the time of Bacon onwards the respect which had been traditionally accorded to classical thought and, in particular, to Aristotle's philosophy, had begun to decline. In a passage in the *Advancement of Learning* devoted to medieval philosophy, Bacon writes:

> "This kind of degenerate learning did chiefly reign among the Schoolmen: who, having sharp and strong wits, and abundance of leisure, and small variety of reading but their wits being shut up in the cells of a few authors (chiefly Aristotle their dictator) . . . did out of no great quantity of matter and infinite agitation of wit spin out unto us those laborious webs of learning which are extant in their books."

It is true that a distinction was often made between the authority of Greece in science and her authority in letters; Gildon in his *Modern Poets Against the Ancients* (1694), for example, writes as follows:

> ". . . the poetry of *Greece* was her most valuable Learning, for that still maintains its Share of Glory and Esteem, whilst her Philosophy is now exploded by the Universal Reason of Mankind . . . the *Stagyrite* with all his Volumes, is now shrunk from his Ostentatious Title of the *Philosopher*, to that of a good *Critic*, or *Grammarian*."

Yet the difference between this and what had once been said of Aristotle is tremendous.

The decline of Aristotle's reputation was all the swifter because many English critics were also men of science. In France, the Ancients and Moderns controversy had been fought out over the issue whether the authors of classical antiquity or those of modern times were the better writers, but both sides in the dispute agreed that the 'rules' were to be taken for granted and assumed that the issue left their authority untouched. In England, on the other hand, the critics were men often deeply interested in science whose dislike of the Aristotelian philosophy made them more ready to throw over the 'rules'. The last thirty years of the seventeenth century were remarkable for the number of men who combined literary scholarship with scientific interests. The Royal Society, which had been founded in 1662, exerted a tremendous influence upon the intellectual life of the nation. Attacks were made upon it, for as Wotton wrote in his *Reflections Upon Ancient and Modern Learning*, 1694,

"Though the Royal Society has weathered the rude attacks . . . yet the sly Insinuations of the Men of Wit . . . that every man they call a virtuoso must needs be a Sir Nicolas Gimcrack . . . have . . . taken off the Edge of . . . a love of learning." (*Conclusion*.)

Yet it took more than such jibes to stop the onward march of science; besides famous men of letters such as Pepys, Evelyn, Cowley, Sprat and Dryden, the membership of the Royal Society included Richard Bentley, Humfrey Wanley, the great Anglo-Saxon scholar, Thomas Birch, who contributed so many biographies to the *General Dictionary*, and a considerable number of other scholars and antiquarians.

These scholars had immense respect for the classics, but their philosophical and scientific knowledge would not allow them to regard the writers of classical antiquity as authorities in matters of philosophical principle. They insisted that the criterion in such matters must be conformity to the laws of nature, and that the precepts of Aristotle and Horace should submit to this test. Their influence led to a diminution of authority in criticism and the emergence of a spirit of free and impartial inquiry: criticism, in their hands, began to evince a more liberal temper of thought and a common-sense attitude that corresponded very much to the free and empirical approach of the Baconian tradition in science.

The novelty of this is brought out very clearly when we compare English criticism at this time with its counterpart in France. The difference is, perhaps, one of emphasis more than of kind, but there can be no doubt that the French were intent on inner consistency and logical coherence, and regarded the rules as a means to this end; the English, on the other hand, were more interested in conformity to experience, and found it easier to disregard the 'rules' if they wished, since they had a criterion which needed no such justification. This puts the matter with a theoretical precision that did not always obtain in fact, but brings out the difference brought about by a rationalist tradition of thought in France, and an empirical one in England. Saint-Évremond, who could speak with authority on the national temperament of both countries at this time, sums up the difference very happily when he says:

"A la vérité, je n'ai point vû de gens de meilleur entendement que les *François* qui considerent les choses avec attention, et les *Anglois* qui peuvent se détacher de leurs trop grandes meditations, pour revenir à la Facilité du discours et à certaine Liberté d'Esprit qu'il faut posséder toujours, s'il est possible." (*De la Comedie Angloise.*)

It is not sufficient, of course, simply to set French and English criticism in opposition, for France at this time exerted a considerable influence upon English letters and her critics may be said to have brought a conservative element into English criticism and to have stiffened opposition to the more liberal tendencies at work. It was not only fashions in dress and manners, but literary conventions and taste, that the exiled Charles had brought back from the French Court.

II

The two most representative French critics of the late seventeenth century were Boileau and Rapin. It is convenient to deal with them together, for not only were their views similar, but they wrote at the same time; Boileau's *L'Art Poétique* and Rapin's *Réflexions sur la Poétique* both appeared in 1674. Both critics understood the function of poetry to be an imitation of nature, and by this meant that the poet should concern himself with general truths rather than particular; should endeavour to exhibit in his work a regard for the universal laws of both physical and human nature. The work of the Ancients, for them, embodied these laws; to follow the Ancients was a short cut to following nature. The first part of this argument is summed up in Rapin's statement concerning the 'rules'.

"Enfin c'est par ces règles que tout devient juste, proportionné, naturel: estant comme elles sont fondées sur le bon sens et sur la raison, plus que sur l'autorité et sur l'exemple." (*Réflexion XII.*)

The second part is added when he continues:

"Je dis seulement, qu'à bien considérer ces règles on trouvera qu'elles ne sont faites que pour réduire la nature en méthodes." (*ibid.*)

The classical insistence on harmony and design is seen in the writings of both, but it would be a mistake to think that either of them resolved poetic composition into a mere matter of applying the 'rules'. Both saw quite clearly that genius as well as application is needed and that there is a quality in art which goes beyond the 'rules'. The opening lines of *L'Art Poétique* are alone sufficient to give the lie to the belief that a poet is made and not born, and the following passage shows that Boileau was as much an enemy of cold and formal correctness as any Romantic critic.

"Je hais ces vains auteurs dont la muse forcée
M'entretient de ses feux, toûjours froide et glacée;
Qui s'affligent par art, et, fous de sens rassis,
S'érigent, pour rimer, en amoureux transis."

(II, 45–8.)

Rapin is equally insistent that art defies rational analysis; that there is something which is incapable of definition, something borrowed from nature, which art can only imitate without fully comprehending.

"Il y a encore dans la Poësie, comme dans les autres arts, de certaines choses ineffables, & qu'on ne peut expliquer: ces choses en sont comme les mysteres. Il n'y a point de preceptes, pour enseigner ces graces secretes, ces charmes imperceptibles, & tous ces agrémens cachez de la Poësie qui vont au coeur. Comme il n' y a pas de methode pour enseigner à plaire, c'est un pur effet du naturel." (*Réflexion*, XXXV.)

We must not spend more space on Boileau and Rapin, for to do so would be to exaggerate their importance to English criticism at this time. Contrary to what is often said, there seems, indeed, little evidence that Boileau attained any great popularity in England as a critic until the early years of the eighteenth century. In 1711, the year when the *Characteristics* was published, there appeared Pope's *Essay on Criticism*, which was really the first English work to show any considerable debt to Boileau's critical theory. There were plenty of references to Boileau throughout the last quarter of the seventeenth century, but these were nearly all concerned with his poetry. In 1680–3, Dryden collaborated with Sir William Soame in producing a translation of *L'Art Poétique*, but his own *Essay of Dramatic Poesy*, which was undoubtedly influenced by French criticism, was written a few years before Boileau's treatise and his debt was mainly to Corneille. Most of Dryden's remarks on Boileau are contained in the essay *The Original and Progress of Satire* (1693), where the English poet pays generous tribute to his French contemporary.

> "... if I would only cross the seas," he writes, "I might find in France a living Horace and a Juvenal, in the person of the admirable Boileau; whose numbers are excellent, whose expressions are noble, whose thoughts are just, whose language is pure, whose satire is pointed, and whose sense is close." (*Essays of Dryden*, ed. Ker, II, 26.)

Dryden's *Apology for Heroic Poetry* mentions both Boileau and Rapin as the "best of modern critics" and there are some further scattered references, but for the greater part these are concerned not with Boileau's criticism, but his satire.

It may be that the war with France did something to detract from Boileau's reputation in England. Dryden, in 1693, warned his countrymen not to allow nationalist sentiments to interfere with their critical judgment: writing of Louis of France, whose patronage of the arts he compares with that of Augustus Caesar, he observes:

> "Let this be said without entering into the interests of factions and parties, and relating only to the bounty of that king to men of learning and merit; a praise so just, that even we, who are his enemies, cannot refuse it to him." (*ibid.*, II, 26.)

Though perhaps some were ready to be animated by this spirit, many were only too ready to seize upon the war as an occasion for the sort of scurrilous writing that best suited their talents. Many of the allusions to Boileau and his countrymen were in the vein of burlesque which we encounter in Prior's *English Ballad on the taking of Namur* (1695), perhaps the best-known example and certainly one of the few worth preserving.

It has been contended that it was Boileau's influence which brought about the decline of the Christian epic in England, and one of the few allusions made by Dryden to Boileau as a critic is in the course of a discussion of Christian 'machinery' in epic poetry.

> " 'Tis objected by a great French critic, as well as an admirable poet, yet living, and whom I have mentioned with that honour which his merit exacts from me, I mean Boileau, that the machines of our Christian religion in heroic poetry, are much more feeble to support that weight than those of heathenism." (*ibid.*, II, 31-2.)

Sir William Temple and a number of other critics also quoted Boileau in support of their denunciation of Christian epic. Dennis in his *Remarks on Prince Arthur* (1696) sets out the argument which Boileau had popularized.

> "Boileau tells us," he writes, "with a great deal of reason in the Third Canto of his Art of Poetry, though it is spoken in rhyme: 'That the terrible mysteries of the Christian faith are not capable of delightful ornaments, that the Gospel offers nothing to us but repentance on the one side or eternal torments on the other, and that the criminal mixture of poetical fictions gives a fabulous air even to its most sacred truths.' "

Now, there is no doubt that Boileau did do something to cause the Christian epic to lose favour, but it is more likely that he gave impetus to a movement that had already started and did not himself initiate the movement. His arguments had already been anticipated in Davenant's *Preface to Gondibert*, and the decline of the Christian epic can probably be attributed more to the steady growth of rationalism and the decline of authority, than to any purely literary forces. In other words, Boileau's attack was more a symptom of what was happening than the cause; he was only one of many who saw and pointed out what was regarded as the 'improbability' of Christian 'machines'. The supernatural was not an easy topic for poetry in an age characterized by scientific habits of thought, and not only Christian doctrine, but pagan mythology as well, was suspect. As

Hurd was to say, many years later, in his *Letters on Chivalry and Romance*,

"The Pagan Gods and Gothic Faeries were equally out of credit when Milton wrote." (*Letter X.*)

Rapin appears to have been more influential than Boileau in seventeenth-century England. Rymer, who translated the *Réflexions sur la Poétique d'Aristote* into English in the year of its publication, was an almost fanatical devotee of Rapin, while Gerard Langbaine, Jeremy Collier, Sir Thomas Pope Blount and Charles Gildon all knew and quoted the *Réflexions*, either in translation or the original. The other French critic who enjoyed something of the same reputation in England was Le Bossu. This is a little difficult to explain, for he was the most stereotyped of the French critics, lacking the independence and individuality of both Boileau and Rapin; yet his *Traité du Poème Épique* (1675) became the standard work on the subject of heroic poetry and there were frequent references to it, even before its translation into English in 1695. Le Bossu was praised by Dryden, and Addison is obviously indebted to the *Traité* in his papers on *Chevy Chase* and *Paradise Lost*. Shaftesbury called him "the excellent Bossu" and said that he had

". . . presented the world with a view of ancient literature and just writing beyond any other modern of whatever nation." (*Freedom of Wit and Humour, Characteristics*, I, 94.)

It is strange that Le Bossu should have won all this esteem, when a critic like Corneille was comparatively neglected. Corneille, who actually preceded Boileau, Rapin and Le Bossu, had had a great and beneficial influence upon Dryden, particularly upon the *Essay of Dramatic Poesy*, which was probably the greatest critical work of this generation. Yet the allusions to Corneille became pitifully small, in spite of a critical moderation and balanced judgment that allied him more to English writers than to his immediate successors in France. Shaftesbury is one of the few writers after the turn of the century, who even mention him, and the manner in which he does so in his fifth *Miscellany* shows his high regard.

It will already have become evident that the criticism of this period cannot be made the subject of neat generalizations or clear divisions. Even the neo-classical critics whom we have been considering were by no means the reactionary pedants they have often been represented to be; and even in France, where critical principles had not been so weakened by the solvents of scientific method, there began to appear writers who stressed the subjective nature of aesthetic appreciation. The truth is that all over Europe authority in literature was crumbling; the experimental temper that characterized English thought was only part, even if an important part, of a process that was well nigh universal. Writers such as Bouhours, La Bruyère, Saint-Évremond and the Chevalier de Méré, were the French counterparts of the English critics mentioned at the end of the first chapter. Like Temple, Wotton, Gildon and the others who belonged to the English school of taste, these French critics were eager to evaluate a work of literature, not by its observance of the 'rules', but by the sort of emotional appeal it made. They were interested in the evolutionary development of literature rather than in attempting to conserve a static perfection. The Chevalier de Méré put the extreme point of view when he wrote:

> "As for myself I judge things only in accordance with my own taste, and I am therefore often in danger of rejecting what is good and admiring what is bad, because I have not been warned about it. But despite certain great critics whom you may consult, how can you ever succeed in getting beyond your own personal opinion in judging the work of good writers?" (*Oeuvres*, Amsterdam, 1692, II, 72. Quoted by Spingarn in the Introduction to *Critical Essays of the Seventeenth Century*.)

There were comparatively few references to these French critics of taste by English writers and this itself suggests that what was taking place in England was a parallel movement rather than the result of French influence. It is true that Saint-Évremond's writings, besides being quoted by Dryden, were translated into several English editions in the last decade of the seventeenth century, and their author appears to have been known personally to many Englishmen; while Lord Lansdowne's *Essay upon Unnatural Flights in Poetry* (1701), was very much indebted to Bouhours. Yet few other English critics appear to have mentioned these Frenchmen. Shaftesbury is one of the exceptions; he refers to La Bruyère and cites a work of Saint-Évremond in his *Second Characters*, and though he does not mention it by name, a comparison of the *Characteristics* with *La Manière de bien penser* of Bouhours shows some striking similarities of thought.

III

The most eminent English critic of the period we are considering was, of course, John Dryden. It would be wrong to suggest that Dryden is a representative figure, for he had qualities both of style and judgment that raised him above the common level; nevertheless, at this higher level of achievement, his writings provide a most useful guide to the various schools of thought in the criticism of the time. This can rightly be called the Age of Dryden in criticism, for his flexible and sensitive personality seems to have been susceptible to nearly all the current ideas. His was far from being a simple and uncomplicated mind, nor was it merely fickle; yet he seemed to react with the sensitivity of a barometer to the prevailing climate of opinion. On the one side, he was a member of the Royal Society; very interested, if only as an amateur, in scientific research and discovery; in certain respects a disciple of Hobbes and prepared to welcome the new psychological approach to literature. On the other side, he had a profound respect for the writers of classical antiquity and a truer appreciation of their aim and spirit than many of the more pedantic upholders of modernity.

There is no doubt that in the Ancients and Moderns dispute Dryden was on the side of the Moderns. In the verses addressed to his antiquarian friend, Dr. Charleton, he declaims against the authority of Aristotle as a critic:

> "The longest tyranny that ever swayed
> Was that wherein our ancestors betrayed
> Their free-born reason to the Stagirite,
> And made his torch their universal light."

This was but a corollary of the support he gave the new tradition of scientific thought; part of his conviction that

> "The World to Bacon does not only owe
> Its present Knowledge, but its future too."

For Dryden was a Modern, a liberal critic who placed a higher value upon personal judgment and the practical test of whether a work of art succeeded in its intention, than upon formal correctness. His writings carried on the tradition of which Corneille had been an architect, a tradition which was now broadened and enlivened by the school of taste.

Yet Dryden had a tremendous admiration for the achievements of classical literature. He was prepared to judge classical literature by the same standards as the modern, and believed that it survived this comparison honourably. Certain of the Moderns, however, were intent only on showing that contemporary literature obeyed the canons of Aristotle and Horace even more closely than the old masterpieces had done. They were interested only in contending that the Moderns were more strictly classical than even the classics; that the Moderns could beat the Ancients at their own game. With these Dryden had no sympathy. In many ways he was too big for the narrow confines of contemporary controversy and turned aside with a dignified indifference from the petty squabbles that had obscured the larger issues.

Shaftesbury, as we might have expected, had little regard for Dryden. The caricatures that Dryden had made of his father and grandfather in *Absalom and Achitophel*, could have been sufficient of themselves to mean bitter and unrelenting hostility on Shaftesbury's part. When he does deign to refer to him, it is nearly always as "Mr. Bayes", the name by which Buckingham had pilloried Dryden in *The Rehearsal*. Some idea of Shaftesbury's contempt can be gained from a note to *Miscellany V*, in which he refers to the *Preface* to *Don Sebastian* in the following harsh terms.

"To see the incorrigibleness of our poets in their pedantic manner, their vanity, defiance of criticism, their rhodomontade and poetical bravado, we need only turn to our famous poet-laureate, (the very Mr. Bays himself) in one of his latest and most valued pieces, writ many years after the ingenious author of the Rehearsal had drawn his picture." (*Characteristics*, II, 328.)

Yet is it not too easy to ascribe Shaftesbury's dislike of Dryden simply to personal animus? Shaftesbury was not the man to allow prejudice to overcome fair-mindedness in matters of this sort. It is significant that his references to Dryden's name are few and even more significant that in the *Second Characters*, in a context that does not involve critical principles, he writes of him without any acerbity. The real point we must grasp is that for Shaftesbury a man's critical opinions were not accidental; they could not be separated from his beliefs in politics and religion. Dryden's Catholicism, his belief in the divine right of kings, his rigid Tory doctrines, all of which were anathema to Shaftesbury, implied that his critical theories must be suspect; the division between Whig and Tory, Protestant and Catholic, at this time, meant far more than a difference of political opinion or religious conviction. Now obviously this can be pushed too far and it would be wrong to exaggerate Shaftesbury's attitude; the reasons for his dislike of Dryden are never expressed explicitly and all that we can do is to hazard an explanation of this dislike in rational terms. Yet we are probably right in trying to get behind mere personal feelings to account for Shaftesbury's attitude, for behind the disarming figure of Dryden there lurked the evil genius of Hobbes.

Dryden would have contended in all innocence that his critical opinions were quite independent of philosophical presuppositions; that he spoke the truth as he saw it, and was guided by his own heart. To some extent, of course, he was quite right; Dryden is at his best when making practical judgments and when free of theoretical considerations. Nevertheless, it would be naïve not to recognize that at the back of his critical utterances there are many assumptions which cannot be taken for granted. We have already seen in an earlier chapter that he follows Hobbes in reducing the poetic imagination to a mere operation of memory; perhaps the most far-reaching intellectual decision that a critic could make, and carrying with it a whole range of implications in the field of day-to-day judgments. Nor was Dryden's allegiance to Hobbes merely a matter of literary criticism; his narrow conception of the function of monarchy and his belief in an authoritarian form of government found a measure of support in the arguments of the *Leviathan*. When we remember also that he gave dramatic presentation to Hobbes's pessimistic theory of human nature, there is little need to bring forward prejudice as a reason for Shaftesbury's dislike.

If Dryden were on the side of the Moderns, then we should have to place Shaftesbury on the side of the Ancients; at any rate he had little sympathy with many of the beliefs of the Moderns. He viewed with distaste and suspicion the activities of the members of the Royal Society; their scientific interests, though he would probably have had nothing against them as such, were, after all, inspired by the tradition of thought which had nurtured Hobbes and his hated brood of mechanists. Equally, their antiquarian interests had taken criticism out of polite society and made it a business of technical scholarship, conducted by people like Addison's Tom Folio, who carried, in Pope's famous phrase, "a lumber house of books in every head." Yet, if we count Shaftesbury among the Ancients, we should bear in mind that, as in Temple's case, he was not simply an adherent of the classical 'rules'. He knew not only the literature of Greece and

Rome, but had drunk at those well-springs of classical philosophy which had watered and refreshed liberal thought throughout every age of European civilization. His was a generous and cultivated mind, with little sympathy for pedants, whether ancient or modern. He knew and admired not only the neo-classical critics of France and England, but also the modern writers who took taste as their guiding principle.

Shaftesbury, in fact, was too great to be fitted into this over-neat classification of Ancients and Moderns; he stood at the beginning of a new period in criticism which had left this dispute of the seventeenth century behind. Mere authority in literature had gone; that much was clear. Was it good enough, however, for criticism to proceed simply as if it could manage without any sort of principles? Those like Dryden, who seemed to think that it could, were simply playing into the hands of the disciples of Hobbes; accepting without question assumptions that were by no means matters of fact. To make things worse, there had grown up a class of professional critics, who exploited literature simply as a means of earning their bread and butter. With the development of journalism, London seemed to be swarming with those who made a business out of the tittle-tattle of the stage-door and the gossip of the coffee-house. If these camp-followers of the literary world were going to cheapen the *obiter dicta* of Dryden, by popularizing them with the piquancy of literary feuds and slander, the outlook for criticism would not be bright. In a passage in his *Miscellany V* Shaftesbury gives an ironical picture of these superficial followers of Dryden, gathered together in mutual admiration.

> "This is the young fry," he writes, "which you may see busily surrounding the grown poet or chief playhouse author, at a coffee-house. They are his guards, ready to take up arms for him, if by some presumptuous critic he is at any time attacked. They are indeed the very shadows of their immediate predecessor, and represent the same features, with some small alteration perhaps for the worse. They are sure to aim at nothing above or beyond their master, and would on no account give him the least jealousy of their aspiring to any degree or order of writing above him. From hence that harmony and reciprocal esteem, which, on such a bottom as this, cannot fail of being perfectly well established among our poets: the age, meanwhile, being after this manner hopefully provided and secure of a constant and like succession of meritorious wits, in every kind!" (*Characteristics*, II, 327.)

The common sense of a Dennis or Rymer, and the covert Hobbism of a Dryden, left criticism in a dangerous position. The decline of classical authority had left a vacuum which had to be filled, and if the new mechanical philosophy were not to take its place, some more satisfactory substitute had to be found. It was not that Shaftesbury wished to provide a systematic aesthetics, but simply that he wanted a comprehensive philosophy which took into account and explained man's desire to create and enjoy art; a philosophy which took literature seriously and which would provide a standard of judgment. This philosophy would have to comprehend the whole of man's life and provide a basis for religion, society, and morals as well as art. It was to Platonism that Shaftesbury turned for this philosophy; not indeed to a codified structure of thought which had lost its relevance, (for this would be completely to misunderstand Platonism), but to a living tradition which could embrace modern discoveries and accommodate itself to contemporary needs. As we shall see, he did not always find the problem of accommodation easy to solve in practice, but he was perhaps on surer ground than many of his contemporaries, who were willing to forsake the *philosophia perennis* of Plato for what might be the superficial charms of more modern thought.

CHAPTER V

THE CREATIVE IMAGINATION

"... Imagination, which, in truth,
Is but another name for absolute power
And clearest insight, amplitude of mind,
And Reason in her most exalted mood."
Wordsworth: *The Prelude*, Bk. XIV.

I

SHAFTESBURY'S purpose of reforming the morals, taste and manners of the age is clearly seen in his consideration of literature and the arts. Most of his writings have a bearing on literature and criticism; throughout the *Characteristics* we encounter remarks on authors and books, while his *Advice to An Author* and the third *Miscellany* are specifically concerned with literary questions. His real importance to literature, however, consists not in judgments of particular authors or discussions of actual books, but in the general principles of his philosophy. His comments on Shakespeare, Milton and other writers are always interesting and one gets in his work a shrewd and balanced opinion about the literary movements and fashions of the day, but such comments are not without parallel in the other enlightened criticism of his time. It is his philosophy that determines his place in literature and decides his influence as a critic, for his criticism is concerned with aesthetic issues rather than the evaluation of works of literature. His opinion of individual authors may often be no more profound than that of many of his contemporaries, but his philosophy was a formative influence in deciding the development of subsequent criticism. He was among the first of English critics to deal with aesthetics, and his work gave to criticism a new framework of reference and a new orientation.

We have seen that the new philosophy of ideas had turned criticism towards psychology. Instead of concerning itself with the poem or play, solely as a work of art explicable in its own terms, criticism was beginning to ask questions about the mental processes involved in composition. There had always, of course, been discussions of how far genius and how far reason governed poetic composition and Hobbes's more recent distinction between the judgment and fancy was simply a contribution to this controversy that possessed greater psychological awareness. In fact, it was not the distinction itself which was so important, for that had always been made; what mattered was the content put into any theory that took this distinction as its basis. What mattered was the detailed account of how the poet's mind worked. According to Hobbes the fancy was a mere process of association which formed compound images from the sense impressions stored in the memory; some of the elements in these images could have entered the mind on one occasion and others on another occasion, but the images could be assembled only from the totality of sense experience. Properly speaking, the process that Hobbes envisaged consisted in nothing but one memory image itself calling up another image, simply because the two had previously been associated or because they were similar. Furthermore, the whole process was subordinate to the judgment; it was the judgment which was responsible for the design of a poem and which used the compounded images as decorations for the structure it had designed.

It has already been observed that this theory was adopted by critics such as Dryden, Rymer and Dennis. Nor is this surprising, for it was a psychological account that readily lent itself to what was the general conception of poetry at the time. Most of the critics of the late seventeenth century accepted Aristotle's doctrine of *mimesis* to the extent, at any rate, that they regarded poetry as in some way an imitation of nature, though nearly all of them agreed that it did not mean just copying in any literal or naïve sense. It was a doctrine, in fact, that could be given many different interpretations, as is seen from the long history of criticism. In the early days, even Neo-Platonism had adopted and transformed it; a fact that may appear strange, for Plato, in a well-known passage in the *Republic*, had condemned art as being two degrees removed from reality and had declared that poetry was an imitation of an imitation. This objection had been met, however, by the theory that art does not imitate the objects of the present world of appearances, but the world of Ideas. By such a distortion of Plato's teaching, Proclus and St. Augustine were able to redeem the arts and to recall the poet from his banishment from the Republic. Their version of Platonism might have been found useful at a time like the seventeenth century when Aristotle was so influential in the field of literary criticism, for it was one that could be easily grafted on to the Aristotelian tradition. Poussin in France, and Bellori in Italy, had, indeed, attempted to work out a theory of art in

Neo-Platonic terms, but in England the only well-known evidence of such a theory was the echo of Bellori we catch in Dryden's *Parallel of Poetry and Painting*.

There was a good deal in the Aristotelian doctrine itself, of course, which might have been used in support of a conception of art as an idealization of nature, but in England the doctrine tended to become the suggestion that poetry was merely generalization. Art was regarded less as an imitation of an ideal order only imperfectly apprehended, than as a generalized picture of this world purged of all peculiarities and grossness. The Hobbesian psychology reinforced this suggestion until it became a belief. It led some critics to think that the poet, instead of copying the actual and particular person or event, brings together elements from a number of persons and events and makes a general representation of them; a representation that is devoid of all particularities and which only in this restricted sense might be called an idealization. Sometimes in the criticism of the period this is mingled in a curious manner with the Neo-Platonic theory, as in the following passage from Dennis's *Remarks on Prince Arthur* (1696):

> "... a Poet is not so much to consult Nature in any particular Person, which is but a Copy, and an imperfect copy of Universal Nature; he is to examine that Universal Nature, which is always perfect, and to consult the Original Ideas of things, which in a Sovereign manner are beautiful. ... Thus if a Poet is to draw a King or a great Captain ... if History has given that King or that Captain, any shameful Frailty, or low Vice, which are unworthy of the Majesty of the one, and of the high Command of the other; the Poet is obliged to conceal that Frailty and to dissemble that Vice." (Part II, Ch. 1.)

More frequently, however, there existed simply a belief that generalized representation was the only alternative to copying. One of the best known quotations which was later to express such a view is the famous passage from Johnson's *Rasselas*:

> " 'The business of a poet,' said Imlac, 'is to examine, not the individual, but the species, to remark general properties and large appearances; he does not number the streaks of the tulip, or describe the different shades of the verdure of the forest.' "

Shaftesbury followed most of his contemporaries in regarding poetry as in some sense an imitation, but he avoided both the interpretation that would reduce it to copying and that which identifies it with generalized representation. Poetry is certainly concerned with this present world and must use the material provided by it; in that sense it can be thought of as imitation, but it is not merely a copying of nature, for, he writes in *Miscellany V*,

"They are mean spirits who love to copy merely, nothing is agreeable or natural but what is original." (*Characteristics*, II, 319.)

Moreover, the truth of art is not the truth of real life, and art does not simply hold a mirror to reality; Shaftesbury agrees with Aristotle that a probable impossibility is better than a possible improbability.

"'Tis not the possible but the probable and likely which must be the poet's guide in manners." (*ibid.*, II, 318.)

Poetry is not literal copying, but on the other hand it is not a generalized imitation of nature. Art is concerned with particulars. The dramatist's task, for instance, as Shaftesbury outlines it in the *Advice to an Author*, is not to bring generalized figures on to the stage, that is, characters which are an amalgam of qualities found in several particular persons. Dramatic characters must be real people.

"Nor is it enough that the persons introduced speak pertinent and good sense at every turn. . . . For the understanding here must have its mark, its characteristic note, by which it may be distinguished. It must be such and such an understanding; as when we say, for instance, such or such a face; since Nature has characterized tempers and minds as peculiarly as faces. And for an artist who draws naturally, 'tis not enough to show us merely faces which may be called men's: every face must be a certain man's." (*ibid.*, I, 132.)

It is clear that imitation of nature means for Shaftesbury something different from what the followers of Hobbes understood it to be. For the Hobbists nature was a mechanism. For Shaftesbury, on the other hand, art is an imitation of an ideal world only partly realized in the natural order. He believes that beyond the present world there is an ideal order with which the reason can make contact. Yet in apprehending this ideal the reason must work in and by the senses, for art can imitate the ideal only by using the temporal and spatial forms in which the ideal manifests itself. But this is not all; for Shaftesbury the ideal world is not caught and fixed in dead and immutable symbols. It is a living force working in the changing forms of this world; the natural order is not fixed and dead, but a living organic growth.

Just as the mechanistic interpretation of nature bore fruit in an associationist psychology, so Shaftesbury's interpretation produced its own characteristic theory of the mental processes involved in art. For if nature is not a mechanical but a creative process, then, since it imitates nature, artistic invention itself must be creative. We have seen Shaftesbury's dislike of the results of an associationist psychology in ethics, but he is equally aware of its disastrous implications for aesthetics. The view that the mind is a *tabula rasa* and that knowledge derives wholly from sense experience had led to a mechanical account of the imagination.

Empiricism need not, of course, adopt the belief that the mind is passive either in perception or in art, but there is no doubt that this was the position it found itself in at the beginning of the eighteenth century. In Shaftesbury's eyes, Locke was to be identified with Hobbes not only in ethics, but in art. In the notes which constitute *Treatise IV* of the *Second Characters* he writes:

"Hence Hobbes, Locke etc. still the same man, same genus at the bottom.—'Beauty is nothing.'—'Virtue is nothing.'—So 'perspective nothing—Music nothing.'—but these are the greatest realities of things, especially the beauty and order of affections. These philosophers together with the anti-virtuosi may be called by one common name, viz. barbar[ians]." (*Second Characters*, 178.)

Shaftesbury detests the suggestion that the human mind is a passive receptacle of ideas which join together by association, and also the view that sees it as a machine working according to the laws of motion. He sees the human mind as analogous to the mind of God.

"This self of mine . . . is a real self, drawn out from and copied from another principle and original self (the Great One of the World)."

As the human mind is analogous to the divine one, so the work of art is analogous to nature; both art and nature are the product of a creative energy which gives them being. The second-rate artist, the mere contriver and artificer, may work by assembling the bits and pieces of the artistic material; his work is the outcome of "an injudicious random use of wit and fancy."

"But," writes Shaftesbury in his *Advice to An Author*, "for the man who truly and in a just sense deserves the name of poet, and who as a real master, or architect in the kind, can describe both men and manners, and give to an action its just body and proportions, he will be found, if I mistake not, a very different creature. Such a poet is indeed a second *Maker*; a just Prometheus under Jove. Like that sovereign artist or universal plastic nature, he forms a whole, coherent and proportioned in itself, with due subjection and subordinacy of constituent parts." (*Characteristics*, I, 135—6.)

We should fail to understand this passage if we regarded it just as a fine piece of rhetoric which pays lip-service to the high calling of the poet, for it provides us with a conception of the poetic imagination which cuts right across the Hobbesian aesthetics. Shaftesbury is far from uttering a pious platitude when he says that the relation between the poet and his work is analogous to the relation existing between God and His creation. Shaftesbury holds a particular doctrine of the relationship between God and nature and we must look at this again more closely before we can appreciate the sort of claim he is making for the poet. Properly understood, the claim he makes leads directly to a theory of creative imagination. It is significant that Coleridge, whose great work in aesthetics was to insist on the creative nature of the imagination, should also have based his theory on what he called 'the divine analogue'. In a letter to Thomas Poole in March 1801, in which he expresses his dissatisfaction with Locke and his belief that Newton's philosophy is false, Coleridge writes:

"Newton was a mere materialist. *Mind*, in his system, is always *passive*,—a lazy *Looker-on* on an external world. If the mind be not *passive*, if it be indeed made in God's Image, and that, too, in the sublimest sense, the *Image of the Creator*, there is ground for suspicion that any system built on the passiveness of the mind must be false, as a system." (*Letters*, ed. E. H. Coleridge, I, 352.)

Shaftesbury believes that nature was created by the impress of the divine mind on unformed matter and that natural phenomena are symbols in a world of change of an ideal which is eternal and changeless. The divine ideas are not, indeed, patterns in the sense that natural objects are mere copies of them; they have a perfection which lies beyond being and this world is only the inadequate expression of a greater glory which transcends this earthly life. The impress of the divine ideas on matter is not like the impress of a seal on wax, however, for nature is something that grows and changes. It is wrong, in fact, to speak of nature as having been *created*, for it is always in process of creation by the divine will. Shaftesbury adopts the principle of a plastic power, which animates the natural world and seeks to evolve from matter shapes and forms approximating ever more closely to the divine ideas. He believes that this shaping power is part of the divine activity, but this is not to say that he identifies it with God; it is rather, he suggests, one of the aspects, though not the sum total, of God's nature.

We can now understand what Shaftesbury means by likening the poet to "that universal plastic nature" and calling him "a just Prometheus under Jove." By substituting the poet for God in the above account we arrive at a view of poetry that sees it as a creative process in which the poet expresses his thought by impressing it on the raw and unformed material of his mind. Corresponding to the plastic principle in nature, it would be argued, there is a power of the mind which operates on the raw stuff of the poet's consciousness and elaborates new forms from it. The poet's thought is not stamped on his sense experience as a seal is impressed on wax, but is realized in particular forms which are the products of an active principle. This active principle which is analogous to the forming power in nature, is the imagination which gives sensible shape to the poet's thought. The products of the imagination are not like the products of a machine which must always be reproductions of an original prototype, but resemble the members of the natural creation which are all unique and particular. If we wish, we can press Shaftesbury's analogy even further. Just as the plastic power in nature is not to be identified with God, so it could be maintained that the creative imagination of the artist is only an agent of the reason and not identical with it.

The analogy leads us to the point where it might be said that as natural objects can be regarded as symbols of God's thought, so the products of the poetic imagination may be described as symbols of the poet's. By symbols we do not mean here the arbitrarily chosen signs which are used as part of an agreed and conventional terminology. Symbols of this kind form a large part of language and are used in the naming of things as when, for instance, we use the word 'table' to denote the objects we choose to call by that name. But poetic symbolism is something quite different from the assigning of labels to things: it is not arbitrary or conventional, and though exact, is not exact in this kind of way. The symbolism of the poetic imagination is an attempt to express thought which cannot be put in the conventional language of logical or scientific statement. A poet's thought can be expressed only in the symbolism of his imagery. The reader cannot become acquainted with the thought in any more direct way, though it is sometimes possible for him to go behind the symbols and to perceive what is being symbolized. To translate the poetic symbols into conceptual statement is not a substitute for the symbols, however, and only a lesser and not a greater appreciation of the poet's thought is gained in this way. The symbols are the most exact way in which the poet can express himself. An example of what we mean can be seen in the famous line where Wordsworth invokes duty as

"Stern Daughter of the Voice of God."

To some extent we can go behind the imagery to something that can be expressed in such conceptual terms as 'duty' and 'conscience', but to do so does not bring us nearer Wordsworth's meaning, for his thought is such that it cannot be exactly equated with such statements.

It could be argued that nature and art are alike in this and that both are symbolic of their creator's thought in such a way that the meaning of the symbols can never be satisfactorily expressed in exact language. Unless the symbols are to be meaningless, however, the human mind must make some attempt at interpretation. In other words, although a poet's imagery may embody the kind of thought that cannot be adequately translated into conceptual terms, yet the task of translation must be attempted. Because the attempt will never be wholly successful all poetic imagery is indeterminate; any statement that tries to comprehend it will at best contain only part of its meaning and even a whole series of statements can only approximate to the poet's thought and can never exhaust it. For this reason there can never be any one exact and determinate meaning attached to a poetic image. The poet is always in search of an exactitude he can never attain and constantly wrestling with new forms of expression. A contemporary writer has described very well the feeling of dissatisfaction that the poet must feel at the inadequacy of his imagery to express his thought.

> "So here I am, in the middle way, having had twenty years—
> Twenty years largely wasted, the years of *l'entre deux guerres*—
> Trying to learn to use words, and every attempt
> Is a wholly new start, and a different kind of failure
> Because one has only learnt to get the better of words
> For the thing one no longer has to say, or the way in which
> One is no longer disposed to say it. And so each venture
> Is a new beginning, a raid on the inarticulate
> With shabby equipment always deteriorating
> In the general mess of imprecision of feeling,
> Undisciplined squads of emotion."[1]

II

It is interesting to find that Coleridge elaborated very much the sort of aesthetic theory sketched above, and even more noteworthy that he based his theory on the kind of analogy that Shaftesbury drew between art and nature. In that curious essay *The Statesman's Manual* Coleridge compares poetic imagery with the symbolism of nature. Part of the argument in this "lay-sermon, addressed to the higher classes of society", is that the Scriptures must be regarded as works of the imagination. The facts and persons of Old Testament history have a two-fold reference. The Bible is concerned with individual men and women, and yet in the story of God's dealing with them we are given much more than a literal and historical narrative; it is concerned with universal truths and yet truths which cannot be put in the form of conceptual statements. The weakness of contemporary histories, Coleridge considered, was that they consisted of generalized statements, mere abstractions and conceptualizations. The Scriptures, on the other hand, provide both "Portraits and Ideals".

"The histories and political economy of the present and preceding century," he writes, "partake in the general contagion of its mechanistic philosophy, and are the *product* of an unenlivened generalizing Understanding. In the Scriptures they are the living *educts* of the Imagination; of that reconciling and mediatory power, which incorporating the Reason in Images of

[1] T. S. Eliot, *East Coker*, Faber and Faber.

the Sense ... gives birth to a system of symbols, harmonious in themselves, and consubstantial with the truths, of which they are the *conductors*.... The truths and the symbols that represent them move in conjunction and form the living chariot that bears up (for us) the throne of the Divine Humanity."

The Bible for Coleridge is in truth the Word of God, expressing in its people and stories God's truth in an imaginative medium; it is artistic and not scientific writing. Coleridge would have denied that even purely historical writing can be wholly scientific, and in the case of the Bible we are confronted, not merely with history, but with an attempt to apprehend those truths of God's being and nature which can be grasped only imaginatively. Moreover, the Bible is not the only manifestation of God's truth. In the notes appended to this section of the *Statesman's Manual* he develops the suggestion that God is seen also in the works of nature.

"Let it not weary you if I digress for a few moments to another book, likewise a revelation of God—the great book of his servant Nature. That in its obvious sense and literal interpretation it declares the being and attributes of the Almighty Father, none but the *poor in heart* has ever dared gainsay. But it has been the music of gentle and pious minds in all ages, it is the *poetry* of all human nature, to read it likewise in a figurative sense, and to find therein correspondencies and symbols of the spiritual world."

Coleridge expresses the same thought in verse, both in *Frost at Midnight* where he calls nature God's "eternal language", and also in the *Destiny of Nations* where he declares,

> "All that meets the bodily sense I deem
> Symbolical, one mighty alphabet
> To infant minds; and we in this low world
> Placed with our backs to bright reality,
> That we might learn with young unwounded ken
> The substance from the shadow."

These quotations raise the interesting question of how far Coleridge's theory of the imagination can be developed from Shaftesbury's starting-point of the poet as "a just Prometheus under Jove." Both men had very much the same attitudes; both distrusted the associationist psychology and based their thinking on the realization that this gave a completely wrong account of the writing of poetry. It is significant, too, that Coleridge chose to call the imagination by the name of the 'esemplastic power'. There is no doubt that Coleridge had been influenced by the Neo-Platonic tradition, for in the *Biographia Literaria* he refers to Henry More, Plotinus, Proclus and the mystical writers Jacob Boehme and William Law: it was their influence, he tells us, which had kept him faithful to a nobler conception of poetry while still under the domination of Hartley and the associationists. Such considerations make it more than idle speculation to ask how much Coleridge had in common with Shaftesbury.

Shaftesbury does not make any formal distinction between fancy and the imagination. Like most of his contemporaries he uses the two words as more or less interchangeable. This, however, is unimportant, for the formal distinction made between the two by Coleridge is a matter of mere terminology. Imagination (or fancy) can be used to denote two things, (*a*) the compounding of the elements of mental experience by some process of association; (*b*) the bringing into being, by a process other than association, of a created whole. The former of these is an explanation of poetry in terms of mechanical causation. Shaftesbury's great merit is that he realizes that this has nothing to do with the poetic imagination, but that it has confused the issues and done positive harm to poetry. His recognition of this fact is tantamount to making the distinction Coleridge made more formally, and must place Shaftesbury amongst the most important of the aesthetic writers of the eighteenth century.

There is more in Coleridge's theory, however, than his distinction between the associative faculty of the fancy and the creative power of the imagination. Having made this initial distinction he proceeds to distinguish between what he calls the 'primary imagination' and the 'secondary imagination'. His theory is based on an account of perception. He shows that perception is more than what is given to the human mind by sensation. The human mind in apprehending an object receives from the five senses colour, shape, tactual sensations of softness or hardness, and sometimes taste and smell. The associationists had maintained that our perception is merely the compounding of such sense-data. A classic statement of this doctrine can be found in John Stuart Mill's *System of Logic*, where in his presentation of their psychology, he writes:

> "Our idea of an orange really *consists* of the simple ideas of a certain colour, a certain form, a certain taste and smell, etc.,

because we can by interrogating our consciousness, perceive all these elements in the idea." (1862 edition, II, 33.)

Coleridge would have denied the truth of this and said that the sum of such sense-data would never bring about our perception of an orange; to make this possible there is needed an active power of the mind itself. The mind is not a passive receptacle which merely receives sense-data, nor is it a blank screen on which the outside world reflects an image. The mind is actively engaged in perception and amalgamates the sense-data by a power which he calls the 'primary imagination', so that they are seen *as an object* and not merely the sum of the constituent elements. What the mind receives through the senses is an unordered mass of sensory material, and in perception the mind itself imposes form upon this flux. In doing this the human mind acts analogously to the divine activity in creation, for the process is, in the words of the famous passage of Coleridge's *Biographia Literaria*,

"a repetition in the finite mind of the eternal act of creation in the infinite I AM." (Chap. XIII.)

Coleridge's 'secondary imagination', the faculty concerned with the process of artistic composition, is an extension of this 'primary imagination'. It is alike in kind, he tells us, and differs only in degree and in the mode of its operation. The other difference is that it acts in accordance with the will. By this he means that the 'primary imagination' operates involuntarily; we perceive whether we wish to or not. The poetic imagination, on the other hand, is one that can be held in check or allowed to act by our own deliberation. The remainder of Coleridge's account is not as clear as we would wish: he tells us that as part of its operation the 'secondary imagination' "dissolves, diffuses and dissipates"; that before creation can take place there must be a process of disintegration. This would seem to suggest that the perceptions, which have already been created out of sense-data, must be melted down again as it were, into their original form and that the 'secondary imagination' uses this raw stuff of consciousness as material for its constructive work. The products of the 'secondary imagination' are like the objects of perception: they are concrete and particular, sensible and not conceptual. Yet, quite clearly the products of the poetic imagination, although they may be similar, cannot be absolutely the same as the objects of perception. If they were, there would be no difference between perception and art. There must be a difference between the two kinds of imagination, but what this is we are not told precisely. All we are told is that the 'secondary imagination' is free in a way that the 'primary' is not. Presumably, however, it is not absolutely free. It is not free, for instance, to create forms that bear no relation at all to the objects of sense perception. In fact its similarity to the 'primary imagination' suggests, if anything, that it must be governed to some extent at least, by the laws which govern our sensory experience.

What Coleridge is trying to convey by describing the poetic imagination as free, is better understood from a study of Kant's aesthetics. Early in the *Biographia Literaria* he tells us that although his argument had been worked out independently, it had been confirmed by the writings of the German philosopher, who had taken possession of his mind "as with a giant's hand." A brief consideration of what Kant has to say will help us not only to understand Coleridge but also to appreciate Shaftesbury's contribution to the subject, for Kant's theory was influenced considerably by eighteenth-century English thinkers, Shaftesbury among them.

Kant distinguishes three types of imagination. In the first place, there is the reproductive imagination which is not free, but is governed by the laws of sense experience; this corresponds to Coleridge's fancy. Secondly, there is the productive imagination, which again is not free but is governed by the *a priori* laws of the understanding. This is parallel to Coleridge's 'primary imagination' which moulds sense-data into perceptions and by bringing sensation and the understanding together makes it possible for the latter to frame concepts and to carry on its work of discursive reasoning. Lastly, for Kant, there is the aesthetic imagination, which is not reproductive (as is the fancy), but productive and also free (that is, independent, to some extent at least, of the laws of the understanding). It is not absolutely free according to Kant, for it is related in an indeterminate sort of way to the understanding.

Kant's analysis of the aesthetic imagination becomes clear when we know what he means by the understanding and how it differs from the reason. The understanding for Kant is the faculty which forms concepts; the discursive faculty that corresponds to what we would call the reasoning. Above this is the reason, a faculty concerned not with the application of concepts to particulars, but with giving the mind regulative principles (what Kant calls 'Ideas') which are independent of sensory knowledge and not empirically verifiable. There are two sorts of Ideas according to Kant, rational and aesthetic. Rational Ideas he describes as "transcendent concepts," which differ from the concepts formed by the understanding in that their application cannot be verified by experience. An aesthetic Idea, on the other hand, is not a concept. No concept, he tells us, is adequate to express the content of an aesthetic Idea.

> "But, by an aesthetic idea," he writes, "I mean that representation of the imagination which induces much thought, yet without the possibility of any definite thought whatever, i.e. *concept*, being adequate to it, and which language, consequently, can never get quite on level terms with or render completely intelligible." (*Critique of Judgment*, trans. Meredith, Oxford, 1911, 175–6.)

The human mind will always endeavour to translate the representations of the aesthetic imagination into conceptual forms, but will always be doomed to failure since no merely logical statement can adequately express the fullness of an aesthetic Idea.

We have already seen that according to Kant the aesthetic imagination is related to the understanding in an indeterminate way. We can now comprehend the meaning of this. Although the products of the aesthetic imagination cannot be translated into concepts, the attempt to do so must always be made and the aesthetic imagination can never be completely free of the understanding. But conceptual statement is no substitute for artistic expression, for it is an organization of experience for a different and more practical purpose. It thus becomes the function of the artist to make real and urgent, features that might be overlooked or thought unimportant in such an organization; part of this function being, for instance, the artist's insistence on the particularity of every situation and event, a feature of experience which is not the special concern of the conceptual thinker. The artistic imagination is free in a sense in which Coleridge's 'primary imagination' (and Kant's productive imagination) are not, for it can produce representations that need not conform exactly to sense experience. Nevertheless, it is not entirely free since though it can go beyond conceptual knowledge it must be related to it.

It is sometimes said that Coleridge owed most of his theory of the imagination to Kant. There are good grounds for taking Coleridge's own statements at their face value and accepting his assertion that Kant only made more systematic and explicit what he had already worked out for himself. It has been suggested that Coleridge was led away by Kant and because of his influence confused the imagination and reason. Actually Coleridge never identifies the imagination with the reason: he calls it the agent of the reason and he does so with a clear realization of what he is about. Reason for Coleridge is a faculty of insight and not of ratiocination, or conceptual thinking. It arrives at truth by direct awareness and not by argument. There is no need, however, to go to Kant for a justification of such a position. Coleridge is careful to remind us that a distinction had been drawn between the reason and the understanding by the philosophers and divines of the seventeenth century. He brings not the Cambridge Platonists, but Milton himself to bear witness to this. In the *Biographia Literaria* he writes,

> "I have cautiously discriminated the terms, the reason and the understanding, encouraged and confirmed by the authority of our genuine divines and philosophers before the Revolution:
>
>> 'both life, and sense,
>> Fancy and understanding; whence the soul
>> Reason receives, and reason is her *being*,
>> Discursive or intuitive: discourse
>> Is oftest yours, the latter most is ours,
>> Differing but in degree, in kind the same.' "
>
> (Chap. X.)

Coleridge might have added that the distinction did not entirely disappear with the passing of the seventeenth century. Although the distinction between the reason and understanding was not drawn so sharply as by Kant, the recognition of a difference between them was characteristic of the Platonic tradition in philosophy. Shaftesbury was aware of a power of reason which is more than discursive reasoning. He believed it to be a faculty which apprehends the truth by an immediate act of awareness. We have already seen that he does not consider moral judgments a matter of inference but of direct awareness. Moreover, when he speaks of the reason as if it were responsible for artistic creation, he means by it a power greater than the discursive faculty. Neither moral judgments nor the products of the artistic imagination are arrived at by inference, nor do they require to be proved valid in the way that scientific truths do. If we ask the ground of their truth the answer is that if our experience is to make sense they demand to be accepted as true. "Reason," in Coleridge's words, "is the source and substance of truths above sense, having their evidence in themselves."

A belief in poetry as the expression of truths which cannot be comprehended by the discursive reasoning became less frequent after the appearance of Locke's *Essay Concerning Human Understanding*. Reason, for Locke, meant little more than the understanding: it is true that he recognized an intuitive knowledge the certitude of which is greater than that given by the discursive reasoning, but whatever he might have meant by this, it is clear that he did not regard poetry as its instrument. The fact that words sometimes have indeterminate meanings was something which Locke deplored, and the ambiguity of poetry, as far as he was concerned, was precisely what was wrong with it.[1] It would be silly, however, to think that a belief in the high calling of poetry ceased to exist. The poets themselves were loath to accept philosophical notions that robbed their work of its true significance, and it is interesting to find Thomas Parnell distinguishing the poetry of fancy (the mere outcome of a passive associative process) from the poetry of imagination which is illumined by a divine fire and springs from the active power of the reason. The lines in which he makes the distinction are not themselves very inspired, but his point is clear enough.

> "My God! from whom proceeds the gifts divine,
> My God! I think I feel the gift is thine.
> Be this no vain illusion which I find,
> Nor Nature's impulse on the passive mind,
> But Reason's act, produc'd by good desire,
> By grace enliven'd with celestial fire;
> While base conceits, like misty sons of Night,
> Before such beams of glory take their flight."
>   (*The Gift of Poetry*.)

III

One big difference between Shaftesbury's and Coleridge's contributions, apart, of course, from the greater detail and profundity of Coleridge's account, is that Shaftesbury's theory is not a psychological one. Coleridge may not have been merely writing psychology, but Shaftesbury made no attempt to do so and, in fact, was always scornful of the new way of ideas in philosophy. All that Shaftesbury really gives us is a picture of the poet as a creator, but

[1] cf. Warton, *Essay on the Genius and Writings of Pope*: "Locke, to his other superior talents, did not add a good taste. He affected to despise poetry, and he depreciated the ancients; which circumstance, as I am informed from undoubted authority, was the source of perpetual discontent and dispute betwixt him and his pupil Lord Shaftesbury." (*Section XII*.)

this is not to be counted entirely against him. No account of the psychological processes involved in writing poetry can validate poetry itself, any more than a psychological analysis of the moral consciousness can justify the validity of our moral judgments. In likening the mind of the poet to the mind of God, Shaftesbury is not making a psychological analysis of the art of writing poetry, nor is his description of the poet something which can be directly and empirically verified as scientific statements can be. He gives us a guiding idea which orders and explains our experience of poetry, though this may, of course, lead to statements about the nature of poetry and the poet's mind which are capable of scientific testing and proof. In other words, we may elaborate from this key-idea psychological theories concerning both the appreciation and the writing of poetry, but we should realize that the idea itself cannot be substantiated directly by scientific means. We accept it or reject it, according to whether the theories which issue from it square with our aesthetic experience or not.

Our main purpose has been to demonstrate Shaftesbury's dissatisfaction with the mechanical account of reality, particularly in its attempt to explain the nature of poetry. He may not have been very successful in persuading his readers of the truth of his view, not because he was wrong, but because the philosophical temper of the time was unsympathetic and because the achievements of science had led to the adoption of scientific presuppositions even in fields where they were manifestly out of place. Coleridge was attempting the same task as Shaftesbury, after nearly a century of experience had demonstrated the truth of the *Characteristics*. The guiding idea behind his philosophy of art was the same as Shaftesbury's. Drawing his inspiration from the same Platonic tradition of English thought, he built up his aesthetic theory on the belief that nature is a work of art and that the poet is made in the image of God.[1]

Although nearly a century passed before Shaftesbury's views were developed into a full-grown theory it would be wrong to suggest that his interest in the imagination was the only one at this time. Addison, Hutcheson, Akenside, Reynolds and Blake are only some of those who concerned themselves with the subject in the eighteenth century. This is not the place in which to examine their writings in detail, but a brief glance at the work of Addison and Akenside is necessary for the present study. Addison's papers *On the Pleasures of the Imagination* appeared in the *Spectator* in the year

[1]For a fuller treatment of this contention, see the present writer's *Coleridge's Theory of the Imagination*, in *English Studies*, 1949.

1712, while the *Moralists* was published in 1709 and the complete *Characteristics* in 1711, so that it is not unlikely that Addison had read and was influenced by Shaftesbury's work. Akenside, whose poem *The Pleasures of the Imagination* appeared in 1744, was a confessed disciple of Shaftesbury (as the notes to his poem reveal) and also an admirer of Addison, and the two main sources of his poem's inspiration are the *Characteristics* and the *Spectator*.

Both Addison and Akenside regard the imagination as not so much the faculty of artistic creation as the source of that aesthetic pleasure which we gain in apprehending not only beauty, but also greatness and novelty. For them it is a faculty of appreciation rather than of invention or creation. According to Addison the imagination lies between the understanding and the senses, and the pleasures it gives rise to, he believes, are not so gross as those of sense or yet so refined as those of the understanding. Akenside's version makes a slight modification, for he places imagination between the senses and what he calls moral perception, but it is clear that his theory is substantially the same as Addison's.

Addison and Akenside are more interested in the nature of the aesthetic judgment than in the processes of artistic creation, and the next chapter, which is concerned with this subject, will take further account of their theories. The ability to make an aesthetic judgment, however, is not the same as that needed to create a work of art, and while their theories of the imagination show considerable insight into the nature of aesthetic appreciation, they are not sufficient to explain artistic creation. It has sometimes been argued that when we appreciate a work of art we reproduce the mental processes that brought it into being and so become artists ourselves, for the time being. That this is not so becomes clear if we treat the theories of Addison and Akenside not as ones about aesthetic judgment, but as ones concerned with aesthetic creation. Viewed in this way they take us a good way, but in the end will prove unsatisfactory.

In placing the imagination between the senses and the understanding Addison and Akenside realize something of the nature of art. They see that it stands between the particulars of sense perception on the one side, and the conceptualizations of the understanding, on the other. To say this, however, is to get no further than recognizing a power identical with Coleridge's 'primary imagination'. For the understanding to work at all some such power must exist, for how could the senses and the understanding ever be reconciled without such an intermediary? Without such a power we should be merely creatures capable of sense experience, but lacking the ability to think or argue. Even our sense experience would be chaotic, being merely a mass of sensation without the organization that is given to it by the higher cognitive processes. To identify this power with the aesthetic and creative imagination, however, is not enough. The importance of the contribution made by Kant and Coleridge was the assertion that there is a power higher than that of the understanding and that this power is the servant not of the understanding, but of the reason. The 'primary imagination' may enable the mind to think conceptually and to organize its sense experience, but this is not the same as the ability to create works of art. We can all perceive and can all think but we are not all artists. What is peculiar to the artistic imagination is its ability to create representations which go beyond both perception and argument. The weakness of Addison and Akenside is that they do not recognize any power higher than the understanding: because of this their account of the imagination fails to do justice to the creative processes involved in art, though, as we shall see, it does say something important about the aesthetic judgment.

Shaftesbury's description of the poet as "a just Prometheus under Jove", on the other hand, is one that bears witness to the really creative nature of the artistic imagination. The Neo-Platonic belief that the natural world is symbolic of the thought of God and that such thought cannot be fully apprehended by conceptual statement can be developed by analogy into a profound theory of aesthetics. The theory, it is true, has its dangers, as we can see in some of the extremer forms of romanticism which sprang from it. The excesses we have in mind, however, were the result of extravagant interpretations of the belief in the first place and are not intrinsic to the belief itself. The Neo-Platonic tradition, as disciplined by Christian thinking, only claimed that man's mind was made in the image of the divine mind and did not contend that it was identical with God's mind. Certain forms of philosophical idealism were sometimes willing to make such a claim and were prepared to hold that all reality falls within the processes of the human mind. Similarly, underlying some forms of romanticism was the assumption that the artistic imagination is really divine and that reality can be comprehended by the constructions of art.

Shaftesbury's use of the Prometheus myth to describe the poetic imagination is itself significant in this connection, for the myth was one that had a peculiar and compelling power for romantic poetry.[1] In England it was generally given a humanitarian, or even a political,

[1] *vide*, for example, Douglas Bush, *Mythology and the Romantic Tradition*.

interpretation, but it was not confined to this. Romanticism saw that the legend could have implications for poetry itself and with writers such as Shelley, for instance, the rebel against tyranny is always associated in some way with the poet:

> "Most wretched men
> Are cradled into poetry by wrong,
> They learn in suffering what they teach in song."
> *(Julian and Maddalo.)*

In Germany especially the myth was interpreted in this way and Prometheus represented as not so much the spirit of striving mankind, as the poet himself. Goethe himself, for example, in one of the earlier poems of his *Sturm und Drang* period, pictures the poet as Prometheus hurling defiance at Jove.

> "Here sit I, forming mortals
> After my image,
> A race, resembling me,
> To suffer, to weep,
> To enjoy, to be glad,
> And thee to scorn,
> As I!"   *(Prometheus*, trans. by E. A. Bowring.)

This conception of the poet as a kind of superman, the products of whose imagination are ultimate truth and reality, is not one that necessarily springs from Shaftesbury's theory. We should remember that in the classical forms of the myth, which would have been Shaftesbury's background, a final reconciliation was achieved between Prometheus and Jove. Indeed, Shaftesbury's own phrase implies a subordination of Prometheus to Jove, not a usurpation by the poet of the divine nature.

Certain other types of romanticism have rested on the assumption that while man himself may be fallen, the rest of the natural world does not share this fall. The suggestion that nature is symbolic of another world can easily be turned into loose talk about a sacramental principle in nature and become the doctrine that the contemplation of natural beauty provides some sort of peculiar and superior access to reality and truth. It could easily become the view that God is nature.

The Neo-Platonic tradition, at least in the Christian form that Shaftesbury knew, would make no absolute claim for the beauty of either nature or art, for it believed that the natural order, including the human mind, was fallen. Nevertheless, it would claim that, while lacking any absolute validity, the apprehension of beauty affords us something for which there is no substitute. In the first place, the beauty of both nature and art is the expression of thought which cannot adequately be grasped by discursive reasoning. By the contemplation of beauty we become aware of other minds and finally of the divine mind which is the author of all beauty and truth. In the second place, the contemplation of beauty gives us a pleasure which is *sui generis*; we contemplate it for its own sake and not because it will make us richer, or more powerful, or will give us useful knowledge.

If the fault of Addison and Akenside is to relate the artistic imagination too closely to the understanding, the fault of the extremer forms of Romanticism is to separate them too sharply. It is the great merit of Kant's account that he avoids both extremes and makes the relationship between the two an indeterminate one. While it is undoubtedly true that a poem cannot be translated into other terms without suffering loss, we must still maintain that an attempt to do so is possible and, indeed, even necessary as a part of our understanding of it. If there is nothing in poetry which can be communicated in terms that have a common meaning then poetry would cease to exist. The belief of certain Symbolist poets of our own time would appear to be that poetry can communicate private experiences without recourse to common meanings and their poetry puts this belief into practice, for its symbolism seems to have a purely private significance. Surely such a belief is mistaken. Even purely lyrical poetry, which professes to say nothing beyond the expression of emotion, must communicate this emotion by reference to some sort of common meaning. No doubt, poetry which tries to express experiences which are novel, or very personal, will be especially handicapped by the seeming lack of any suitable medium of communication, and new forms of poetry of any kind have to develop the taste and understanding necessary to their appreciation. Yet the fact that a medium of communication is sought for so strenuously is an indication, not only that the poet is trying to say something unique and particular, but that he is obliged to express this to some extent in terms which are general and common. If this were not so, the poet would not struggle to make his meaning clear in the logical sense. The appeal of poetry would consist in its pattern of sounds and nothing else.

Some modern poets and critics have had recourse to a theory of a group unconsciousness, thinking that this justifies the view that the meaning of poetic imagery can be communicated before it is understood. But this is no way out of the dilemma. No recourse to psychological doctrine, no talk of primordial images, can ever get over the fact that meaning is something that implies understanding on the conscious level, whatever else in addition it might imply. To be sure, poetry can move one before it is fully understood; no one would wish to deny that. But however important such an element in our appreciation may be, the reader of poetry will not be satisfied with this alone; he will wish to interpret the imagery, to translate the symbolism, so far as he is able, into the terms of his own experience and thinking. Such efforts may never be wholly successful, but this is not to say that they can have no success at all.

Miss Rosemary Freeman's study of English emblem books, to which I have already referred, shows that there was a long tradition in England which used symbolical pictures and diagrams for the expression of ideas. These emblems, as they were called, generally endeavoured to point some moral truth or to demonstrate some maxim of practical wisdom by means of rebuses, allegorical figures, and other symbolical devices. This tradition failed to survive the development of new modes of thinking which assigned little value to the expression of abstract thought in this way, but Shaftesbury realized that though emblems in this old sense might have been banished by scientific categories, there was still a highly important rôle in thinking which symbolism alone could play. Emblems of the old sort were gone never to return, but Shaftesbury continued to use the word and gave a great deal of thought to the grounds on which their real importance could be demonstrated. In the notes which form part of the *Second Characters* and which were left by him for the unwritten essay on *Plastics*, Shaftesbury distinguishes between three kinds of symbols, or 'characters'. Firstly, there are arbitrary signs such as words or the symbols of mathematics and shorthand. Secondly, there are imitations of actual life; in other words, symbols which are literally copies of natural objects and people. Besides these, however, there is a third sort, which Shaftesbury calls emblematic; a 'middle or mixed' form of symbolism, standing between the other two and having something of the nature of both of them. This he regards as the truly imaginative form of symbolism which belongs to real art. It is not, on the one hand, merely the use of arbitrary signs to explicate thought which has already been formulated, nor, on the other hand, is it merely a mirror image of the natural world containing no thought at all;

yet it combines what is valuable in both of these. It is related to conceptual thought sufficiently to avoid being idiosyncratic or meaningless, and yet it manifests itself in concrete and particular forms, like the objects of real life.

The older emblem books had used the first kind of symbolism; they contained merely mechanically-contrived pictures and designs for the communication of thought that was not integral to the emblems themselves. But the emblems with which Shaftesbury embellished the second edition of the *Characteristics* were real works of art illustrating not only something which could be communicated separately, but embodying in themselves what could be expressed in no other way. They were a reinforcement of what Shaftesbury had said in the text, not a substitute. They were allegorical, certainly, and meant to have a reference and meaning beyond themselves, but this does not matter. For allegory is an ambiguous term: while some kinds of allegory are, indeed, only mechanically-contrived products of the fancy, others are indisputably works of the imagination. Shaftesbury's emblems were not only illustrations of his general philosophical principles, but the imaginative and allegorized embodiment of his teaching.

CHAPTER VI

THE AESTHETIC JUDGMENT

"Thus doth Beauty dwell
There most conspicuous, even in outward shape,
Where dawns the high expression of a mind."
(Akenside: *Pleasures of the Imagination*.)

I

WHEN writers of the Augustan period asserted that the function of poetry was to imitate, they did not have in mind the imitation of past works of literature so much as the imitation of nature. The importance of the great writings of classical antiquity was that they exemplified what a close observation of nature could do; the precepts of Aristotle and Horace alike were "those rules of old discovered not devis'd", which owed their authority precisely to the fact that they could be found in nature. Dryden indicated the relation that was felt to hold between nature and the great classical writers, when he wrote in his *Apology for Heroic Poetry*,

"Thus I grant you, that the knowledge of Nature was the original rule; and that all poets ought to study her, as well as Aristotle and Horace, her interpreters. But then this also undeniably follows, that those things, which delight all ages, must have been an imitation of Nature; which is all I contend." (*Essays*, ed. Ker, I, 183-4.)

What the critics of the time did not appear to realize was that while clarifying the term 'imitation', they were still using the word 'nature' imprecisely. 'Imitation of nature' can mean many things: the direct representation of external objects; a concern with man's social life; a desire to base literature upon experience; or simply a demand for internal consistency and coherence in a work of art. The development of scientific method in the seventeenth century in stressing the order and rationality of nature, had given the concept a new emphasis; an emphasis that made the most characteristic feature of nature its conformity to the laws which science had discovered. It followed that if poetry were to be an imitation of nature it, too, should demonstrate the same order and symmetry, should obey the same laws and possess the same coherence as were now seen to characterize nature. Dennis put the matter as succinctly as anyone in *The Epistle Dedicatory* to his *Advancement and Reformation of Modern Poetry* (1701).

> "But, as both Nature and Reason, which two in a larger Acceptation, is Nature, owe their greatness, their Beauty, their Majesty, to their perpetual Order . . . so Poetry which is an Imitation of nature must do the same thing. It can neither have greatness or Real Beauty, if it swerves from the Laws which Reason severely prescribes it, and the more Irregular any Poetical composition is, the nearer it comes to Extravagance and Confusion, and to Nonsense, which is Nothing."

To call the Augustan age an age of rationalism, however, is an over-simplification, for its main tendency in religion, morals, metaphysics, and literature was to make the criterion 'reasonableness' rather than 'reason'. The two are not, of course, the same thing; and in literature the appeal was rather to 'good-sense' than to abstract rational principles. Moreover, while the Augustan critics expected a literary work to exhibit symmetry and proportion and to obey rational principles, it would be a mistake to suggest that they regarded reason as the sole faculty of poetic creation. As we have already seen, the generally accepted view was the one elaborated by Hobbes, which rested poetic composition on fancy as well as judgment. The same balance is encountered when we consider aesthetic appreciation, though here the two elements of fancy and judgment were more difficult to reconcile.

Certainly the critic at the end of the seventeenth century did not think that in judging a poem he was employing only his reason. In nearly all criticism at this time there was a recognition that some element beyond the scope of reason enters into our appreciation of poetry, and there were features which together formed a tendency to emphasize taste to a much greater degree than previous ages had yet done. This tendency sprang out of and was reinforced by a growing relativism in literary criticism and it is significant that those critics who emphasized taste also popularized the belief that literature is the product of economic, social and climatic forces. In the Ancients and Moderns dispute, critics on both sides had brought forward arguments based on the view that changes of external circumstance had affected literature for better or worse. Temple, Wotton,

Dryden and others had all expressed a belief that there is an evolutionary process in literature which, although it cannot be described in exact scientific terms, nevertheless gives rise to change and development, and Pope, who once thought of writing a history of English poetry, subscribed to the same doctrine in his *Essay on Criticism*. Later in the eighteenth century the belief flowered into the historical method of criticism; one of the best known products of this method was Thomas Blackwell's *Enquiry into the Life and Writings of Homer* (1735), and the first critical work really to be based upon the historical outlook was Thomas Warton's *Observations on the Faerie Queene* (1754). Warton's account of the *Faerie Queene* was an attempt to evaluate the poem in relation to its historical *milieu*, and the experience he thus accumulated proved invaluable when he came to write his *History of English Poetry*. Joseph Warton, who shared his brother's critical outlook and opinions, used the same approach in his *Essay on the Writings and Genius of Pope* (1756), where he made his starting-point the belief that

> "We can never completely relish, or adequately understand any author, especially any Ancient, except we constantly keep in our eye, his climate, his country and his age."

The historical method in criticism was inspired and strengthened by the revival of interest in antiquarian research, which in many cases had been fostered by the very writers who had popularized the concept of taste; it was, in fact, part of that whole liberalizing movement in criticism, of which the believers in taste were the chief originators.

These critics insisted, as all good critics have insisted, that there is a beauty in poetry unattainable by any mere application of the rules, but they reformulated the age-old distinction between genius and application. Genius, or this "certain Air and Spirit which perhaps the most Learned and judicious in other Arts do not perfectly apprehend" and which is not "attainable by any Study or Industry"[1] was considered to be the prerogative of the man of taste. Temple, Gildon, Farquhar, Dennis and others emphasized this in varying degrees. Dennis declared that

> "that which is commonly called good sence, is not sufficient to form a good tast in Poetry, tho' the good sence should be joyn'd with an inclination for Poetry, and with a tolerable share of

[1] Edward Phillips, Preface to *Theatrum Poetarum*, 1675.

experience in it: For if this were sufficient, it would undeniably follow, that all who have this Experience, this Inclination, and this good Sence, would have the same tast: whereas it is manifest that they who are not without these qualities, differ very considerably in their opinions and in their tasts of Verses and Poems."
(*Remarks Upon Prince Arthur*, 1696, Pt. II, Ch. I).

It was soon felt, however, that there must be a standard by which taste itself could be judged and which would raise it from the level of mere liking and disliking: otherwise the result would be critical anarchy. George Farquhar, with more than a hint of irony, drew the attention of his fellow writers to the position in which criticism had placed itself, when he wrote in his *Discourse upon Comedy*,

"Now here are a multitude of Criticks, whereof the twentieth Person only has read *Quae Genus*, and yet every one is a Critick after his own way; that is, Such a play is best, because I like it. A very familiar Argument, methinks to prove the Excellence of a Play, and to which an Author wou'd be very unwilling to appeal for his Success: Yet such is the unfortunate State of Dramatick Poetry, that it must submit to such Judgments; and by the Censure or Approbation of such variety it must either stand or fall."

Yet, significantly, it was not any *a priori*, rational principle that was called in to decide the standard of taste; nor, still more surprisingly, was the consensus of opinion through the ages, or even an appeal to men's experience, chosen as the final arbiter. The only way, it was felt, by which a standard of taste or criterion of judgment could be established was to ground it upon artistic sensibility. The opinion of those who can enter into and share, to some extent at any rate, in the act of literary creation was considered the only sure one. Dennis and Farquhar both came to the same conclusion in essays which were published in 1702. Dennis, in *A Large Account of the Taste in Poetry*, makes the point with an engaging forthrightness.

"This, I think, Sir, need not be disputed, that for the judging of any sort of Writings, those talents are in some measure requisite, which were necessary to produce them."

and Farquhar asks:

"Is it reasonable that any Person that has never writ a Distich of Verses in his life, shou'd set up for a Dictator in Poetry; and without the least Practice in his own Performance, must give Laws and Rules to that of others?"

Not only should the critic be one who can enter into the creative processes of the poet's mind, but he should be cultivated, a man of refinement and discernment. No longer was the critic required to be a philosopher who could lay down laws for poetic composition; the essential requirements were acquaintance with the arts and aesthetic sensibility. Farquhar continues, in the *Discourse upon Comedy*, with a long tirade against Aristotle's claim to be a critic and ends with these words:

> "I have talk'd so long to lay a Foundation for these following Conclusions; *Aristotle* was no poet, and consequently not capable of giving Instructions in the Art of Poetry."

This disregard of the rules and the Ancients, and the new emphasis on effectiveness, had become increasingly popular by the time Shaftesbury began to write. In the conception of the critic as a man of liberal culture, with sensibility, or with actual experience, of creative writing, can be seen an approach to the Romantic attitude, which regarded criticism as a re-creation of the emotional experience of the artist himself. This, together with the growing belief in a sense of historical development, made Augustan criticism much more liberal than is generally supposed; the extreme neo-classicist exists more frequently in text-books than in fact. The truth is that literary criticism had only recently become emancipated from the authority of classical antiquity and was still looking for principles on which it could base its inquiries. Criticism was becoming self-conscious and examining the scope, the assumptions and the methods of its own work, and it was from this increase of self-consciousness that the study of aesthetics was born in England.

With the breakdown of traditional authority it was natural that criticism should turn to the new philosophy of ideas and substitute psychological explanation for the dictates of Aristotle; and even Shaftesbury, though he had little sympathy with psychological analysis, was obliged to work within the framework of con-temporary thought. This psychological bias can be seen in the question which underlies a good deal of his and subsequent aesthetics; the question whether a work of art appeals to our reason or feelings. At first sight there would appear to be plenty of evidence to suggest that Shaftesbury makes reason the ultimate criterion. The appeal to reason certainly holds a higher place in his theory than the Ancients and the rules, but it is not as strongly emphasized as in the work of the majority of his contemporaries, and it is rather in the concept of taste that he finds his guiding principle. He thus follows in the tradition of writers such as Dennis, Temple, Gildon and Farquhar.

That quality in a work of art which defies analysis and can be described only in terms of the effect it produces, Shaftesbury calls the *je ne sais quoi*. He never seeks to make this a mysterious or esoteric quality and says simply that it is a charm captured from nature.

> "Though his [i.e., the poet's] intention be to please the world, he must nevertheless be, in a manner, above it, and fix his eye upon that consummate grace, that beauty of Nature, and that perfection of numbers which the rest of mankind, feeling only by the effect whilst ignorant of the cause, term the *je ne sçay quoy*, the unintelligible or the I know not what, and suppose to be a kind of charm or enchantment of which the artist himself can give no account."
>
> (*Advice to An Author, Characteristics*, I, 214.)

Shaftesbury never succeeds in defining it and, indeed, the significance of such a phrase lies precisely in the fact that a new critical awareness had arisen which could not yet be expressed in precise terminology. Such phrases are slogans and not detailed marching orders. Pope suggests the same sort of belief in the well-known lines of the *Essay on Criticism* where he says that the task of the poet is to

> "... snatch a grace beyond the reach of art,
> Which, without passing thro' the judgment, gains
> The heart, and all its end at once attains."

The origin of the term *je ne sais quoi* is not easy to trace. Bouhours, the French critic, discusses the phrase in his *Les Entretiens d'Ariste et d'Eugène* (1671), where he says,

> "Les Italiens, qui font mystère de tout, emploient en toutes rencontres leur *non sò che*: on ne voit rien de plus commun dans leurs poètes."

He devotes more space to it than do any of his contemporaries, and Shaftesbury probably borrowed it from him; but whether he did so, or not, the term was not much in vogue in England before Shaftesbury's day and it was undoubtedly the *Characteristics* that made it fashionable.

We meet quite frequently in the *Characteristics* the idea that literature is influenced by national, political, economic and even climatic forces. Literature, for Shaftesbury, takes different forms according to the changes of man's historical development. He would have agreed with Ruskin that good art can be produced only in a healthy society and that beauty and morality are causally related. Furthermore, he believes that each nationality has its own genius and that literature will flourish or decline as this genius manifests itself in sound, or corrupt, political institutions. An instance of his use of this idea is seen in the way he constantly attributes the differences between English and French literature to the temperaments and institutions of the two countries.

> " 'Tis evident our natural genius shines above that airy neighbouring nation, of whom, however, it must be confessed that with truer pains and industry they have sought politeness, and studied to give the Muses their due body and proportion, as well as the natural ornaments of correctness, chastity and grace of style." (*Advice to An Author, Characteristics*, I, 142.)

In England the national temperament insisted on mixing comedy with tragedy, whereas, in France, the lack of political freedom killed the tragic spirit altogether. The "variableness and inconstancy of our weather" must be the reason, he ironically declares, for the sudden changes and lack of unity of so much English writing. He also realized quite clearly the part that economic factors play in literature. The system of patronage had for long encouraged sycophancy, but there was an equal danger of insincerity in the pamphleteering wars of the time: booksellers, for example, were anxious to maintain a controversy and to encourage disputants to further efforts, not because of public spirit, or an interest in the truth, but for personal gain.

> "So have I known a crafty glazier," he writes, "in time of frost, procure a football to draw into the street the emulous chiefs of the robust youth." (*Miscellany* I, *Characteristics*, II, 165.)

Whatever might be said about the theory of criticism, its practice for Shaftesbury was not a matter of philosophical speculation. It demanded sensibility, taste and an acquaintance with the arts, and the critic, in his view, needed to be a *virtuoso* rather than a systematic thinker. By this he did not mean that the critic should be a scholar and antiquarian, which is what the word generally meant in his day. He had little patience with the sort of specialist scholarship that had grown up in the age of Anne.

"I am persuaded that to be a *virtuoso* (so far as befits a gentleman) is a higher step towards the becoming a man of virtue and good sense than the being what in this age we call a scholar." (*Advice to An Author, Characteristics*, I, 214–5.)

The *virtuosi* are "the real fine gentlemen, the lovers of art and ingenuity, such as have seen the world." They must not become too specialized in their interests, or devoted to out-of-the-way researches, or they will become 'inferior virtuosi', who

"in seeking so earnestly for rarities . . . fall in love with rarity for rareness' sake." (*Miscellany* III, *Characteristics*, II, 253.)

Criticism, he thought, needed to be liberated from its academic bondage and to be much more a creative art in its own right, nourished by a direct acquaintance with the arts themselves and informed by a wide and liberal culture.

II

Although Shaftesbury belonged to the group of critics who made taste their dominant idea, he believed in a universal standard of judgment. He did not regard each person as a rule to himself and he never used the word 'taste' as meaning mere personal liking or disliking. The word 'taste' is, of course, ambiguous. The popularity of such an ambiguous term generally betokens some shift of emphasis or some change of ideas in the field where the word is used, and the popularity of the word 'taste' in the early eighteenth century is no exception to this rule. 'Taste' is a word which is not only ambiguous, but when applied to literature, is fraught with all the dangers of metaphorical language. It can mean, on one side, mere personal preference or, on the other, it can signify a universal standard of judgment; in other words, it can be used to describe things precisely opposite. As a matter of historical fact, there can be no doubt that the concept of taste stressed the emotional rather than the rational element in the aesthetic judgment and did much to lessen the objectivity of critical standards in men's eyes. Shaftesbury himself, would have deplored this result and yet, paradoxically, he was one of those chiefly responsible for it.

The ambiguity of the word 'taste' bore witness to a real difficulty and a difficulty that was not merely the practical one of trying to hold in balance judgment and fancy, reason and taste, in evaluating a work of art. It was a logical problem which was of the utmost importance and which was to haunt critical theory for a long time to come. Those who upheld taste recognized that aesthetic pleasure is a feeling, whereas the supporters of reason claimed that if the aesthetic judgment were to be universally valid it must be made at the bar of the reason. When one man says that he considers a picture beautiful, he implies that other people should consider it beautiful as well: he is not merely concerned with his own reactions. Similarly, when two people disagree about the aesthetic quality of a piece of music, it is felt that one of the parties must be right and the other wrong and that they are not merely stating their personal preferences. In other words, we think that aesthetic judgments have a universal application and validity. But how can this be if aesthetic pleasure is the concern only of the feelings, and if the aesthetic judgment is formulated by them? It was this question which perplexed so many of the eighteenth-century critics and which shaped the critical theory of the period. Many of these writers failed to see the problem clearly, of course, but all recognized a difficulty in the apparently irreconcilable claims of the feelings and the reason.

The way out of the *impasse* lay in the doctrine of an aesthetic sense. Shaftesbury had popularized the idea of a moral sense in his *Inquiry Concerning Virtue* and it is clear that in using such a notion he was attempting to solve a similar problem in morals. Though he never really describes accurately what he means by a moral sense, and though he tries to make it partake of both the reason and the feelings, nevertheless his theory does justice to what is undoubtedly a feature of moral experience. In many cases our moral judgments are made immediately and in such a way that they appear as a spontaneous reaction. The moral sense is something that satisfies this claim of immediacy. We see a character, or action, and at once we make a moral judgment almost as if it were a matter of sensation. The same thing happens with judgments of beauty according to Shaftesbury and, indeed, he believes it to be the same sense that operates in both cases; for, according to him, beauty and goodness are the same and taste is as much concerned with morals as with the arts.

"Is there then ... a natural beauty of figures? and is there not as natural a one of actions? No sooner the eye opens upon figures, the ears to sounds, than straight the beautiful results and grace and harmony are known and acknowledged. No sooner are actions viewed, no sooner the human affections and passions discerned (and they are most of them as soon discerned as felt) than straight an inward eye distinguishes and sees the fair and shapely, the amiable and the admirable, apart from the deformed, the foul, the odious, or the despicable." (*Moralists, Characteristics*, II, 137.)

This theory of a special sense which apprehends beauty immediately the latter is presented to it, does not really solve the problem. For one thing, he never fully discusses the relation of this sense to the reason, although he would not seem to dissociate it from the reason altogether. On the other hand, if it is a sense in the same way as our other senses of sight, smell, physical taste, and so on, our aesthetic judgments would be as relative as our tastes in food and there would be no possibility of setting up a standard of taste. In fact, *de gustibus non est disputandum* would be as true of our artistic opinions as of our physical appetites.

Yet in spite of its failure to provide a real answer to the philosophical question, Shaftesbury's theory was seized upon with enthusiasm by the critics as a solution of their problem. It is surprising how many subsequent writers accepted the belief in a special aesthetic sense. The term was not used with any great precision, and often the writers who adopted it were vague about its exact meaning. Leonard Welsted, for example, tells us, in the *State of Poetry* (1724), that

"Many of the Graces in Poetry may, I grant, be talk'd of in very intelligible Language, but intelligible only to those who have a natural *Taste* for it, or are born with the Talent of judging: To have what we call *Taste*, is having, one may say, a new Sense or Faculty superadded to the ordinary ones of the Soul, the Prerogative of Fine Spirits!"

Shaftesbury's disciple, Hutcheson, in his *Inquiry into the Original of our Ideas of Beauty and Virtue* (1725) bases a belief in this sense upon the immediacy of our aesthetic appreciation and its apparent independence of reasoning.

> "This superior Power of Perception is justly called *a Sense*, because of its Affinity to the other Senses in this, that the Pleasure does not arise from any Knowledge of Principles, Proportions, Causes, or of the Usefulness of the Object; but strikes us at first with the Idea of Beauty: nor does the most accurate knowledge increase this measure of Beauty, however it may super-add a distinct rational Pleasure from prospects of Advantage, or from the Increase of Knowledge." (*Treatise I*, Sect. I).

That the doctrine had a long life is seen from its appearance in Blair's *Lectures on Rhetoric and Belles Lettres* which appeared as late in the century as 1783. In the second of these *Lectures* Blair defines taste as an internal sense distinct from any rational process.

> "The first question that occurs concerning it is, whether it is to be considered as an internal sense, or as an exertion of reason? Reason is a very general term; but if we understand by it, that power of the mind which in speculative matters discovers truth, and in practical matters judges of the fitness of means to an end, I apprehend the question may be easily answered. For nothing can be more clear than that Taste is not resolvable into any such operation of Reason. . . . Hence the faculty by which we relish such beauties seems more a-kin to a feeling of sense, than to a process of the understanding."

Blair is firmly of the opinion that there is a standard of taste and that it is possible to say whether a man's taste is good or bad, and yet he wishes to give due recognition to individual preference. Truth, he tells us, is one, but beauty can be many.

> "It is not in matters of Taste, as in questions of mere reason, where there is but one conclusion that can be true, and all the rest are erroneous. Truth which is the object of reason is one; Beauty which is the object of Taste, is manifold."

But this does not get him out of the difficulty and applies only when men are discussing different objects: when they are discussing the same object and come to different conclusions one must be right and the other wrong. Blair himself is uneasy with his own answer, for he goes on to suggest that the solution is to set up as a criterion the general consensus of opinion throughout the ages.

"That which men concur the most in admiring must be held to be beautiful."

This is the view which Dryden and others had expressed, and is a good working principle; but it comes to grief eventually, for one man may be right against the majority and in such a case there must be some other criterion by which the general consensus of opinion itself is judged.

We saw in the last chapter that Addison, too, was interested in the same question. His *Spectator* papers on *The Pleasures of the Imagination* are concerned with the nature of the aesthetic judgment, and imagination for him is the faculty of appreciation. Like Shaftesbury's aesthetic sense, Addison's imagination is a *tertium quid*, which attempts to make the best of both the worlds of reason and the feelings. According to Addison the pleasures of the imagination are not so gross as those of sense, or so refined as those of the understanding. Now this, though it might be in accordance with observation and experience, puts him straightaway in the same paradoxical position as his contemporaries. He is faced with the same question of whether the imagination is the agent of the senses or of the understanding; or, to put it in the terms we have been using, of the reason or the feelings. Instead of trying to resolve the dual nature of his imagination Addison accepts its twofold reference and divides beauty itself into two kinds, each of them corresponding to one aspect of the faculty. In *Spectator* 412, he writes,

". . . there are several modifications of matter which the mind, without any previous consideration, pronounces at first sight beautiful or deformed. . . . There is a second kind of Beauty that we find in the several products of art and nature, which does not work in the Imagination with that warmth and violence as the beauty that appears in our proper species, but is apt however to raise in us a secret delight, and a kind of fondness for the places or objects in which we discover it. This consists in either the gaiety or variety of colours, in the symmetry and proportion of parts, in the arrangement and disposition of bodies, or in a just mixture and concurrence of all together."

Hutcheson takes over this distinction from Addison and makes it much more explicit: of the two kinds of beauty, the one is what he calls Original or Absolute, the other is Comparative or Relative. The first is apprehended in an immediate act of awareness by the aesthetic sense, or the feelings: the other belongs only to the imitative arts and becomes manifest when a work of art is compared with its original; it is perceived by the reason, since it is dependent upon our awareness of a relationship between two objects.

> "We therefore by Absolute Beauty understand only that Beauty, which we perceive in Objects without comparison to any thing external, of which the Object is suppos'd an Imitation, or Picture; such as that Beauty perceiv'd from the Works of Nature, artificial Forms, Figures, Theorems. Comparative or Relative Beauty is that which we perceive in Objects, commonly considered as Imitations or Resemblances of something else." (*Treatise I*, Sect. I).

The two kinds of beauty described by Hutcheson are not identical with those distinguished by Addison, but both witness to the fact that in some cases beauty is apprehended immediately and in others is perceived only after reflection. The latter kind of beauty is larger in scope than Hutcheson's comparative beauty, for it is not limited to art. When we contemplate natural beauty, such as in a landscape, our appreciation is often heightened by relating the parts to each other and to the whole, by grouping and balancing the various elements; that is, by an act of reason. The distinction was not only an attempt to interpret experience, however, but the outcome of a desire to reconcile the claims of the reason and the feelings and to give a due place to both.

The distinction, once made, can be found in a great many critical writings of the eighteenth century. It appears in Hume's youthful work, *A Treatise of Human Nature* (1738), which distinguishes between the beauty of the imagination and the beauty of sense, in John Gilbert Cooper's *Letters Concerning Taste* and in William Shenstone's *Essays on Men and Manners*. Henry Home, Lord Kames, puts it as precisely as anyone in his *Elements of Criticism*:

> "Considering attentively the beauty of visible objects, we discover two kinds. The first may be termed *intrinsic* beauty, because it is discovered in a single object viewed apart without relation to any other.... The other may be termed *relative* beauty, being founded on the relation of objects." (I, 244.)

As we might expect, the distinction became a feature of critical practice as well as of theory. James Forrester, the author of *The Polite Philosopher*, found it useful, for example, in describing Inigo Jones's Banqueting Hall in Whitehall, of which he made the somewhat curious judgment:

> "It fills our minds with rational delight,
> And pleases on reflection, as at sight."

III

It is not too much to say that the development of critical theory throughout the eighteenth century was determined by this question of whether the faculty of aesthetic judgment is the reason or the feelings. It is a question that is always in the background and it may be truly said that the history of eighteenth-century aesthetics is the chronicle of the attempts made to answer it. It remained, indeed, a sort of skeleton in the philosophical cupboard. Not until Kant faced the problem was any satisfactory solution found and then it became clear that the question had not been precisely formulated. Both those who insisted that aesthetic pleasure is a feeling and those who held that if the aesthetic judgment were to be universally valid, it must be the product of the reason, were to some extent right; but it needed Kant to go beyond the two points of view and to reconcile them.

Much of Kant's thought may be said to deal with the perennial problem in philosophy of the relation between particulars and universals and his contribution to the discussion of the nature of beauty and how we judge it can be viewed as part of this problem. We have already seen that the products of the artistic imagination must be regarded as particular objects which cannot be adequately comprehended in logical form. Similarly, all objects when viewed aesthetically are, for Kant, particulars in the same way. In the ordinary course of things we group, classify and compare objects by making logical judgments about them, but when we look at things aesthetically this is not so. In artistic appreciation we are concerned with the actual, particular and individual object. As Kant says,

> "There can, therefore, be no rule according to which any one is to be compelled to recognise anything as beautiful. Whether a dress, a house, or a flower is beautiful is a matter upon which one

declines to allow one's judgment to be swayed by any reasons or principles. We want to get a look at the Object with our own eyes, just as if our delight depended on sensation." (*Critique of Judgment*, trans. Meredith, 56.)

It is true, of course, that we can make a general statement such as that all roses are beautiful. In such a case, however, Kant shows that we are making a judgment which is founded upon several aesthetic judgments. As a matter of experience every rose that we have seen, we have judged beautiful, but on each of the several occasions we have done so, what we were concerned with was a particular rose.

Yet, strangely enough, every time that we make an aesthetic judgment we assume that other people ought to agree with us; we are not content to believe that we are merely recording our own reactions, or expressing a personal preference. It is this which distinguishes the beautiful from the merely pleasant. When we express a preference for tea rather than coffee, we do not presume that everyone else should do the same; we are quite content to leave this as a matter of subjective taste. When, however, we say that a play by Shakespeare is superior to one by Mr. Priestley, we imply that everyone should agree with us. But how does this come about, if we have agreed that our judgment is independent of objective and conceptual thinking? It cannot be because of some objective quality in the thing we judge which regulates and determines our judgment, for if there were such a quality it could be made the object of logical statements. We thus arrive at Kant's solution to the problem put to him by the eighteenth-century English thinkers. The aesthetic judgment, he tells us, is universal; something which must be valid for everyone. It is not objective, however; for there is no objective quality which we can point to and say, "This is why you must consider it beautiful".

Kant maintains that our aesthetic judgments have a universal validity, but that their universality is a subjective and not an objective one. We must not misunderstand him, however, for he does not mean that what is universally valid is the feeling of pleasure we get from looking at a beautiful object. He does not mean that we obtain pleasure from the contemplation of an object and *because* of this pleasure judge that it must be beautiful. Kant is most emphatic on this point. The judgment of beauty comes first. It is because we consider a thing beautiful that we obtain aesthetic pleasure from it. What is universally valid is the state of mind which gives rise to the pleasure, that is, the aesthetic judgment. Everyone contemplating the same beautiful object should have the same state of mind and consequently should experience the same aesthetic pleasure.

What this state of mind is, is not very clear in Kant's account. On the one hand, he does not hold that an object of beauty can be regarded as food and drink are: the appreciation of beauty is not merely a matter of sensation, a private relation between a particular person and a particular object. On the other hand, beauty is not something which can really be handled in logical forms as an item of knowledge. Like Addison, Kant puts aesthetic appreciation between sensation and the understanding. But he goes farther than Addison and draws out the fundamental nature of our aesthetic judgments by contrasting them with our logical judgments. As we saw in the last chapter, Kant's belief is that we organize the material given to us in sensation by means of the productive imagination, which acts as a sort of bridge between our senses and our reasoning powers. This productive imagination, by bringing sensation and the understanding together, makes it possible for us to order our sense experience. In the case of logical judgments, there is a clear and determinate relationship between the imagination and the understanding. Now Kant advances the view that some sort of relationship must exist between sensation and the understanding in our aesthetic judgments. When we speak of a work of art or a natural scene, as being beautiful, we do not regard the pleasure they give us merely as a matter of sensation. We speak of our aesthetic appreciation as if it were a form of knowledge and as if it had an objective validity. This can only be because there is some sort of relationship between the imagination and the understanding. It is not a determinate relationship as in the case of logical judgments, but rather a subjective harmony, a sense of well-being because two faculties of our minds have come together. This is the state of mind which gives our aesthetic judgments universal validity. Everyone, in contemplating beauty, should be conscious of such a harmony and should derive aesthetic pleasure from the consciousness that his understanding has come to terms with the interpretation of sense experience made by his imagination.

Kant's doctrine is difficult and this has been an inadequate expression of it. What perhaps is the most fundamental principle in the whole of its complex structure is his assertion of the disinterestedness of the aesthetic judgment. We have seen already that he distinguishes sharply between the judgment that something is beautiful and the judgment that something is merely pleasant. While the aesthetic judgment is subjective, it never owes its validity to this fact, and it is in spite of its subjectivity, not because of it, that it holds good for all men. When I read a poem, or look at a picture, if I am sufficiently impressed, I say that I think it beautiful. I do not say, "I think it beautiful for me"; to do so, would be to bring in a partiality which would at once undermine the claims of the real aesthetic judgment. For this reason Kant also distinguishes between aesthetic and moral judgments. When we say that a thing is good we imply that it ought to exist. We are not disinterested in the face of moral issues, but at once include in our judgments the desire to see the better supplant the worse. It is not so in our strictly aesthetic judgments. We may say that we would like more beautiful things to exist, but this is not in itself an aesthetic judgment. Kant brings out the disinterested nature of the aesthetic judgment by a simple illustration. If we were confronted with a fine palace we might make all sorts of statements. We could say that it should never have been built; that it is the product of sweated labour; or, that we envy the owner and that we should like to possess it; but none of these observations is an aesthetic judgment. All we are asked to say is whether it is beautiful and all other considerations are irrelevant.

It is surprising how much of Kant's aesthetics has its source in eighteenth-century England. As Hume was said to have aroused him from his dogmatic slumbers in theory of knowledge, so it could be maintained with equal truth that the English writers were his starting-point in aesthetics. The problems leading Kant to a consideration of art were those which had been propounded mainly by the tradition of thought started by Shaftesbury and continued by Addison, Hutcheson, Hume, and Burke. Kant, indeed, owed to these thinkers more than the formulation of the questions, for in many instances he built on the foundations they had laid. That the aesthetic judgment must be disinterested, for example, was a principle first clearly enunciated by Shaftesbury and developed by later English writers. Shaftesbury is most emphatic that to desire a thing, or to find it pleasant, is quite different from saying it is beautiful. In the *Moralists* (in the person of Theocles) he puts this most forcibly as something central to his whole work.

"Imagine then, good Philocles, if being taken with the beauty of the ocean, which you see yonder at a distance, it should come into your head to seek how to command it, and, like some mighty admiral, ride master of the sea, would not the fancy be a little absurd? ... Let who will call it theirs, replied Theocles, you will own the enjoyment of this kind to be very different from that which should naturally follow from the contemplation of the ocean's beauty. The bridegroom-Doge, who in his stately Bucentaur floats on the bosom of his Thetis, has less possession than the poor shepherd, who from a hanging rock or point of some high promontory, stretched at his ease, forgets his feeding flocks, while he admires her beauty." (*Characteristics*, II, 126-7.)

By making the faculty of aesthetic appreciation a sense, Shaftesbury does not wish to imply that the enjoyment of beauty is merely sensuous. With Addison and Kant, he places the aesthetic judgment between the sensuous and the intellectual. He emphasizes, for instance, the non-sensuous quality of the pleasure which we derive from pure mathematics, for he says,

"There is no-one, who, by the least progress in science or learning, has come to know barely the principles of mathematics, but has found, that in the exercise of his mind on the discoveries he there makes, though merely of speculative truths, he receives a pleasure and a delight superior to that of sense. When we have thoroughly searched into the nature of this contemplative delight, we shall find it of a kind which relates not in the least to any private interest of the creature, nor has it for its object any self-good or advantage of the private system." (*Essay Concerning Virtue and Merit, Characteristics*, I, 296.)

Shaftesbury perhaps goes much farther than is generally popular in minimizing the sensuous element in beauty. Few today would agree, for instance, with his contention that colour is subsidiary to design in painting. He is in good company, however, and Kant for one would have agreed with the argument in *A Notion of the Historical Draught of Hercules*, that the pleasure of colour

"is plainly foreign and *separate*, as having no concern or share in the proper delight or entertainment." (*Second Characters*, p. 61.)

Akenside, following Shaftesbury in this, as in so many other matters, draws up a scale in which the sensuous beauty of colour is put below the intellectual beauty of mathematical forms.

". . . . Of degree
The least and lowliest, in th' effusive warmth
Of colours mingling with a random blaze,
Doth beauty dwell. Then higher in the line
And variation of determin'd shape,
Where truth's eternal measures mark the bound
Of circle, cube, or sphere."

Highest in the scale is the beauty of nature where colour and formal excellence combine; nature is infused with a life that proceeds from God, and its beauty is the sensuous manifestation of divine reason.

> ". . . But more lovely still
> Is nature's charm, where to the full consent
> Of complicated members, to the bloom
> Of colour, and the vital change of growth,
> Life's holy flame and piercing sense are giv'n,
> And active motion speaks the temper'd soul."
> (*Pleasures of the Imagination*, I, 442-80.)

With Kant the disinterestedness of the aesthetic judgment is bound up with what he calls the 'purposeless purposiveness' of beauty. If our judgments about the beautiful are really disinterested then they must be quite free from any notion of purpose: the mere contemplation of the beautiful is sufficient to delight us and we do not ask whether the beautiful object serves any end. To ask such a question is to cease to view the matter aesthetically and to engage in a utilitarian or moral concern. Yet it must be recognized that from a purely subjective point of view beauty does seem to have a purposiveness as far as our own minds are concerned. Does not the fact that beauty brings about a harmony between our mental faculties suggest that our aesthetic pleasure, in part at any rate, springs from the realization that the objects of perception fit our human understanding? Is there not a reciprocity between nature and our own minds? Kant would agree, but he would argue that this must not be taken to imply that beautiful objects declare a purposiveness related to the demands of man's mind. The only purposiveness they have is purely subjective and consists in the ability of the human mind to come to terms with experience. It is this to which Wordsworth refers when he writes:

> "How exquisitely the individual mind,
> (And the progressive powers perhaps no less
> Of the whole species) to the external world
> Is fitted:—and how exquisitely, too,
> (Theme this but little heard of among men),
> The external world is fitted to the mind,
> And the creation (by no lower name
> Can it be called) which they with blended might
> Accomplish." (*Preface* to *The Excursion*, 63-71.)

In Wordsworth's lines, however, there is more than a suggestion that the reciprocity of the human mind and nature is part of a divine purpose. God speaks in the beauty of a nature which can be comprehended by the human mind, for both have their ground of being in God. The appreciation of beauty involves not merely the subjective purposiveness of Kant, but the recognition of one mind by another, an awareness by the finite mind of the Mind of God. This is what Shaftesbury means when he declares in *The Moralists*,

> "That the beautiful, the fair, the comely, were never in the matter, but in the art and design. . . . What is it but the design which strikes? What is it you admire but mind, or the effect of mind? 'Tis mind alone which forms. All which is void of mind is horrid, and matter formless is deformity itself." (*Characteristics*, II, 132.)

Beauty, for Shaftesbury, is always the expression of mind and this is as true of nature as of art, for natural beauty is the expression of the divine mind. Our delight in nature comes from

> "the contemplation of those numbers, that harmony, proportion, and concord which supports the universal nature." (*ibid.*, I, 296.)

Shaftesbury is not concerned here to proclaim the majesty of the natural order as laid bare and explained by scientific laws. By beauty he does not mean a merely mechanical symmetry of parts related to a whole. The beauty of nature is of a higher kind than "mere mechanic beauties", such as "the plans of gardens and the ordering of walks, plantations, avenues". Natural beauty will "discover itself on a thousand occasions, and in a thousand subjects", but wherever it does so, it will be part of "that happier and higher symmetry of a mind".[1] Nature is beautiful not because it works according to scientific laws, but because it is the expression of mind.

> "Whatever in Nature is beautiful or charming is only the faint shadow of that first beauty." (*ibid.*, II, 126.)

Professor Willey, in his *Eighteenth Century Background*, declares that,

> " 'Nature' may be conceived rationally or emotionally. Indeed the history of the idea in the eighteenth century can be

[1] *Freedom of Wit and Humour*, *Characteristics*, I, 92.

described in the most general terms as its development from a rational into an emotional principle. Nature and Reason are normally associated in the earlier part of the century, Nature and Feeling in the later."[1]

As a general statement this may be true, but it fails to do justice to Shaftesbury. Shaftesbury tries to make the best of both worlds; to reconcile the claims of both the reason and the feelings. His picture of the universe is not that of a great machine; for him nature is a work of art fashioned by the divine artist, and as a work of art it can be properly apprehended only by the reason and feelings working together.

The difficulty was that his doctrine of an aesthetic sense seemed to suggest that only feeling mattered and that there could be no standard of taste, only personal likes and dislikes. Shaftesbury saw that this was the position to which the more radical members of the School of Taste had allowed themselves to be committed, and his dislike of their critical arbitrariness often gave him the appearance of fighting in the last ditch with the die-hard neo-classicists, for they, indeed, did recognize that criticism could not be a chaos of personal sensibility. It is this which has led Irving Babbitt to write of Shaftesbury,

"He undermines insidiously decorum, the central doctrine of the classicist, at the very time that he seems to be defending it."[2]

Shaftesbury was no neo-classicist. The trouble was that he found it difficult to advance a Platonic philosophy in an age dominated by the thought of Hobbes, Locke, and Newton. At a time when reason meant no more than the understanding, it was useless to assert that beauty was the sensuous representation of rational ideas. To do so was to be misunderstood, for this would be interpreted as tricking out in verse the products of discursive argument.

There was one point, however, where this ambiguity could not exist. In his attitude to nature it is clear that Shaftesbury is not a neo-classicist; that he did not regard beauty as something which can be expressed in clear-cut conceptual terms. It is not only the order and symmetry of nature that declare it to be the artistic expression of divine thought; for, says Shaftesbury,

[1] Willey; *The Eighteenth Century Background*, Chatto and Windus, p. 207.
[2] Babbitt, *Rousseau and Romanticism*, Houghton Mifflin Co., Boston and New York, 1919, p. 45.

"Even the rude rocks, the mossy caverns, the irregular unwrought grottos and broken falls of waters, with all the horrid graces of the wilderness itself . . . appear with a magnificence beyond the formal mockery of princely gardens." (*Moralists*, *Characteristics*, II, 125.)

Were there not certain features in nature that baffled the understanding? Were there not awful and terrible aspects of the natural scene that did not bring a feeling of harmony, but disturbed the mind with strange yet stimulating thoughts, with fearful but somehow pleasing feelings? When Shaftesbury introduces his notion of the sublime it is evident that criticism has moved right away from neo-classicism and is speaking with a new and compelling voice.

CHAPTER VII

THE SUBLIME

"To the poet nothing can be useless. Whatever is beautiful, and whatever is dreadful, must be familiar to his imagination; he must be conversant with all that is awfully vast or elegantly little."

Johnson: *Rasselas*.

I

FROM the year 1674, when Boileau translated the treatise of Longinus *On the Sublime*, there began what might almost be called a cult of sublimity in France and England. A few years later, Boileau published his *Réflexions sur Longin* and Rapin had followed, in 1686, with *Du Grand et du Sublime dans les Moeurs et dans les différentes conditions des hommes*. In England the references to Longinus became almost irritatingly frequent and at the time when the *Characteristics* were being written, most critics knew the treatise *On the Sublime*, either in Boileau's translation or in the original Greek. John Dennis, who led the fashion perhaps too enthusiastically, earned for himself the nickname 'Sir Longinus', while Pope, who had already referred to Longinus in his *Essay on Criticism*, later felt compelled to parody the whole business in his ironical *The Art of Sinking in Poetry*.

Most writers before the turn of the century used the word 'sublime' with a critical indifference that signified little consideration of its meaning. Generally it was used with reference to points of style and in fact expressed a rhetorical rather than an aesthetic concept. In this respect critics were merely following Longinus himself, to whom the Greek word meant something like 'elevation of style'. Longinus does not penetrate into the aesthetic implications of what we understand by sublimity; as Bosanquet says in his *History of Aesthetic*,

"The philosophical importance of the treatise is rather in its evidence that consciousness has become sensitive in this direction than in any systematic insight into the nature of the sublime."[1]

[1] Bosanquet, *A History of Aesthetic*, London, Swan, Sonnenschein, 1910 edn., p. 104.

Shaftesbury, himself, most often uses the word 'sublime' in connection with style. His view of sublimity in style is that it consists in emotional appeal wedded to loftiness of thought and expression, a sublime style being one in which the fusion of high feeling and thought imparts to the language an eloquence that defies analysis. The falsely sublime, the pompous, or "what commonly passes for sublime", is merely a matter of stylistic devices, but the truly sublime is beyond the reach of criticism.

"The sublime can no way condescend thus, or bear to be suspended in its impetuous course . . . though it be often the subject of criticism, it can never be the manner or afford the means." (*Advice to An Author, Characteristics*, I, 168–9.)

Shaftesbury's importance, however, does not lie in his discussion of style, but in the fact that he was influential in transforming the idea of sublimity from a rhetorical to an aesthetic one. It is not that he himself gave a new meaning to the word, so much as the fact that he drew attention to a realm of experience with which the word was to become increasingly associated. Before Shaftesbury the word 'sublime' was used almost always in connection with style; after the appearance of the *Characteristics*, it increasingly betokened a specific sort of feeling in the face of the awful and great. Shaftesbury does not, indeed, consistently identify the word with this sort of feeling and in this he is at one with Addison, who also used it in a stylistic sense, as when he wrote of the sublimity of Milton's *Paradise Lost*. Both of them, however, drew attention to the special emotional quality of sublimity and described the circumstances which called it forth. Addison, there can be little doubt, was following the guidance given him by the *Characteristics*, and it is to Shaftesbury that the credit must be given of enlarging the whole idea of sublimity by relating it to the context of his thought.

The novelty of Shaftesbury's approach to the sublime is that he connects it with the idea of infinity; a subject to which the disputes between Hobbes and the Platonists must have drawn his attention. In a passage in the *True Intellectual System*,[1] where the writer obviously has Hobbes's remarks on infinity in mind, Cudworth is concerned to refute the notion that because we have no clear sense-image of infinity the whole idea is nonsense. The idea of infinity may be, of course, unimaginable in the sense that we can attach no clear-cut

[1] Vol. II, 521, Harrison's edition, 1845.

mental image to it, but this does not make it nonsensical. In Hobbes there is the suggestion that anything of which we have no clear sensory image is unreal, as when he writes:

> "Whatever we imagine is finite. There is therefore no idea or conception of any thing we call *Infinite*. . . . When we say that any thing in infinite, we signify only that we are not able to conceive the ends, and bounds of the the thing named; having no conception of the thing, but of our own inability."

Moreover, there is probably a hint of irony when Hobbes continues,

> "And therefore the Name of God is used, not to make us conceive him; (for he is incomprehensible; and his greatness, and power are unconceivable;) but that we may honour him." (*Leviathan*, Pt. I, Ch. 3.)

Locke did not consider the idea of infinity to be nonsense, but for him it was based on sense experience, and was a negative rather than a positive idea. The perception of a sensible object is finite, he argued; if, however, we go on extending indefinitely such an object we derive the idea of something infinite. In other words, Locke does not deny the validity of the idea of infinity, but waters it down to mean an idea which is built up from sensation. Moreover, the tradition of philosophy to which he belonged tended to suggest that all knowledge must submit to empirical verification; anything which could not be expressed in empirical concepts must be bogus. Kant put his finger on the weakness of the empirical account of knowledge when he censured the way in which Locke used the word 'idea'. In a passage in the *Critique of Pure Reason*, devoted to Plato's theory of Ideas he ridiculed the way in which the empiricists had used the word to refer to sense-data. Ideas of reason in Kant's philosophy are not derived from sense experience and yet they are not mental figments, for reason in the Kantian sense transcends the limits of experience. The idea of infinity may not be derived from experience, but it is not, on this account, useless: it is a rational Idea and, as such, regulates our experience. It is not something we can prove true, nevertheless there is something in our experience which seems to demand that we accept it as true.[1]

[1] It is also part of Kant's theory that the opposite view, i.e., that the world had a beginning in space and time, is an Idea of the reason. Both are opposite sides of an Antinomy which arises because our knowledge is only of a world of appearances and is phenomenal.

The empirical philosophy, in making the idea of the infinite suspect, robbed poetry of one of its main sustaining forces. Poetry no longer felt at ease in concerning itself with the great themes of religion, of death and immortality and of human life seen *sub specie aeternitatis*. John Dennis noted the change that had occurred, in *The Grounds of Criticism in Poetry* (1704), where he writes,

> "And I have reason to believe, that one of the principal Reasons that has made the modern Poetry so contemptible, is, that by divesting itself of Religion, it is fallen from its Dignity, and its original Nature and Excellence; and from the greatest Production of the Mind of Man, is dwindled to an extravagant and a vain Amusement." (Ch. V.)

In so far as poetry adopted religious themes it tended to deal with them conceptually and not symbolically. It took over the findings of philosophy and theology, but did not attempt to explicate the infinite by analogy or symbol. The religious poetry that was written often lacked that numinous quality which distinguishes what is really religious poetry from what is only theological poetry. It was clear, precise, and conceptual; failing to appreciate the truth of Burke's dictum that

> "It is one thing to make an idea clear, and another to make it *affecting* to the imagination." (*Of the Sublime and Beautiful*, II, iv.)

Shaftesbury himself, like Dr. Johnson later, felt that the truths of religion were too high for poetry. This suggests a disappointing conception of poetry, but, in Shaftesbury's case, it sprang from the view that there are certain experiences which are so sublime that even art cannot express them. It was left to later generations to give the reasons why poetry could legitimately attempt to express this sort of experience. Poetry, of course, had always made the attempt and always would, and it would be stupid to suggest that poetry began to concern itself with subjects beyond empirical verification only with the advent of nineteenth-century romanticism. But one of the novel features of romanticism was that philosophical reasons were advanced to justify the attempt; practice was vindicated by theory, as it had not been before, and it was seen that poetry might essay what science could never even hope to do. Shaftesbury's concern with the sublime, however, was in the sphere of nature rather than of art. He believed that in trying to comprehend aspects of nature too great for the understanding the human mind receives a particular aesthetic pleasure. This was his great contribution to the study of the sublime and the point had to be made before it could be realized that poetry, too, may be inspired by the endeavour to express what lies beyond the ordinary categories of thought.

In Longinus there had been the hint that sublimity is related to the kind of experience which comes to us when we contemplate the wonderful and tremendous in nature. With Longinus it had been no more than a hint, but with Shaftesbury it is a major and recurring theme. He follows Longinus in relating such an experience to religion, for he believes that it follows upon a conviction that such phenomena are the manifestation of divine power. Throughout *The Moralists* the awe-inspiring aspects of nature are praised in almost extravagant language. When we contemplate the vastness of the interstellar spaces we are filled with wonder, and a wonder that is deepened into awe as the vastness is associated with the Author and Finisher of the universe.

> "How glorious is it to contemplate him in this noblest of his works apparent to us, the system of the bigger world! ... Besides the neighbouring planets ... what multitudes of fixed stars did we see sparkle not an hour ago in the clear night, which yet had hardly yielded to the day? How many others are discovered by the help of art? Yet how many remain still beyond the reach of our discovery! Crowded as they seem, their distance from each other is as unmeasurable by art as is the distance between them and us. Whence we are naturally taught the immensity of that being who, through these immense spaces, has disposed such an infinity of bodies." (*Characteristics*, II, 112-13.)

But it is in his conception of the sublime as that experience which comes to us in contemplating natural phenomena that are too large to be comprehended by the senses or the imagination, that Shaftesbury gives a newer and profounder content to the term. It is in the attempt to embrace infinity that we experience sublimity. In the following passage, in which Theocles addresses the Creator, we encounter a doctrine that was to develop in importance as the eighteenth century wore on.

> "Thy being is boundless, unsearchable, impenetrable. In thy immensity all thought is lost, fancy gives over its flight, and wearied imagination spends itself in vain. ... Thus having oft essayed, thus sallied forth into the wide expanse, when I return

again within myself, struck with the sense of this so narrow being and of the fulness of that immense one, I dare no more behold the amazing depths nor sound the abyss of Deity. Yet since by thee, O sovereign mind, I have been formed such as I am, intelligent and rational, since the peculiar dignity of my nature is to know and contemplate thee, permit that with due freedom I exert those faculties with which thou hast adorned me." (*ibid.*, 98.)

The sublime, when used in this sense of being something too vast for the senses or the imagination, belongs properly to nature and not to art. Shaftesbury uses the word 'sublime' in discussing art, but it is clear that he does not consider art sublime in this way. Art must be acceptable to the imagination; must present "a simple, clear, and united view." In fact, the sublime, when used with reference to art, is identical with the beautiful in Shaftesbury's view.

". . . the τὸ καλόν, the beautiful, or the sublime . . . is from the expression of greatness with order: that is to say, exhibiting the principal or main of what is designed, in the very largest proportions in which it is capable of being viewed." (*Freedom of Wit and Humour, Characteristics*, I, 94, n. 3.)

But in his description of the sublime in nature, as something too big for the capacity of the imagination, Shaftesbury was laying the foundations for an inquiry which lasted throughout the century. The passage from *The Moralists*, quoted above, contains a pattern of thought which is seen again in Addison, Burke and Kant. It removes sublimity from the rhetorical context in which the tradition of Longinus had placed it and makes it the subject of aesthetic inquiry.

II

The reader of *The Moralists* is at once struck with the similarity between Shaftesbury's views and what Addison has to say about the sublime in the *Spectator*. Addison, like Shaftesbury, finds that the vast is something which excites the mind with a peculiar pleasure and that, in particular, the idea of God, as a Being infinitely beyond our understanding, is most potent in this way.

"Our Admiration, which is a very pleasing Motion of the Mind, immediately rises at the Consideration of any Object that takes up a great deal of room in the Fancy, and, by consequence, will improve into the highest pitch of Astonishment and Devotion when we contemplate his Nature that is neither circumscribed by Time and Place, nor to be comprehended by the largest Capacity of a Created Being." (*Spectator* 413.)

In the previous number of the *Spectator*, Addison had come very near to reproducing Shaftesbury's analysis of the sublime. There are three sources of aesthetic pleasure for Addison; the beautiful, the novel, and the great. The great is Addison's way of referring to the sublime, and in elaborating his point he says very much what Shaftesbury had already said.

"Our Imagination loves to be filled with an Object, or to grasp at any thing that is too big for its Capacity. We are flung into a pleasing Astonishment at such unbounded Views, and feel a delightful Stillness and Amazement in the Soul at the Apprehension of them. The Mind of Man naturally hates everything that looks like a Restraint upon it."

In *The Genesis of Romantic Theory*, Professor J. G. Robertson suggests that Addison, in writing his papers on the Pleasures of the Imagination, was influenced by the Italian critic, Muratori, though he admits that there is little specific evidence to support this suggestion. Addison, it is true, had been in Italy some time between 1700 and 1702, but then many other young Englishmen had also made the tour to Italy without becoming acquainted with Italian thought and criticism. Addison, indeed, like many Englishmen of the time, seems to have had a low opinion of Italian culture. Professor Robertson rests his case on two main points. The first is that Addison speaks of taste as a specific 'faculty of the soul', as Muratori had done; but, as we have seen, the notion that there is a faculty of aesthetic judgment, a special sense which can be identified with taste, had already been advanced in the *Characteristics*. The other contention is that Addison's division of the ground of aesthetic pleasure into beauty, novelty and greatness also came from Muratori's *Perfetta Poesia*. That the same three elements should appear in both critics is perhaps striking; on the other hand, the importance of novelty had already been recognized by both Bacon and Hobbes, while Shaftesbury's treatment of the sublime would have provided Addison with a source nearer home for his remarks on greatness.

The tracing of influences in the history of ideas is a risky and often a futile business. A perusal of the *Spectator* will soon convince the reader that Addison was susceptible to every wind of critical doctrine, and there were a good many of these blowing at the beginning of the eighteenth century. Nevertheless, Shaftesbury's influence on the papers on the Pleasures of the Imagination seems unmistakable. Particularly is this so in Addison's concern with sublimity. Both of them thought of the sublime as something more concerned with nature than art; both were overwhelmed at the thought of infinite space and the spectacle of the starry heavens, which, later, coupled with respect for the moral law, was so to impress Kant; both thought that we experience a sense of the sublime particularly in contemplating the infinity of God. The following passage from *Spectator* 420 might have come straight from the *Moralists*.

"Nothing is more pleasant to the Fancy, than to enlarge itself by degrees, in its contemplation of the various proportions which its several objects bear to each other, when it compares the body of man to the bulk of the whole earth, the earth to the circle it describes round the sun, that circle to the sphere of the fixed stars, the sphere of the fixed stars to the circuit of the whole Creation, the whole Creation itself to the infinite space that is everywhere diffused about it. . . . The Understanding, indeed, opens an infinite space on every side of us, but the Imagination, after a few faint efforts, is immediately at a stand."

Addison's influence was perhaps wider than Shaftesbury's, great as was the vogue of the *Characteristics* in the early eighteenth century, but together they formed an overwhelming force in popularizing the sublime. From the first decades of the century onwards the idea continues to recur in terms that unmistakably reveal its origin. David Mallet's *Excursion*, for instance, which in spite of the brevity of its two cantos undertakes a survey of the entire Universe, after a description of the earth ascends to the heavens to describe the sublimity of the starry spaces in language that by now is quite familiar to the reader.

"Endless the wonders of creating power
On Earth, but chief on high through Heaven display'd
There shines the full magnificence unveil'd
Of Majesty divine: refulgent there
Ten thousand suns blaze forth, with each his train
Of worlds dependent, all beneath the eye
And equal rule of one eternal Lord."

In the end, imagination has to give up her flight; the attempt to comprehend the First Cause is impossible, for God

> "Endures, and fills th' immensity of space;
> That infinite diffusion, where the mind
> Conceives no limits; undistinguish'd void,
> Invariable, where no land-marks are,
> No paths to guide Imagination's flight."

The starry heavens were also to figure in the accounts of sublimity by Burke and Kant, though in both these writers we get a far profounder conception of the sublime than at the beginning of the century. Burke saw that the insistence on clear and distinct ideas was inimical to art. The appeal of the infinite was precisely in its lack of any clear idea which could be attached to it. He sweeps aside the Cartesians and the followers of Locke with something like impatience, when he writes,

> ". . . hardly anything can strike the mind with its greatness, which does not make some sort of approach towards infinity; which nothing can do whilst we are able to perceive its bounds; but to see an object distinctly, and to perceive its bounds, is one and the same thing. A clear idea is therefore another name for a little idea." (*Of the Sublime and Beautiful*, II, iv.)

Kant, however, was to crown the endeavours of all previous writers in the systematic treatment he gave the subject in the *Critique of Judgment*. We have seen that, for Kant, the beautiful implies a harmony between the imagination and the understanding: the beautiful object displays form and order. While aesthetic creation depends upon a power higher than that of the understanding, aesthetic appreciation demands nothing more than the interplay of the imagination and understanding. It is not that the beautiful can be expressed conceptually; but, nevertheless, there is an indeterminate relationship between the imagination and understanding. In the case of the sublime, however, even in appreciating it one goes beyond the understanding. The sublime lacks form: it is too large, or is made up of too many parts, for the imagination or the understanding to cope with, and calls forth the powers of the reason. Just as our aesthetic judgments about the beautiful depend upon an indeterminate relationship between the imagination and the understanding, so our aesthetic judgments about the sublime depend upon an indeterminate relationship between the imagination and the reason. The main point to grasp in this very brief summary is that, for Kant, the sublime is something which baffles the understanding and can be comprehended only by the reason. He puts the matter in one sentence,

> "The sublime is that, the mere capacity of thinking which evidences a faculty of the mind transcending every standard of sense." (*Critique of Judgment*, trans. Meredith, 98.)

Mr. E. F. Carritt has shown[1] that many features in Kant's analysis of the sublime are derived from eighteenth-century English thought and that some go back to Addison. Yet some features of Kant's thought are foreshadowed more by Shaftesbury than Addison. For Addison, who took over his philosophy in the main from Locke, there was no power of the mind higher than that of the understanding. It was this which weakened his aesthetics in a fundamental manner. Because of this he depicts the entire human mind at a loss to grapple with the sublime, and his account emphasizes the element of astonishment. He sees that the infinite is too great for the imagination, but he never considers the place of reason. The pleasure the human mind obtains from the sublime springs in his view entirely from its failure to comprehend the infinite. The delight lies in the feeling of astonishment mingled with the lack of any restraint upon the mind.

This is not Kant's belief. Kant taught that the human mind, while at first baffled by the sublime, proceeds to recover itself and to assert its supremacy. The beholder, on first looking at the sublime, is conscious of his own limitations and the greatness of the object he contemplates. He feels the inadequacy of his own imagination and his own smallness as a creature of sense. But then the rational side of his being asserts itself. He becomes aware that as a rational being he is superior to any sensible object, however large, and realizes that the rational Idea of infinity can comprehend the largest object of the senses. There is thus, in Kant's account, a movement and a countermovement of the mind. The feeling of sublimity is at first a feeling of awe and inadequacy at the sight of the tremendous; the imagination boggles and we are conscious of our own smallness. Then we recover ourselves and remember that we have a rational power which transcends all sensible standards. It is this pattern, first of a feeling of inferiority then of superiority, which constitutes the Kantian sense of sublimity.

[1] *Addison, Kant and Wordsworth*, in *Essays and Studies*, 1936.

While Addison speaks of a 'movement of the mind' it is clear that he does not establish the same pattern. His account rests on the mind's inadequacy in the face of the infinite. In the *Characteristics*, on the other hand, as can be seen in the passage already quoted, there is an anticipation of the analysis made in the *Critique of Judgment*. The initial failure of the imagination is followed by the realization of the superiority of man's reason:

> "Yet since by thee, O sovereign mind, I have been formed such as I am, intelligent and rational . . . permit that with due freedom I exert those faculties with which thou has adorned me."

The sublime goes beyond the limits of the understanding, but this does not defeat us. The fact that we can have a sense of sublimity at all means that we have a power of mind above the senses. The sublime gives pleasure because it reminds us that we are creatures of reason and belong to a supersensible as well as a sensible world.

According to Kant, our judgments about the sublime are entirely subjective. When we call something sublime we do not suggest that it possesses a certain quality, but only that it evokes in us a certain state of mind. Even this perhaps would be going too far on Kant's view. According to him,

> "All that we can say is that the object lends itself to the presentation of a sublimity discoverable in the mind." (*op. cit.* 92.)

It is not even that the object has a quality which evokes a feeling of sublimity, but simply that the feeling arises because the object reminds us first of our limitations as sensible beings and then of our superiority as rational beings.

> ". . . the feeling of the sublime is a pleasure that only arises indirectly, being brought about by the feeling of a momentary check to the vital forces followed at once by a discharge all the more powerful." (*ibid.*, 91.)

This again was a point at which Kant gave philosophical confirmation to what had been developed in English thought. The eighteenth century in England was a period during which an increasing emphasis was put upon the emotions in aesthetic appreciation. We have already seen that the idea of taste at the beginning of the eighteenth century had gone a long way towards equating aesthetic judgment with personal sensibility. In fact, so strong was this movement, that aesthetics by the middle of the century had to concern itself largely with the question of how a standard could be erected on the shifting sands of taste, and the criticism of the age of Johnson had tended once more to become conservative. Nevertheless, throughout the century, the forces of sensibility were breaking down the barriers of a decorum which was never as strong as some have believed.

One of the strongest of these forces was the concept of sublimity. The beautiful was generally considered as an objective quality and the judgment of the beautiful was never wholly identified with the feelings. With the sublime, on the other hand, feeling was emphasized from the beginning. The word itself came increasingly to refer not so much to a certain sort of scenery, as the feeling of mingled awe and delight evoked in the human breast by the spectacle of such scenery. From being a descriptive term it came to connote increased sensibility and self-consciousness. The association of grandeur in natural scenery with a feeling of sublimity was one of the chief characteristics of what is called romanticism. But it was not something which came, as is sometimes supposed, with *The Lyrical Ballads*, heralded by a few so-called precursors of romanticism. It grew steadily from the very beginning of the century.

III

Shaftesbury was the first English writer really to relate sublimity to nature. Dennis had expressed his 'delightful Horrour' and 'terrible Joy' at the sight of the Alps in his *Miscellanies in Verse and Prose* (1693), but had never developed the aesthetic implications of this experience. Addison, of course, had also made the tour to Italy and reported (in *Remarks on Several Parts of Italy*, 1705), much the same sort of feeling, on passing over the Alps, as Dennis had experienced. With Addison, however, sublimity never becomes emancipated from its literary associations. *Paradise Lost* can be sublime as well as can "open Champagne country, a vast Desert, a huge Heap of Mountains, high Rocks and Precipices, or a wide Expanse of Waters." The growth of feeling for nature and, in particular, for the grand and terrible aspects of nature, is by now a well-known story in the history of eighteenth-century literature. There is no need to chronicle the remarks of the many travellers who followed Dennis and Addison through the rocks and snows of Alpine scenery, or to investigate again the cult of the Gothic, the fashion for ivy-mantled towers and artificial ruins, or the flight of poetry from the town to the country. Our task is only to show the significance of Shaftesbury in this change of taste.

Shaftesbury's attitude to nature springs from his philosophy of optimism in which everything in the natural order reveals the goodness of God and has its own beauty. According to this philosophy there was nothing in nature which could not be appreciated and even the terrible and frightening were aesthetically valuable. Here is the crucial ambiguity of Shaftesbury's position as a critic, for his judgments of works of art tend on the whole to be neo-classical. Beauty for him consists of harmony, proportion and symmetry, qualities very dear to the neo-classicist. In nature, on the other hand, we encounter features which lack these qualities and are awful and even terrifying. At first these were not considered to have any intrinsic aesthetic value. They were valued only as parts of a larger whole which was harmonious and proportionate. If by definition the beautiful consists of proportion, form and symmetry, they could not be beautiful. Nevertheless, the philosophy of optimism led to their being valued for their own sakes and in doing so brought about the distinction between the beautiful and the sublime. It regarded these features as a revelation of God's majesty; not merely were they parts, but necessary parts of the larger whole. Thus the grand and even terrible aspects of nature were appreciated, not because they were beautiful in the ordinary sense, not only because they were part of a larger beauty, but because of some special quality all their own. It was this quality which came to be known as the sublime, or, more accurately, as the quality which evoked feelings of sublimity. Shaftesbury, for instance, finds a landscape of mountains, ravines, waterfalls and hanging forests an object of aesthetic appreciation in its own right and not merely tolerable because it is part of a larger and more acceptable whole. The "vast deserts of these parts" although

"ghastly and hideous ... want not their peculiar beauties. The wildness pleases." (*Moralists, Characteristics*, II, 122.)

In this way the neo-classicist in art could be romantic in his attitude towards nature. This, indeed, largely explains how the development from neo-classicism to romanticism came about. The change of taste took place first in regard to nature; the change in poetry and the other arts was an extension and development of this.

We see with Shaftesbury, himself, how his attitude to nature influenced his taste in art. In literature, for the most part, he displays a classical temper, but in painting, the most naturalistic of the arts, his taste was more romantic. Before Salvator Rosa's landscapes became the fashion of the middle of the century, we find him praising the wild and gloomy scenes of this painter, and, as we saw in an earlier chapter, he was one of those responsible for encouraging an appreciation of such paintings in England.

Shaftesbury found the prospect of mountains, torrents and wild skies, something he liked for its own sake and not merely on philosophical grounds, though the latter doubtlessly tutored his taste.

In an imaginary tour of the universe (something which was to become a popular feature of the poetry of the following years), Theocles in the *Moralists*, rhapsodizes upon "the darkest and most imperfect parts of our map"; after traversing the frozen wastes and sandy deserts, he ends with a description of a mountain scene which is felt to be a revelation of God as much as the "many bright parts of earth".

> "But behold! through a vast tract of sky before us, the mighty Atlas rears his lofty head covered with snow above the clouds. Beneath the mountain's foot the rocky country rises into hills, a proper basis of the ponderous mass above, where huge embodied rocks lie piled on one another. ... See! with what trembling steps poor mankind tread the narrow brink of the deep precipices, from whence with giddy horror they look down, mistrusting even the ground which bears them, whilst they hear the hollow sound of torrents underneath, and see the ruin of the impending rock, with falling trees which hang with their roots upward and seem to draw more ruin after them."

The imaginary travellers are encouraged by the scene to speculate on neo-Platonic lines concerning the transitoriness of material beauty, and are led to feel that this is a world of appearances and not of reality. As they descend to the forests, "the ever green and lofty pines, the firs, and noble cedars, whose towering heads seem endless in the sky",

> "... a different horror seizes our sheltered travellers when they see the day diminished by the deep shades of the vast wood, which, closing thick above, spreads darkness and eternal night

below. The faint and gloomy light looks horrid as the shade itself; and the profound stillness of these places imposes silence upon men, struck with the hoarse echoings of every sound within the spacious caverns of the wood. Here space astonishes; silence itself seems pregnant, whilst an unknown force works on the mind, and dubious objects move the wakeful sense." (*ibid.*, 122–3.)

It might seem strange at first sight to find the author of the *Letter Concerning Enthusiasm* writing in such an enthusiastic manner, but Shaftesbury's *Letter* was never an attack on enthusiasm as such. It was an attack, as he makes clear in his second *Miscellany*, on false enthusiasm, or fanaticism. Shaftesbury is an ardent admirer of the "kind of enchantment or magic in that which we call enthusiasm." Philocles, after listening to the rhapsodizing of Theocles quoted above, declares:

"... all sound love and admiration is enthusiasm: The transports of poets, the sublime of orators, the rapture of musicians, the high strains of the virtuosi—all mere enthusiasm! Even learning itself, the love of arts and curiosities, the spirit of travellers and adventurers, gallantry, war, heroism—all mere enthusiasm!... 'Tis enough; I am content to be this new enthusiast in a way unknown to me before." (*ibid.*, 129.)

The *Moralists* was an important factor in the changing attitude towards nature, preaching, as it did, an optimism which saw everything as good and which upheld a theory of ethics based upon a belief in the essential goodness of man. Original sin smacked too much of Hobbes and was discarded, while the world of nature was no longer a fallen world, but a revelation of the goodness and beauty of the Godhead. Moreover, the *Moralists* provided not only an aesthetic, but a style and language in which admiration for nature could be fittingly expressed. Amongst the poets, Thomson and Akenside, in particular, were inspired by Shaftesbury. They, more than any others, were perhaps responsible for the growth of that attitude which came finally to speak of 'Nature' and 'Poetry' as almost synonymous terms. Both of them made nature the subject of their verse, only because they accepted a body of philosophical doctrines which entailed and justified the rightness of their attitude: their love of nature was not just personal whimsy, but part of a philosophical system. Shaftesbury was as important to them as

Godwin to Wordsworth,[1] and, furthermore, they borrowed not only the philosophy of the *Moralists*, but even its language and style. The *Characteristics* was not, of course, the only source of their ideas, for we find traces of the writings of Addison, Locke and Newton in their poetry, but Shaftesbury's philosophy, and especially his theory of the sublime, was the most powerful of these forces.

Thomson showed his indebtedness at an early age in his fragmentary *Works and Wonders of Almighty Power*. His description of the sublimity of nature is no more than a verse paraphrase of the passage from the *Moralists*, which has already been quoted.

> "Gladly would I declare, in lofty strains,
> The power of Godhead to the sons of men.
> But thought is lost in its immensity;
> Imagination wastes its strength in vain;
> And fancy tires, and turns within itself,
> Struck with the amazing depths of Deity."

With his friend, Mallet, he used the device employed in the *Moralists*, of an imaginary tour of the universe, ranging from the sandy wastes to the snow-covered mountains, but emphasizing always the awful and grand. The animal kingdom, in spite of appearances to the contrary, is the creation of a good and all-wise God. Thomson's description, in the *Seasons*, of the tropical river with its prolific mudbanks, spawning a myriad forms of life, is almost identical with Shaftesbury's; even the crocodile (Shaftesbury's "noted tyrant of the flood and terror of its borders") receives special mention.

> "Prodigious rivers roll their fattening seas;
> On whose luxuriant herbage, half-concealed,
> Like a fallen cedar, far diffused his train,
> Cased in green scales, the crocodile extends."
> (*Summer*, 705–8.)

Akenside, too, surveys the cosmic scene with an optimistic eye; he is more directly interested in aesthetics than Thomson and is a closer follower of Shaftesbury. *The Pleasures of the Imagination*, it is true, owes a great deal to Addison, but the influence of Shaftesbury

---

[1] S. H. Monk, *The Sublime*, which is a study of eighteenth-century theories of the sublime, takes an opposite view. Monk considers that "creative art led the way, and theory, ever a laggard, followed behind" (p. 87). He regards Burke's and other critical treatises of the mid-century as "attempts to explain the age to itself", that is, as rationalizations of artistic practice. I hope I have said enough about Shaftesbury's influence to show that this was not always so.

is manifest and there is a neo-Platonic strain in the poem, which is quite foreign to the *Spectator*. He believes that the natural world is a shadowing forth of the eternal forms which have been in God's mind since before the creation.

> "There lived the Almighty One: then, deep retired
> In his unfathom'd essence, view'd the forms,
> The forms eternal of created things,
>
> . . . . .
>
> . . . till in time complete
> What he admired and loved, his vital smile
> Unfolded into being. Hence the breath
> Of life informing each organic frame." (I, 64–74.)

According to Akenside some minds have a bent to the sublime and others to the beautiful; Shakespeare being an example of the first and Waller of the second.

> ". . . one pursues
> The vast alone, the wonderful, the wild;
> Another sighs for harmony and grace,
> And gentlest beauty." (III, 547–50.)

But the beautiful and the sublime are both aesthetic aspects of a whole, all of whose features are good. Akenside is an optimist with the rest.

IV

The logical conclusion of philosophical optimism was that not only the great and awe-inspiring, but even the terrible and ugly aspects of nature must have an aesthetic appeal. The whole of nature is a revelation of God's goodness and bounty, and everything must be, if not beautiful, at least aesthetically valuable. Aesthetic theory did, in fact, follow this line of logical development. On ceasing to be a merely rhetorical concept, the sublime first became associated with the feeling of awe, but eventually became related to the feeling of terror. The conception of beauty as 'unity in variety', had to make room for aesthetic categories which recognized the appeal of the terrible as well as the appeal of greatness. The sublime with Addison had been connected with the great, but by the time of Burke it had become a matter of terror.

Burke in his *Philosophical Inquiry into the Origin of our Ideas of the Sublime and Beautiful*, as the title suggests, was making a psychological analysis of the sublime. Taking the distinction made by eighteenth-century psychology between the emotions of pleasure and pain, he erected on it a theory of sublimity. The beautiful is that which arouses a feeling of pleasure, whereas,

> "Whatever is fitted in any sort to excite the ideas of pain and danger, that is to say, whatever is in any sort terrible, or is conversant about terrible objects, or operates in a manner analogous to terror, is a source of the *sublime*." (I, vii.)

The pain and danger must not be too real, or too pressing, however; only when they are at a distance, or more apparent than real, do we derive any delight from them. But it is not introspection, so much as philosophical presuppositions, which causes Burke to associate the sublime with ugliness: to a consistent optimist, even the ugly must have an aesthetic appeal. The appeal could not be based on beauty (for this is the direct antithesis of the ugly), so it came to depend on the sublime.

> "Ugliness I imagine likewise to be consistent enough with an idea of the sublime. But I would by no means insinuate that ugliness of itself is a sublime idea, unless united with such qualities as excite a strong terror." (III, xxi.)

It was these two elements of sublimity, the great and the terrible, deriving from Addison and Burke respectively, which formed the twin pillars of the Kantian sublime. Kant distinguishes between the mathematically sublime and the dynamically sublime. The former refers to those features of nature which seem to possess infinite magnitude, whereas the latter refers to features which seem to possess infinite power. When we think of nature possessing infinite power, according to Kant, we experience something akin to fear; we ourselves seem weak and puny spectators of the infinite might of nature. Yet if the experience is of real sublimity the feeling is not actually of fear, but only a realization that the situation is potentially frightening. On reflection we realize that we belong not merely to the natural order, but are creatures who can transcend physical being. It is clear that Kant's distinction between two sorts of sublimity can be seen as an elaboration of the difference between Addison's and Burke's theories.

Kant brought together the various elements which had been advanced separately by English thinkers throughout the century; he gave system and coherence to their efforts and brought to them a profundity which was all his own. It would be wrong to exaggerate Shaftesbury's contribution to the subject, yet it is clear that it was of supreme importance. Addison and Burke took the sublime farther as an aesthetic idea; Thomson and Akenside expressed more fervently a feeling of the sublimity of nature; yet none of their contributions would have been possible without the background of philosophical optimism which Shaftesbury did so much to popularize. More important still, there is an element in his philosophy which is lacking in both Addison and Burke, but which Kant made the foundation of his aesthetics.

Both Addison and Burke were empiricists: their philosophy was implicitly that of Locke. The feeling of sublimity, in their account, arises when the understanding is confronted with something too big for its comprehension. Kant would agree, but as we have seen, goes farther. According to him, the pleasure we get from experiencing the sublime arises from our consciousness that we have a power of reason; we become aware that we are creatures not only of the sensible world, but also of a supersensible existence. The understanding, for Kant, conceives nature as governed by mechanical laws. It gives rise to the scientific view of nature as a machine, the parts of which have no relationship to each other, apart from being parts of the same machine. The reason, on the other hand, regards nature as more than a machine, and sees it as a whole the parts of which are all related to each other as elements in a work of art. Such an idea of wholeness can only be the product of reason, according to Kant. It cannot be built up empirically, or tested by the evidence of the senses. It can never be proved as objectively valid, yet our aesthetic experience demands that we accept it as true. Coleridge thought that the importance of an education which valued the imaginative awareness given by romantic literature, lay precisely in this impression it built up of supersensible greatness and wholeness. In a letter to Poole he writes,

> "For from my early reading of fairy tales and genii, etc., etc., my mind had been habituated *to the Vast*, and I never regarded *my senses* in any way as the criteria of my belief. I regulated all my creeds by my conceptions, not by my *sight*, even at that age. Should children be permitted to read romances, and relations of giants and magicians and genii? I know all that has been said

against it; but I have formed my faith in the affirmative. I know of no other way of giving the mind a love of the Great and the Whole. Those who have been led to the same truths step by step through the constant testimony of their senses, seem to me to want a sense which I possess. They contemplate nothing but *parts*, and all *parts* are necessarily little. And the universe to them is but a mass of *little things*."

Only an acquaintance with the arts can inculcate this sense of greatness and wholeness; a study of scientific techniques cannot. Coleridge continues:

"I have known some who have been *rationally* educated, as it is styled. They were marked by a microscopic acuteness, but when they looked at great things, all became a blank and they saw nothing . . . and called the want of imagination judgment and the never being moved to rapture philosophy." (*Letters*, ed. E. H. Coleridge, I, 16.)

We can see how Shaftesbury's philosophy was more conducive to a satisfactory aesthetic than was the tradition of Locke. For Shaftesbury viewed nature as something more than a mechanism, as something explicable only by the analogy of art. Only thus could our aesthetic experience be explained, since the aesthetic appeal of nature lay not only in its symmetry and proportion, but in its irregularity and wildness. Nature could be sublime as well as beautiful. Shaftesbury's thought might have seemed reactionary to the scientific minds of the early eighteenth century, but it received full vindication from Kant. The scientific view of nature could perhaps account for the beautiful, if only in the limited terms of mechanical symmetry, but it could not give birth to a satisfactory theory of the sublime: for a machine may possibly be beautiful, but it cannot be sublime.

CHAPTER VIII

THE DOCTRINE OF RIDICULE

"Du sublime au ridicule il n'y a qu'un pas."
(Napoleon Buonaparte to the Polish Ambassador De Pradt.)

"I have read a sermon of a conventual in the church of Rome, on those words of the wise man: 'I said of Laughter, it is mad; and of Mirth, what does it?' Upon which he laid it down as a point of doctrine, that laughter was the effect of original sin, and that Adam could not laugh before the fall."
(Addison: *Spectator*, No. 249.)

I

PERHAPS the one theory of Shaftesbury's which provoked greater protest than any other was his doctrine of ridicule. His remarks on this subject produced more storms in the years following the publication of the *Characteristics* than any other assertion in this controversial book. The reason for this is not far to seek. The very first essay in the book was the famous or, according to some, infamous *Letter Concerning Enthusiasm*, which had been published anonymously as a separate treatise in 1708, a few years previously. The occasion which called it forth, as we have already seen, was the behaviour of the French Protestants from the Cévennes who had sought shelter in England from the severity of the Revocation of the Edict of Nantes. These fanatics by their enthusiastic excesses had brought upon themselves the censure of the supposedly more temperate English, some of whom, nevertheless, had proposed very far from temperate measures of repression.

The purpose of Shaftesbury's *Letter* was to suggest that ridicule was a more potent weapon with which to attack fanaticism. The way to suppress false zeal and bigotry was to laugh it out of court, not to oppose it by a corresponding fanaticism from the other side.

"Let but the search go freely on, and the right measure of everything will soon be found. Whatever humour has got the start, if it be unnatural, it cannot hold; and the ridicule, if ill-placed at first, will certainly fall at last where it deserves."
(*Characteristics*, I, 10.)

Shaftesbury seems to have had some premonition of the abuse this suggestion would produce, for he continues,

> "I have often wondered to see men of sense so mightily alarmed at the approach of anything like ridicule on certain subjects; as if they mistrusted their own judgment."

If there were any doubt in his mind it was soon dispelled, for three pamphlets quickly appeared attacking his *Letter*. One was Dr. Wotton's *Bart'lemy Fair, or an Enquiry after Wit*; the others, published anonymously, were *Remarks upon a Letter by a Lord concerning Enthusiasm, not written in raillery but good humour* (a hit at Shaftesbury's contention that criticism should always be good-tempered and not made in a spirit of querulousness or raillery), and *Reflections upon a Letter concerning Enthusiasm*. Leibnitz, who later was to speak highly of the *Characteristics* was also critical of the anonymous *Letter*, while even Shaftesbury's friend Le Clerc, who reviewed it in 1709 in the *Bibliothèque Choisie*, wrote cautiously that it must be read with care if we were not to misunderstand its purpose.

It is easy enough to see why the *Letter* should have been so unpopular. Ridicule is a dangerous weapon to wield; and it was felt that Shaftesbury's use of it against the French Prophets (as they were called) could be made with equal facility, and just as much success, against the beliefs and practices of more orthodox religion. His case was not helped by the suggestion which is always present in the treatise, that a good deal of organized Christianity would benefit from an application of ridicule. The Age of Anne might welcome such an experiment if its object were the Papists, or non-conformist sects such as the Quakers and Baptists: but where was one to draw the line? It was not only that Shaftesbury had ridiculed one of the bishops for believing in fairies, but the whole supernatural element of religion could be made the object of ridicule. It was feared that by the end of the process the whole of Christianity might be turned into a watered-down and emasculated body of beliefs no different from deism. In fact, for many people Shaftesbury was no more than an unusually clever and sophisticated upholder of deism.

That it was not Shaftesbury's intention to use ridicule as a weapon against true religion is shown in his *Miscellany II*, where he tries to clear up the confusion that had resulted from the *Letter*. In this later work he makes it clear that there are different sorts of enthusiasm and that his purpose had been to hold up to scorn only the false enthusiasm which derives its inspiration from unworthy sources. Speaking of himself, he writes,

> "So far is he from degrading enthusiasm or disclaiming it in himself, that he looks on this passion, simply considered, as the most natural, and its object as the justest in the world." (*ibid.*, II, 176.)

Indeed, Shaftesbury's own glowing description of nature in the *Moralists* could only be described as enthusiastic and he believed that enthusiasm of the right sort was a necessary element in religion. He continues,

> "We can admire nothing profoundly without a certain religious veneration." (*ibid.*, II, 177.)

The trouble is that "all affections have their excess" and enthusiasm, unless it is grounded upon the right sort of philosophy, may get out of control. In particular, the enthusiasm which often accompanies religious conviction may

> "too easily mount into high fanaticism or degenerate into abject superstition."

Upon the whole, therefore, he concludes,

> "enthusiasm is in itself a very natural honest passion, and has properly nothing for its object but what is good and honest." (*ibid.*, II, 178–9.)

Nevertheless, the hostility which Shaftesbury had aroused was by no means assuaged, for his main contention had been left untouched by the explanations vouchsafed in his second *Miscellany*. Not only did Shaftesbury maintain that ridicule is the instrument of reason, to be levelled against convictions which reason had found untenable; this, although its application might have produced resentment, would have been logically unassailable, but Shaftesbury went much farther and maintained that ridicule is itself a test of truth. The second essay of the *Characteristics*, entitled *The Freedom of Wit and Humour* was a prolonged defence of his view that

> "A freedom of raillery, a liberty in decent language to question everything, and an allowance of unravelling or refuting any

argument, without offence to the arguer, are the only terms which can render . . . speculative conversations any way agreeable." (*ibid.*, I, 49.)

In the course of this essay he advances the theory that ridicule is a criterion of the truth: whatever can stand up to ridicule is true, whereas whatever succumbs to its attack will be seen to be false.

"Truth, 'tis supposed, may bear all lights; and one of those principle lights, or natural mediums, by which things are to be viewed, in order to a thorough recognition, is ridicule itself, or that manner of proof by which we discern whatever is liable to just raillery in any subject." (*ibid.*, I, 44.)

He buttresses his argument with a reference to Aristotle's *Rhetoric* that was soon seized upon by his critics as a misrepresentation.

" 'Twas the saying of an ancient sage, 'that humour was the only test of gravity; and gravity of humour. For a subject which would not bear raillery was suspicious; and a jest which would not bear a serious examination was certainly false wit'." (*ibid.*, I, 52.)[1]

It was this theory of ridicule which brought opprobrium on Shaftesbury. The champions of religious orthodoxy, in particular, were quick to concentrate their attacks on this principle of his philosophy. Nevertheless, there were those who supported it, and not only in the ranks of the deists and free thinkers. Hutcheson, who was a devout Presbyterian minister, saw nothing in it to upset the beliefs of true religion. His early work, *Thoughts on Laughter*, which was first contributed as separate essays to *Hibernicus' Letters* (a periodical appearing in Dublin between 1725 and 1727), is an elaboration and defence of Shaftesbury's views. The other conception of comedy then assuming popularity, owing to the support given it in the *Spectator*, was derived from Hobbes's psychological

---

[1] It was pointed out by Brown in his *Essays on the Characteristics* (1751) that this saying of Gorgias, which Aristotle quotes approvingly, merely means that serious argument should be countered with humour and humour with serious argument. The second sentence in Shaftesbury's quotation is his own addition to the text of Aristotle. We must not assume, however, that this was necessarily dishonesty or special pleading on Shaftesbury's part. It may have been a part of the general confusion that existed in the eighteenth century in interpreting Aristotle's remarks on comedy.

inquiry into the nature of laughter, and Hutcheson set himself to refute the Hobbesian theory that laughter springs from

"a sudden glory, arising from a sudden conception of some eminency in ourselves, by comparison with the infirmity of others, or with our own formerly." (*Discourse of Human Nature*, Ch. IX.)

Hutcheson's answer is that the sight of a diseased beggar in the streets should produce laughter according to Hobbes, since we are conscious of our own 'eminency' at such a spectacle. With a fine irony he recommends a visit to the lazar-house as a cure for despondency. Laughter is rather, he suggests, a faculty provided by God to correct the extravagancies of our fancy. The reason is often obstructed and overthrown by conceits and follies which are the product of an excited fancy. The use of laughter is to act as a corrective to these flights of the fancy and to bring back the mind to the ways of sober reason. In other words, ridicule is a practical test of the truth. The affectations and enthusiasms which are deviations from reason will wither at the blast of ridicule and truth will stand forth free and unobscured. To objections that may be raised against the theory, Hutcheson answers:

"This engine of ridicule, no doubt, may be abused, and have a bad effect upon a weak mind; but with men of any reflection, there is little fear that it will ever be very pernicious." (*Letter* III.)

As for the contention that religion and morality may suffer, he retorts that they are impervious to those who "try their mettle in ridiculing the opinion of a good and wise Mind governing the whole universe", or who "try to ridicule integrity and honesty, gratitude, generosity, or the love of one's country, accompanied with wisdom". His point is, of course, the same as Shaftesbury's; not that one cannot ridicule religion and morality, but that ridicule will not prevail against what is true. It is precisely this which allows ridicule to be the criterion of truth.

Hutcheson was followed by Anthony Collins, who in 1729 published his *Discourse concerning Ridicule and Irony*, which supported Shaftesbury's theory. It was not long, however, before an attack was made on the *Characteristics*. The year 1732 saw the publication of Berkeley's *Alciphron, or the Minute Philosopher*, the third Dialogue of which is taken up with an examination of Shaftesbury's philosophy. Berkeley's criticism was far from fair and did a great deal to build up that picture of Shaftesbury as an irreligious scoffer which took the place of an impartial examination of his writings. Most of Berkeley's comments are concerned with Shaftesbury's moral philosophy and whether it is possible to have an ethical theory without religious sanctions. Chapter fifteen, however, deals with ridicule as a test of truth. Alciphron, who in this *Dialogue* represents Shaftesbury, is led to admit that five or six centuries before his day anyone who had believed in the Copernican system, or the circulation of the blood, would have been laughed to scorn. Yet any of Alciphron's contemporaries who did not believe these theories would now be equally ridiculous. If truth has any permanence, Berkeley concludes, ridicule is no criterion of truth and falsehood.

Even the bishops were divided on the issue, however, for in May of the same year, a defence of Shaftesbury against Berkeley's criticism appeared in the *London Journal*. This, according to Joseph Warton, was by Bishop Hoadly. On the other side, the next eminent person to rush into the attack was Bishop Warburton, the friend of Pope and editor of Shakespeare, whose *Dedication to the Freethinkers* prefixed to the *Divine Legation of Moses* was published in 1738. Warburton inveighs at great length, and with many illustrations of his argument, against Shaftesbury's doctrine of ridicule, though he had to confess that

> "In his writings he [Shaftesbury] hath shown how largely he had imbibed the deep sense and how naturally he could copy the gracious manner of Plato."

The *Dedication to the Freethinkers* marked the beginning of a quarrel which developed between Warburton and Akenside, and later Johnson himself was to censure Akenside for his advocacy of ridicule. Book III of Akenside's *Pleasures of the Imagination*, which paraphrases Hutcheson's *Thoughts on Laughter*, is at once an exposition and a defence of Shaftesbury's theory. In it the poet replies to

> "Some in learning's garb,
> With formal band and sable-cinctur'd gown,
> And rags of mouldy volumes;"

lines which though directed specifically at Warburton might well have been meant to include Berkeley as well. In the notes to his poem Akenside tells objectors to the theory that "the practice fairly managed can never be dangerous ... the sense of ridicule always judges right."

The very existence of this God-given sense of ridicule is sufficient proof of its purpose.

> "Ask we for what fair end, the Almighty Sire
> In mortal bosoms wakes this gay contempt,
> These grateful stings of laughter, from disgust
> Educing pleasure? Wherefore, but to aid,
> The tardy steps of Reason, and at once
> By this prompt impulse urge us to depress
> The giddy aims of Folly?" (ll. 259–265.)

The dispute was not, however, ended by these assurances. It is a clear indication of the stir Shaftesbury had raised that the noise of the battle was heard until well after the middle of the century and that its rumblings continued until the end. John Brown's *Essays on the Characteristics* (1751) devoted over four hundred pages to a consideration of Shaftesbury's philosophy and it is significant that the first essay of over one hundred pages was taken up with the subject of ridicule. But the doctrine seemed impervious to criticism and only three years later Leland, in *A View of the Principal Deistical Writers*, again spent a good deal of space and effort in an attempt to refute it.

II

Before we ask the reason for the continued popularity of the doctrine of ridicule in the teeth of so much opposition, we must first try to answer the question why Shaftesbury came to formulate it at all. The theory that ridicule is a test of truth was not something he threw out as a passing notion. It was not just an aphorism; but something he really believed and which he constantly maintained. On reflection we shall see that it was a logical development of his philosophy of optimism. Philosophical optimism of the kind advocated in the *Characteristics* holds, as we saw in an earlier chapter, that evil is illusory. Some of the things we call evil (such as suffering) are a necessary part of a whole that is fundamentally good, and the whole would be less good if this element were lacking. Apart from such evils as suffering there is the evil will, the desire to bring about evil. This exists, indeed, in a contingent sense, but it has no place in ultimate reality for the *ens realissimum* is good. On this view evil is defective being and all things are good in so far as they have real and positive existence. Virtue accords with reality and a man is most truly himself when he is virtuous. Vice, in fact, is against his own interest, "for every vicious action must be self-injurious and ill." Shaftesbury clinches his argument at the end of the *Inquiry concerning Virtue and Merit* with the sentence:

"And thus virtue is the good, and vice the ill of everyone."

Now, according to this optimistic belief evil is logically nonsense. A good deal of what we regard as evil is not evil at all, but only part of a larger good; but in so far as evil does manifest itself it conflicts with what is real. It can thus be laughed at as, strictly speaking, nonsense. Pure and intrinsic evil is self-contradictory, for it can never be said to exist ultimately at all. Evil (and in evil Shaftesbury includes ugliness) is ridiculous, not only in the sense that it is capable of being ridiculed, but also in the sense that it is just silly. This is the belief which forms the foundation of Shaftesbury's remarks on ridicule. One can laugh at evil with safety, for what is good will stand the test, whereas evil will be seen in its true light as foolish. For, he says,

"Nothing is ridiculous, except what is deformed; nor is anything proof against raillery, except what is handsome and just. And therefore 'tis the hardest thing in the world to deny fair honesty the use of this weapon, which can never bear an edge against herself." (*Freedom of Wit and Humour, Characteristics*, I, 85.)

What Berkeley did not appreciate was that in making ridicule a test of truth Shaftesbury was arguing from certain well-defined premises. Ridicule is a test of truth only because he already holds a certain theory of truth. He believes that reality is an organic, harmonious and perfectly congruous whole. Any statement that is true—in other words, any statement that is descriptive of this reality—cannot but refer to these features, and while these characteristics may not give us a definition, they do provide us with a criterion of truth. Anything that lacks the characteristics of organic harmony and congruity will be unreal; any statement that is incongruous, any statement that reveals an internal disharmony, is untrue. Falsehood is characterized by a quality that can only be described as ridiculous. Before we dismiss his theory too summarily we should bear in mind that in certain respects it agrees with more recent accounts of the nature of comedy. Bergson, for instance, defines comedy as an attempt to impose a mechanical explanation upon a reality that cannot thus be explained. It springs from an endeavour to produce a harmony that, though internally consistent, is untrue when we take account of the nature of reality. Comedy is internally congruous, but compared with the real is fundamentally incongruous.

Any belief which holds that the nature of ultimate reality is good must see evil as in one sense stupid. It is not that evil always provides us with a laughable spectacle, for wickedness in its results can be and often is, of course, a dreadful thing to witness. Nevertheless, it must on such a view be also a foolish thing. Mr. C. S. Lewis is right when in his *Preface to Paradise Lost*, he contends that Milton's Satan viewed from a certain angle is a comic character. Any creature whose evil purpose is constantly baffled, whose every endeavour must meet with eventual frustration and who, in his heart of hearts, knows this at the outset, must be a ludicrous figure. As Mr. Lewis says,

"At that precise point where Satan . . . meets something real, laughter *must* arise, just as steam must when water meets fire."

Shaftesbury's purpose was to secure recognition for his conviction that the evil-doer, in the long run, is ridiculous. Not that evil is laughable in its effects, for no one would maintain that such things as illness and pain are laughable subjects. Shaftesbury himself would have had to argue that these things, although distressing, are not evil in the ultimate sense. They are not part of the evil will itself but only elements in a larger whole which would be less good without them. We may indeed imagine that a better world than this is possible, where no evil exists at all, but such a world is only imaginable and not possible. Real evil—the evil will, that is, which sets itself against good—is, on the other hand, laughable. Satan, as Mr. Lewis points out,

". . . is engaged in sawing off the branch he is sitting on, not only in the quasi-political sense . . . but in a deeper sense still, since a creature revolting against a creator is revolting against the source of his own powers—including even his power to revolt."[1]

The same thought is present in Goethe's *Faust* where Mephistopheles describes himself as

[1]*Preface to Paradise Lost*, Oxford, pp. 93-4.

"Ein Theil von jener Kraft
Die stets das Böse will und stets das Gute schafft."[1]

In all fairness, however, it must be admitted that it is a far cry from the 'divine laughter' of *Paradise Lost* and Goethe's *Faust* to the tone Shaftesbury adopts in speaking of religion. Even if their philosophical basis had been tenable, one can understand the resentment occasioned by the three principles of his second *Miscellany*:

> "1st. That wit and humour are corroborative of religion, and promotive of true faith.
> 2nd. That they are used as proper means of this kind by the holy founders of religion.
> 3rd. That notwithstanding the dark complexion and sour humour of some religious teachers, we may be justly said to have in the main a witty and good-humoured religion." (*Characteristics*, II, 217.)

Whatever the philosophical validity of Shaftesbury's doctrine there can be no doubt of its wide reputation. The chorus of criticism it provoked is sufficient demonstration of that. Some idea of the wide currency given to the theory is glimpsed in Lord Chesterfield's letter of the 6th February (Old Style), 1752, in which he warns his son against its pernicious influence.

> "It is commonly said," he writes, "and more particularly by Lord Shaftesbury that ridicule is the best test of truth; for that it will not stick where it is not just."

The only suggestion that will explain this popularity is that it answered some need. My contention is that it provided a philosophical justification for the satiric temper of mind of the eighteenth century and a *rationale* for the literary expression given to this temper of mind.

Not that satire was something new in the history of our literature; it had been practised ever since Horace and Juvenal first provided models for English writers. Nor did Shaftesbury give satire a moral purpose which it lacked before. One has only to read Dryden and other seventeenth-century satirists to confirm the moral purpose of their poetry and in this, too, of course, they were merely following

[1] A part of that power which always produces good, while constantly devising evil.

THE DOCTRINE OF RIDICULE

classical practice. Dryden in his *Discourse concerning the Original and Progress of Satire* (1693) quotes with approval the definition of satire by Heinsius.

> " 'Tis but necessary, that after so much has been said of Satire some definition of it should be given. Heinsius, in his dissertations on Horace, makes it for me, in these words: 'Satire is a kind of poetry, without a series of action, invented for the purging of our minds; in which human vices, ignorance, and errors, and all things besides, which are produced, from them in every man are severely reprehended; . . .' " (*Essays of John Dryden*, ed. Ker, II, 100.)

There is abundant evidence in Dryden's poetry of a high moral purpose, yet it is true to say that it does not possess what we might describe as the metaphysical basis of, say, Pope's satire. The later writer's work manifests a different quality which suggests that a change had come about in what was believed to be the nature and scope of satirical poetry. The question whence Pope derived his optimistic philosophy must wait for the next chapter, but that Pope was an optimist and that this philosophy coloured his satire there can be no doubt.

In the first place optimism shaped Pope's conception of poetry. In the youthful *Essay on Criticism* we find him subscribing to what has been called the 'beauties-blemishes' theory of criticism: the theory that we should judge a work of art not by the faults and blemishes, but by its total effect. The critic, according to this, is not to pick out the deficiencies and to criticize in a merely negative fashion; his function is to judge a work by its total appeal. What may appear blemishes can, in fact, often contribute to the whole and can, indeed, be a necessary part of it. Such a view was not Pope's own; it was becoming popular at the end of the seventeenth century as a justification for the 'mixed' *genres*, and, in particular, for the characteristically English form of tragi-comedy. But the emergence of the view was probably not unconnected with the appearance of optimism as a philosophical creed, and in Pope's case would have been welcomed on that account. We can see its derivation from a larger philosophy which embraces nature as well as art, in the following lines from his *Essay on Criticism*.

> "A perfect Judge will read each work of Wit
> With the same spirit that its author writ:

> Survey the WHOLE, nor seek slight faults to find
> Where nature moves, and rapture warms the mind;
>
> . . . . .
>
> In wit, as nature, what affects our hearts
> Is not th' exactness of peculiar parts;
> 'Tis not a lip, or eye, we beauty call,
> But the joint force and full result of all.
> Thus when we view some well-proportioned dome,
> (The World's just wonder, and ev'n thine, O Rome!)
> No single parts unequally surprise,
> All comes united to th' admiring eyes;
> No monstrous height, or breadth, or length appear;
> The Whole at once is bold and regular."
>
> (233-52.)

Not only Pope's conception of the nature of poetry, but his conception of the poet's task, owes something to optimism. Like Horace, Pope wanted to write an epic, but found the task difficult, for it was an age that was uncongenial to epic poetry and scientific categories of thought had robbed mythology of self-confidence. Like Horace, Pope turned to satire and we may perhaps regard his *Satires and Epistles of Horace Imitated* as in some ways a compensation for his thwarted urge to write epic. The other outlet for this urge that presented itself was the writing of mock-heroic poetry such as the *Rape of the Lock*, where satire could be given some sort of epic expression. Satire, indeed, was a substitute for epic in an age when epic could no longer be successfully achieved. We can understand the nature of eighteenth-century satire only when we have appreciated this. Satire was not merely a literary fashion; it achieved the high dignity and purpose which epic itself had enjoyed. But it was the philosophy of optimism which gave satire the metaphysical status that put it on an equal level with epic. In writing satire the eighteenth century in many cases was attempting to justify God's ways to man as the seventeenth century had tried to do in epic. It is no accident that the opening lines of *The Essay on Man* should echo *Paradise Lost* and that Pope should begin his theodicy with a declaration of his satiric intention.

> "Eye Nature's walks, shoot Folly as it flies,
> And catch the manners living as they rise;
> Laugh where we must, be candid where we can;
> But vindicate the ways of God to Man."

Pope regarded his satire as an instrument of the truth; of that we can be certain. There was, of course, an element of the personal. His attacks on Theobald, Cibber, Lord Hervey and Lady Mary Wortley Montagu have all the rancour of the jealous and irritable personality stung into a sense of resentment; but this does not entirely account for the nature of his satire. There is a disinterested attack on dullness, pedantry, folly, on the social vices of his age as well as its literary faults. It is sometimes said that the difference between Pope's satire and Dryden's is that Dryden writes calmly and dispassionately, while Pope allows his feelings to become engaged and writes in a passion. Now this is not altogether true. Certainly there is a personal element in Pope's satire that is lacking in Dryden's, but this does not explain the chief difference between them. It is true that Pope disliked with all the intensity of his being, some of the people he satirized, but he does not let that influence the manner of his writing. What petulance existed was, in a phrase of Professor John Butt, "petulance recollected in tranquillity".[1] More important is the fact that apart from the maliciousness, there is a difference in Pope's attitude towards satire which marks it off from Dryden's. There is little real moral indignation in Dryden's satire; in the main Dryden satirizes what are follies and foibles. They may be important follies and foibles; nevertheless, they are not seriously evil. Even his arch-villain Achitophel is represented as a man not wholly evil, but as one with real virtues who has been overcome by a turbulent nature; a creature not so much wicked as crazy. Dryden's characters are comic figures in the sense that Aristotle defines comedy:

"an imitation of characters of a lower type [not socially but in respect of virtue], not, however, in the full sense of the word bad, the Ludicrous being merely a subdivision of the ugly." (*Poetics V*.)

With Pope ridicule knows no bounds; it is not something intrinsic to particular topics. Its object is vice, and the whole of evil is something to be ridiculed. It is precisely the greater conviction of moral purpose that gives his satire added intensity. In a letter to Caryll, written on the 27th September, 1732, he says,

"my studies . . . are directed to a good end, the advancement of moral and religious virtue, and the disparagement of vicious and corrupt hearts. As to the former, I treat it with the utmost

[1] *The Inspiration of Pope's Poetry*, in *Essays on the Eighteenth Century Presented to D. Nichol Smith*, Oxford, 1945.

seriousness and respect. As to the latter I think any means are fair and any method equal, whether preaching or laughing ... I shall make living examples, which enforce best." (*Letters*, ed. Elwin and Courthope, I, 334.)

We meet the same attitude pushed to an extreme in the merciless laughter of Hogarth. Pope satirizes not only the peccadilloes of fashionable society (a popular but unfounded interpretation of his purpose), but the political chicanery, the moral laxity, the drunkenness and brutality, which together with the prostitution of literature he regarded as the sins of the age. Ridicule for him is a sacred thing, a defence of the truth. That is why he ends his *Satires* with a declaration of belief in the high calling of the satirical poet.

> "Yes, I am proud; I must be proud to see
> Men not afraid of God, afraid of me:
> Safe from the Bar, the Pulpit and the Throne,
> Yet touch'd and sham'd by Ridicule alone.
> O sacred weapon! left for Truth's defence,
> Sole Dread of Folly, Vice and Insolence!
> To all but heav'n-directed hands deny'd,
> The Muse may give thee, but the Gods must guide:
> Rev'rent I touch thee! but with honest zeal,
> To rouse the Watchmen of the public Weal."
> (*Epilogue to the Satires, Dialogue II*, 208–17.)

III

The direction satire was taking is made even more manifest when we look at Swift's writings. For Swift, to be virtuous is to behave rationally and to act viciously is to be irrational. This notion, certainly, does not necessarily depend upon accepting a philosophy of optimism; it is characteristic of many systems of thought, and with Swift can be associated with the strain of neo-Stoicism that so strongly tempered his theology. It is difficult to escape the conclusion, however, that in giving literary form to this ethical theory his satire was conditioned by the view that vice is not merely irrational, but ridiculous. Indeed, the *Letter Concerning Enthusiasm*, when it first appeared anonymously, was thought by most of the literary world to be by Swift. In a letter to Ambrose Philips, dated 14th September, 1708, he writes,

"There has been an essay of Enthusiasm lately published, that has run mightily, and is very well writ. All my friends will have me to be the author, *sed ego non credulus illis.*"

In the earlier *Battle of the Books* his satire had as its object the claims of the Moderns to rank with the Ancients. It plays around this theme in a manner that is scarcely serious, but in the later works it has become a searching and insistent laying bare of real vices. No one could doubt that *Gulliver's Travels* was written in deadly earnest. Nevertheless, the vices of men as there represented are meant to appear ridiculous. Gulliver himself is a naïve character who does not see that from the standpoint of reason he is a figure of fun. At the very moment when he considers himself to be putting forward the highest endeavours of human achievement he appears most foolish and most contemptible, and what makes the irony of the book so powerful is that man's wickedness is made to appear also his folly. This is brought out very clearly in the passage where Gulliver describes how the human species make war against each other. After offering the King of Brobdingnag the secret of manufacturing gunpowder and describing in glowing terms the wholesale destruction and slaughter which it produces, Gulliver is astounded that the king should refuse his offer with indignation and contempt.

"A strange effect of narrow principles and short views!" he writes, "that a Prince possessed of every quality which procures veneration, love and esteem; of strong parts, great wisdom and profound learning; endowed with admirable talents for government, and almost adored by his subjects; should from a nice unnecessary scruple, whereof in Europe we can have no conception, let slip an opportunity put into his hands, that would have made him absolute master of the lives, the liberties, and the fortunes of his people. Neither do I say this with the least intention to detract from the many virtues of that excellent king; whose character I am sensible will on this account be very much lessened in the opinion of an English reader." (*A Voyage to Brobdingnag*, Ch. vii.)

Shaftesbury was not, of course, the only one of his generation to realize that laughter could be used for a moral purpose. Among his immediate predecessors and contemporaries there were many who made the same suggestion. Rapin, in his *Réflexions* (1674), had argued that the end of comedy was

". . . to shew on the Stage, the Faults of Particulars, in order to amend the Faults of the Publick, and to correct the People thro' a Fear of being render'd ridiculous." (Trans. Thos. Rymer, 1674.)

In a similar manner Jeremy Collier, whose *Immorality of the English Stage* (1698) had recalled the theatre to some sense of its social duties, had contended that

"The exposing of knavery, and making *Lewdness* ridiculous is a much better occasion for Laughter; And this with submission, I take to be the End of *Comedy*." (Ch. IV.)

These were followed by Dennis, whose *Large Account of the Taste in Poetry* (1702) maintained that

". . . without the *Ridiculum* Comedy cannot subsist, for the design of Comedy is to amend the follies of Mankind, by exposing them."

But Shaftesbury's doctrine that ridicule is the test of truth went farther than any of these, or earlier, statements. It did not seek to raise laughter only against evils that were already recognized as such, but believed that it could lay bare evils that masqueraded as virtues and falsehoods that posed as truth. Even more important, his doctrine gave a cutting edge to satire without turning it into personal malice. Satire could be pointed and yet remain objective, for however scornful ridicule became, did it not have a metaphysical and even an ontological basis?

We must not think that the laughter Shaftesbury wished to raise against vice was the laughter that considers all things a subject for jest. His laughter has a serious purpose:

"By this time, my friend," he writes in the last Part of the *Freedom of Wit and Humour*, "you may possibly, I hope, be satisfied that as I am in earnest in defending raillery, so I can be sober too in the use of it. 'Tis in reality a serious study to learn to temper and regulate that humour which nature has given us as a more lenitive remedy against vice, and a kind of specific against superstition and melancholy delusion. There is a great difference between seeking how to raise a laugh from everything, and seeking in everything what justly may be laughed at." (*Characteristics*, I, 85.)

Addison in many numbers of the *Spectator* regretted the growth of raillery and its effects on society, and Giles Jacob later complained in his *Historical Account of the English Poets* (1720) that

> "What has corrupted our modern Poesy is that Ridicule . . . as if nothing pleas'd but what provokes our Laughter. This Custom of Raillery and Ridiculing is very pernicious, not only to all Poetry, but indeed to all Virtue." (*Introductory Essay*.)

This, if it was true, was certainly not Shaftesbury's intention. In the notes on humour contained in his *Philosophical Regimen* he condemns many contemporary practices, such as the false humour of the gaming tables and the brutal and insensitive laughter of those who considered a week-end visit to Bedlam a pleasant diversion. He is quick to censure laughter when it is ill-judged and out of place, and distinguishes between the proper use of wit which issues in ridicule and its improper use which results in burlesque and buffoonery. Swift makes the distinction in the *Author's Apology* for *The Tale of a Tub* (1709), except that the terms used are humour and banter. Banter is ill-informed laughter, whereas humour is the instrument of virtue and truth. Swift concludes with words that Shaftesbury would have willingly accepted as his own.

> "The author cannot conclude this apology without making this one reflection: that, as wit is the noblest and most useful gift of human nature, so humour is the most agreeable; and where these two enter far into the composition of any work, they will render it always acceptable to the world. Now, the great part of those who have no share or taste of either, but by their pride, pedantry, and ill manners, lay themselves bare to the lashes of both, think the blow is weak, because they are insensible; and, where wit has any mixture of raillery, it is but calling it banter, and the work is done."

Optimism may not of itself have given birth to satire, but it provided a theoretical vindication for the natural bent of the age. Furthermore, Shaftesbury's application of this philosophy enabled satire to deepen its moral purpose while becoming even more trenchant. It would be foolish to contend that this gives a complete explanation of what was one of the chief characteristics of the eighteenth century; all that I would claim is that it was one of the factors in what remains a more involved story. Equally, it would be waste of time to attempt to trace in detail Shaftesbury's influence on the growth of satire during the century, for once the fashion had started its own momentum was sufficient to carry it forward. The success which met the satirical writings of Pope, Swift, Mandeville and others was probably reason enough for its continuation as a literary form. When, however, we encounter an author who is not simply content to follow a fashion, but wishes to scrutinize the philosophical basis of his art, we often catch an echo of the *Characteristics*. This is so with the novelist Fielding.

Fielding had been profoundly affected by his reading of *The Characteristics*, and *Tom Jones*, as Fielding's biographer[1] points out, is an attempt to express Shaftesbury's moral theory in fictional form. Tom himself can be regarded as a hero possessing all the natural virtues of Shaftesbury's system, while Square is an avowed exponent of it. In the well-known *Preface* to *Joseph Andrews* (1742) Fielding also uses the same philosophy to support his theory of comedy. Comedy for Fielding is a serious literary form, and the *Preface* opens with a statement of his conviction that the mantle of the epic poet has fallen upon the writer of comedy and romance. He observes that Aristotle made no attempt to define the ridiculous.

> "Indeed, where he tells us it is proper to comedy, he hath remarked that villainy is not its object; but he hath not, as I remember, positively asserted what it is."

His own view is that the ridiculous springs from affectation. Evil such as suffering is not in itself ridiculous; we do not laugh at it but rather, detest it.

> "What could exceed the absurdity of an author," he writes, "who should write *The Comedy of Nero, with the merry Incident of ripping up his Mother's Belly*?"

Vice, on the other hand, is ridiculous when compared with virtue: the basis of comedy, according to Fielding, is incongruity and especially the incongruity of vice masquerading as virtue. Real virtue is different; we laugh at Parson Adams, but he is never ridiculous. As Joseph Andrews says:

> "I defy the wisest man in the world to turn a truly good action into ridicule." (*Joseph Andrews*, Bk. III, Ch. VI.)

[1] *vide* W. L. Cross, *The History of Henry Fielding*, New Haven, 1918.

In this theory of comedy it can be seen that Fielding is borrowing from the tradition of Shaftesbury. Hobbes, it will be remembered, had spoken of laughter as arising from 'a sudden glory', a quick realization of our own present superiority. Hobbes's recognition of an element of incongruity in humour was important and certainly corresponded to something in our experience, but while Shaftesbury agrees with this, the incongruity for him need have no personal reference. It springs, as with Fielding, rather from a realization of the contrast between virtue and vice. For one with Shaftesbury's beliefs, vice must appear laughable when compared with virtue, for the two are incongruous. Vice, since it does not form part of the structure of reality, must be absurd: it is as ludicrous as a false note in the middle of a harmony, as Akenside contended in the *Pleasures of the Imagination*.

> "Wher'er the power of Ridicule displays
> Her quaint-ey'd visage, some incongruous form,
> Some stubborn dissonance of things combin'd,
> Strikes on the quick observer."
>
> (III, 249–52.)

Fielding could not accept Shaftesbury's notion in its entirety. The criticism which had met the view that all evil is ridiculous led him to adopt the more moderate position that the essence of the comic lies rather in the affectation of virtue by those who do not possess it. Yet the accents of the *Characteristics* make themselves unmistakably heard through the cautious tone of Fielding's *Preface*, as they do in so many other pronouncements on the nature of comedy in the Augustan age.

Our own generation tends to think of eighteenth-century satire as rather cruel and to see in it an indication of a lack of sensibility. Yet if we call to mind the bloodshed and fratricidal strife of the preceding age, we see that satire was the means whereby the eighteenth century made great social advances. The fierce contests which tore the country during the Civil War, the feuds which accompanied the Commonwealth and Restoration and which broke out from time to time in open faction, were now transformed into wordy battles, in which the weapons were broadsheets, pamphlets, burlesques and satires. One may censure the lack of manners, the coarseness and unkindness of these literary wars, particularly when waged by the less cultivated tenants of Grub Street. Yet were they not infinitely preferable to open warfare? Were they not accompanied by an increasing regard for the rules of fair debate and impartial argument? Amongst the better writers, at any rate, there was a conviction that satire was not merely a matter of personalities; that comedy was not only entertainment but an instrument of social improvement. The disputes of rival parties turned into a common cause waged against sin and vice, and literature did, in fact, take the direction Shaftesbury had laid down for it when he wrote:

> "The only manner left in which criticism can have its just force amongst us is the ancient comic; of which kind were the first Roman miscellanies or satiric pieces; . . . if our home wits would refine upon this pattern, they might perhaps meet with considerable success." (*Advice to An Author, Characteristics*, I, 169.)

We may doubt whether ridicule can ever be the criterion of philosophical truth, but there is a good deal to support the suggestion that it was a means of establishing moral and social truth. The high purpose of epic poetry did indeed come to be served by comedy; the general belief of the age was that expressed in an essay which has often been attributed to Goldsmith:

> "The design of Comedy is to make vice and folly appear ridiculous, and to recommend virtue." (*The Art of Poetry*, 1762, Ch. XXI.)

What was taking place in the eighteenth century is described in the anonymous *Essay on Gibing, with a Project for its Improvement* (1727):

> "And yet a Spirit of Humour and Raillery seems to have taken Possession of all Orders and Degrees of Men; it reigns in the Country, as well as in the Town, and the illiterates as well as wise profess themselves Members of this extensive Community."

In spite of its possible abuse, the writer warmly supports the use of ridicule and points out that by such means Addison had done more to reform the morals and manners of the time than had countless sermons and books of formal theology. Nor, he might have added, was Addison alone in this. Pope not only brought a new sense of pride into the profession of letters, but achieved an effect far beyond the literary world. The irony of Swift and Hogarth produced a real improvement in both private and public morality, while the *Spectator* and *Tatler*, followed by such periodicals as Fielding's *Covent Garden Journal*, were a mighty social force. Moreover, satire served to reinforce the growing appeal of sentiment, as we can see in the novels of the mid-century, for it betokened not a lack of sensibility, but an increased awareness of evil and wrong-doing. Satire, indeed, could penetrate where sentiment could not; it could reach the more sophisticated classes who were impervious to the sentimental appeal and religious fervour of the Methodist revival. Satire and sentiment, in fact, were both important features of this diverse age; superficially so dissimilar, they were allies in a common cause.

CHAPTER IX

THE INFLUENCE OF SHAFTESBURY'S THOUGHT

> Can Kent design like Nature? . . .
> Can the great artist, though with taste supreme
> Endu'd, one beauty to this Eden add?
> Though he, by rules unfetter'd; boldly scorns
> Formality and method, round and square
> Disdaining, plans irregularly great.
> (Joseph Warton: *The Enthusiast*.)

I

THE tracing of so-called literary influences is a dangerous and generally a profitless pursuit. The influence of one writer upon another is rarely a direct and simple matter, for writers, like other men, live amid a complicated field of forces, personal, social and intellectual, and their work is generally the product of all of these and not of the literary only. Nevertheless, some attempt must be made to estimate the general significance of Shaftesbury's writings and their importance for the eighteenth century. The other point to be borne in mind in making this attempt is that Shaftesbury's influence in literature lay primarily in the appeal of his philosophy. It is true that his works were widely admired as works of art, and, indeed, there were so many who modelled their writing on his prose style that Goldsmith declared that he had

> "more imitators in Britain than any other writer." (*The Augustan Age in England, The Bee*, 1759.)

Nevertheless, it was chiefly as a thinker that Shaftesbury was valued by the literary figures of the day.

An indication of Shaftesbury's popularity is easily gained by a mere glance at the number of editions into which the *Characteristics* ran in the eighteenth century. Five editions had been published by 1732, and by 1790 the total had reached eleven. What this signifies can be seen when we learn that Locke's *Collected Works* went into only nine editions in the same period, while his famous *Essay concerning Human Understanding* (according to his bibliographer, the most frequently published book of the century) achieved only nineteen editions.

Amongst those who responded to the appeal of Shaftesbury's philosophy the poets writing in the first half of the century form a notable group. The extent of their indebtedness has already been commented upon in some detail by Mr. C. A. Moore.[1] In his valuable article he has brought together a wealth of evidence testifying to the influence of Shaftesbury upon such minor poets as Henry Needler, John Gilbert Cooper and James Harris, as well as on the more important figures of Thomson and Akenside. There is no need to cover this ground again. Where I would venture to disagree with Mr. Moore, however, is not in the evidence he produces, but in his assertion that Shaftesbury's popularity was dependent primarily on his ethical teaching. No doubt Shaftesbury's moral philosophy had a considerable influence, but my contention is that this was only a part of the larger appeal his whole philosophy made, especially to the Augustan poets. His moral philosophy gave an order and coherence to moral experience, while allowing moral judgments to remain free of theological authority, and this was welcome to the growing sensibility of the Enlightenment; but more important to the poets of the period was the fact that his philosophy gave them a world-view more acceptable than either that being propagated by science, or that which had been preached by Puritan theology.

Science presented poets with a dead world which was colourless, inanimate and mechanical. All that poets considered valuable, the scent of a hay-field, the cry of the sea-bird, the beauty of dawn, were now subjective modes of apprehending a reality which was scientific and mathematical. Equally, according to Puritan dogma, the world was so debased that it failed to declare the glory of God and could be regarded only as occupied territory over-run by the forces of the Devil. Against both these views Shaftesbury's philosophy re-asserted a belief in the world as a manifestation of a spiritual reality, a belief in nature as something organic and growing rather than mechanical and static. His insistence on the natural and innate goodness of man was only a part of his rehabilitation of the whole natural order. Only when we grasp this do we see why the poets of the time endorsed his moral philosophy. What they wanted was not merely a theory of ethics freed from ecclesiastical restraint, but a universe which confirmed and fulfilled the visions of the

[1] *Shaftesbury and the Ethical Poets in England*, 1700-60, P.M.L.A., XXXI (1916).

artist. The age was one in which poetical theodicies were particularly plentiful, and in those where Shaftesbury's aid is enlisted it is nearly always as one who gives a poetic account of things and not merely as a moralist.

Enough has already been said, perhaps, to exhibit Akenside's indebtedness to the *Characteristics*. All that remains is to point out that Akenside's views on the nature of poetry and criticism, together with his enthusiasm for nature, proceeded from a definite philosophy. He saw the universe as a revelation of God's purpose, worked out by a plastic power in material forms. His philosophy is much the same as Shaftesbury's; a modern version of Platonism incorporating a belief in a principle of growth similar to Cudworth's.

> "Know then, the Sovereign Spirit of the world,
> Though, self-collected from eternal time,
> Within his own deep essence he beheld
> The bounds of true felicity complete,
> Yet by immense benignity inclined
> To spread around him that primeval joy
> Which fill'd himself, he raised his plastic arm,
> And sounded through the hollow depths of space
> The strong, creative mandate. Straight arose
> Those heavenly orbs, the glad abodes of life,
> Effusive kindled by his breath divine,
> Through endless forms of being."
>
> (*Pleasures of Imagination*, II, 307–18.)

It was possible, of course, to believe in such a plastic power and to embrace the findings of modern science, as the great Newton himself did. It was a principle, indeed, that, with the onward march of science, was to become the basis of the new science of biology; but this was not yet. Science for most people still meant mechanism, and when we meet the plastic principle in the poetry of the period it forms part of the desire to establish a universe sympathetic to art and generally betokens a certain suspicion of science.

As with Akenside, so in the many lines of Thomson's poetry we hear the echoes of now distant controversies and the voices of rival systems of thought. Too often today we think of this period as a serene and untroubled one, whereas, intellectually at least, the peace of the Augustans was little more than a truce between fiercely opposed points of view. The quietude of Thomson's poetry is more apparent than real and often is no more than an uneasy equilibrium of contending forces. In his pages we see a desperate attempt to hold together a scientific way of thinking with a spiritual and Platonic interpretation of reality. Beneath the assurance of the *Seasons* can be discerned the difficulty Thomson experienced in trying to serve both Locke and Shaftesbury. Thomson's indebtedness to the empirical philosophy is patent. He shows, in the manner of Locke, how the mind comes to order and assess its ideas, building up knowledge from sense experience; how we

> "Compound, divide, and into order shift,
> Each to his rank, from plain perception up
> To the fair forms of fancy's fleeting train;
> To reason then, deducing truth from truth,
> And notion quite abstract."
> (*Summer*, 1792–6.)

But alongside this is the desire to relate the moral to the natural order and to see both as the expression of a cosmic purpose in which beauty, goodness and truth are aspects of one reality. This desire was satisfied for him mainly by Shaftesbury, whom he describes in glowing terms as

> "The generous Ashley, thine, the friend of man;
> Who scanned his nature with a brother's eye,
> His weakness prompt to shade, to raise his aim,
> To touch the finer movements of the mind,
> And with the moral beauty charm the heart."
> (*Summer*, 1551–5.)

Thomson, unlike many of his contemporaries who wrote verse, was a poet first and foremost, and for him the theories of contemporary philosophy and science were important only because they helped him celebrate the beauty of the natural world. Shaftesbury's ethics appealed to him because it upheld morality as part of that beauty which animates the whole universe. Nature and morality were both aspects of the same eternal beauty to which all things witness. The seasons form such

> ". . . an harmonious whole
> That, as they still succeed, they ravish still."
> (*Hymn on the Seasons*.)

The whole earth, whether in distant and lonely places, or with the more temperate charms of English scenery, manifests its divine origin; and the heavenly bodies, too, are invoked to suport his optimistic creed.

> ". . . I cannot go
> Where universal love not smiles around,
> Sustaining all yon orbs and all their sons;
> From seeming evil still educing good,
> And better thence again, and better still,
> In infinite progression." *(ibid.)*

Though Thomson is indebted to Locke, the rapture with which he describes the beauties of nature owes more to the enthusiasm of the *Moralists* than the cogent reasonableness of the *Essay Concerning the Human Understanding*. The same is true of many other poets of the time; the writers of poetical theodicies, the followers of Thomson, and all who expressed an appreciation of natural beauty within the framework of the cosmic scene.

Even a poet such as William Shenstone, who was not concerned with 'the universal frame of things', but wished to celebrate the pleasures of rural life and to extol the simplicity of the country as compared with the city, was a devoted student of the *Characteristics*. One of Shenstone's poems was *The Judgment of Hercules* (1741.) The source of this poem was undoubtedly Shaftesbury's *A Notion of the Historical Draught of Hercules* and not the original story as told in Xenophon's *Memorabilia*; and some editions of Shenstone's poem were accompanied by a reproduction of the painting which Shaftesbury had commissioned from the Italian artist Paolo de Mattheis. In accordance with the instructions Shaftesbury had given to the artist, Virtue is depicted in this painting as carrying a "lance, or imperial sword". This was not a part of Xenophon's original story, but Shenstone's poem follows Shaftesbury even in this detail.

There is an old tradition in literary history which attributes a debt to Shaftesbury on the part of Pope. Voltaire in his *Lettres sur les Anglais*, 1734, declared that the philosophical system of the *Essay on Man* had been taken over from the *Characteristics* and he could not understand why Pope should not have acknowledged his borrowing.

> ". . . et je ne sais pourquoi M. Pope en fait uniquement honneur à M. de Bolingbroke, sans dire un mot du célèbre Shaftesbury, élève de Locke." (*Lettre* 22, in the 1756 revision.)

Joseph Warton's *Essay on the Writings and Genius of Pope* said that the *Essay on Man* was indebted to

> "the Theodicée of Leibnitz, to Archbishop King's Origin of Evil, and to the Moralists of Lord Shaftesbury." (Section IX.)

Warton quotes many lines from the *Essay on Man*, which he contends are no more than verse paraphrases of passages in the *Characteristics*, but in spite of the similarity, we must not necessarily accept his statement. In the case of Leibnitz, Warton was most probably in error for, writing to Warburton on the 2nd February, 1739, Pope says:

> "It cannot be unpleasant to you to know that I never in my life read a line of Leibnitz."[1]

Nevertheless, the view has persisted that Pope borrowed from Shaftesbury. Fowler, drawing upon this tradition in his *Shaftesbury and Hutcheson*, makes the assertion that Pope mentioned the *Inquiry concerning Virtue* and the *Moralists* as sources of the *Essay on Man*, but there is no warrant for this in any of Pope's writings.

The trouble with this theory is that Pope, in the fourth book of the *Dunciad*, went out of his way to satirize Shaftesbury, and this fact raises an immediate difficulty. As Warton puts it,

> "After borrowing so largely from this treatise, our author should not, methinks, have ridiculed it as he does, in the Fourth Book of the Dunciad."

If, indeed, Pope consciously borrowed from Shaftesbury there would be a great deal of force in Warton's comment; but can we be certain? Two explanations can be put forward to account for Pope's behaviour. The first of these is that the borrowing from Shaftesbury was quite unconscious and that Pope took over material from Bolingbroke which, though he did not know it, came originally from Shaftesbury. This is the more easily understood when we realize that though many features of Bolingbroke's thought derived from the *Characteristics*, there was no love lost between the Whig Shaftesbury and the turn-coat Tory. The shifty policy of Bolingbroke in negotiating a separate peace with France and leaving

[1] First published by A. W. Evans in *Warburton and the Warburtonians*, Oxford (1932), p. 79.

England's allies to fend for themselves, had not only brought the obloquy of Europe upon England's name, but had set the seal upon Shaftesbury's dislike for his political opponent. Equally on Bolingbroke's side there was hostility, for Shaftesbury in the second chapter of his third *Miscellany* had gone out of his way to pour contempt on Bolingbroke's cynical adoption of a Tory and High Church policy for personal ends. It is no wonder then that in Bolingbroke's philosophical writings, in spite of their indebtedness to him, no mention is made of Shaftesbury; and this would account in some measure for Pope's own possible, if unconscious, debt to the *Characteristics*.

The other explanation is that by the time Pope came to write the fourth book of the *Dunciad*, he had changed the philosophical opinions he had held earlier. This explanation would still, of course, leave him to face the charge of ingratitude; but it would be understandable, for Pope seems to have been scared at the accusations of freethinking levelled against the *Essay on Man* and would have been only too ready to dissociate himself from a name as dubious as Shaftesbury's. He was undoubtedly relieved when Warburton came to his rescue and answered *Examen de l' Essai de M. Pope sur l'Homme*,[1] which had been written by the Swiss philosopher Crousaz. We know, in fact, that Pope's views did undergo a change, in the sense that he repudiated any questionable doctrines that might unwittingly have been advanced in the *Essay on Man*; and the later attack on Shaftesbury might well have been inspired both by Warburton's tutelage and his own fervent desire to appear orthodox. For this reason and also because of the source of the report, we must not attach too much importance to the statement made in January 1750, by Bishop Warburton in a letter to Hurd,

> "Mr. Pope told me, that to his knowledge, the Characteristics had done more harm to revealed religion in England than all the works of infidelity put together." (*Letters of a late Eminent Prelate*, p. 27.)

The mistake that most writers on the subject make is to oversimplify the problem: either all the thought of the *Essay on Man* came from Shaftesbury, or none of it did. It is probably rare for an artist to draw his inspiration from a single source. Like any other person, the writer draws upon a varied background of knowledge and in Pope's case the background was especially complex. His

---

[1] An English translation was made by Miss Carter and published in 1738.

Essay on Criticism shows him to have been a wide reader even as a youth, while the *Essay on Man* shows an even wider range of acquaintance with theology and philosophy. The story of Lord Bathurst that Pope worked from a written statement provided by Bolingbroke, is an insult to the poet's intelligence and an indication only of Hugh Blair's gullibility in retailing it to Boswell. Johnson dismissed it with his usual common sense, when he said to Boswell,

> "Depend upon it, Sir, this is too strongly stated. Pope may have had from Bolingbroke the philosophic *stamina* of his *Essay*; and admitting this to be true Lord Bathurst did not intentionally falsify. But the thing is not true in the latitude that Blair seems to imagine."[1]

Pope acknowledged his indebtedness to Bolingbroke and no doubt owed a great deal to discussion with his noble patron; for his knowledge of philosophy was not profound, as can be seen from his relations with Warburton. Nevertheless, Pope would have resented being regarded as a mere versifier of Bolingbroke's thought. Even though he was no philosopher, Pope must have had an acquaintance with the sort of philosophical works that set the intellectual tone of the period. The educated man of the time would have known, for instance, Locke's *Essays* on government, on the human understanding and on education, without perhaps being able to follow all their philosophical complexities. Clearly Pope must have had the layman's knowledge of such subjects as Newton's physics, the philosophy of optimism, the Great Chain of Being, and so on. These were part of the mental furniture of the Augustan mind. It is unlikely that Pope would not have read the *Characteristics* and there are certainly many lines in the *Essay on Man* which would suggest it; but whether a knowledge of Shaftesbury's philosophy reached Pope directly, or through Bolingbroke, or from another source, or from a number of sources, seems to me impossible to determine with accuracy or finality.

More important than this is the fact that Pope exhibits the same strain of thought that we met in Thomson and Akenside; the same mixture of empiricism and what, for want of a better term, we can only describe as Augustan Platonism. Throughout the Augustan period there ran a deep-seated suspicion of scientific method and achievement. On the one side, it is true, there was wonder at the marvellous discoveries of science and admiration of those who had

[1] *Boswell's Life of Johnson*, ed. Birkbeck Hill, 1934 edn., Vol. III, p. 403.

brought them about. The regard for Newton amounted almost to reverence, as we see in Pope's famous couplet,

> "Nature and Nature's laws lay hid in night;
> God said, 'Let Newton be', and all was light."

The reverse side of the coin showed a different picture, however. There was fear at the implications of science and the feeling that human reason was outreaching itself, and Pope displays this attitude even more strongly than the other.

> "Go, wond'rous creature! mount where Science guides,
> Go, measure earth, weigh air, and state the tides:
> Instruct the planets in what orbs to run,
> Correct old Time, and regulate the Sun;
> Go, soar with Plato to th' empyreal sphere,
> To the first good, first perfect, and first fair;
> Or tread the mazy round his follow'rs trod,
> And quitting sense call imitating God;
> As Eastern priests in giddy circles run,
> And turn their heads to imitate the Sun.
> Go teach Eternal Wisdom how to rule—
> Then drop into thyself, and be a fool!
> Superior beings, when of late they saw
> A mortal Man unfold all Nature's law,
> Admir'd such wisdom in an earthly shape,
> And shew'd a NEWTON as we shew an Ape."
> (*Essay on Man*, II, 19–34.)

Though Pope seems to have included the Platonists with the scientists in this castigation, it was to a neo-Platonic type of philosophy that he turned for an answer to the menace of science. It is important to realize that the harmony he celebrates in the *Essay on Man* is an organic and not a mechanical one: the great chain of being which he traces from the Godhead to the meanest order of things, descends in a series of emanations, just as neo-Platonism from the time of Proclus onwards had proclaimed. Nature, for him, is governed and animated by the same plastic principle that Cudworth had elaborated.

> "Look round our World; behold the chain of Love
> Combining all below and all above.

> See plastic Nature working to this end,
> The single atoms each to other tend,
> Attract, attracted to, the next in place
> Form'd and impell'd its neighbour to embrace."
>
> (*ibid.*, III, 6–11.)

Whatever Shaftesbury's place in the story, there can be no doubt that Pope owed a great deal to the tradition which had produced the *Characteristics*. Whether they were transmitted through Bolingbroke, Archbishop King, or Shaftesbury, many of the ideas of the *Essay on Man* derived ultimately from the rational theology of the Platonists, and this is certainly so with the doctrine of a plastic nature.[1] How was it then, that in the fourth book of the *Dunciad* published in 1742, Pope should not only attack Shaftesbury, but should deride this very doctrine? The only convincing answer is the one I have suggested: that Pope had been flirting, though perhaps unwittingly, with intellectual opinions, which, if not deistical, bordered on a liberalism in theology that was looked at askance. The influence of Warburton is everywhere evident in the *Greater Dunciad*, and Pope's abandonment of his old mentors is sufficiently explained by his adoption of the bishop as his new philosophical guide. We know that Warburton disliked both Shaftesbury and the Cambridge Platonists, and it is natural that the text of the *Greater Dunciad* should reflect this dislike. This is even more so with the notes to Pope's poem, for here the hand may be the hand of Pope, but the voice is unmistakably Warburton's.

II

In the age of Anne the relationship between literature and the other arts was closer than our own generation can easily understand. It was quite possible, for instance, for Vanbrugh to be a dramatist, as well as the architect of Blenheim and Castle Howard; for Burlington to be a friend of Pope as well as of Kent; for Kent himself to be not only an architect, but a painter, landscape-gardener and designer of furniture. It was natural for Pope and Addison to write about the design of the great country houses that were being erected and to discuss the principles underlying landscape-gardening.

---

[1] That Pope knew Cudworth's writings is clear from Bolingbroke's *Fragments or Minutes of Essays*. The first of these is concerned with Cudworth's *Eternal and Immutable Morality*, which Bolingbroke says Pope had sent him.

Not even in the time of Ruskin or the Pre-Raphaelite Brotherhood were literature and her sister arts more closely related. For Shaftesbury it was part of his declared belief that this should be so. To be a man of breeding—indeed, to be fully virtuous according to his system of morals—it was necessary to cultivate a taste in the arts. Not that one should endeavour to become a narrow specialist in a particular branch of the arts, for that was to become eccentric and one-sided.

> "The mere amusements of gentlemen," he writes, "are found more improving than the profound researches of pedants." (*Advice to An Author, Characteristics*, I, 215.)

The fully developed personality will be a virtuoso, one with a fine taste and sensibility in all branches of culture.

> "Thus are the Arts and Virtues mutually friends; and thus the science of virtuosi and that of virtue itself become, in a manner, one and the same." (*ibid.*, 217.)

We shall not understand either Shaftesbury or his age, if we fail to realize that the growing political and social self-confidence of the early eighteenth century had brought about a new interest in the world of art. The Settlement of 1688 had produced at length a peace and stability during which the strife and commotion of the seventeenth century could be forgotten and society could turn once more to constructive pursuits. Nor was this peace merely a smug complacency. The Whigs, in particular, looked to the increased liberty which had accrued to the commoners, as the source of a great revival in the arts. In the *Letter Concerning Design*, which he addressed to Lord Somers in 1712, Shaftesbury takes stock of the artistic state of the nation. Writing at the conclusion of the war with France he looks forward to an era of great achievement.

> "From what I have observed of the rising generation of our nation," he declares, "if we live to see a peace any way answerable to that generous spirit with which this war was begun and carried on for our own liberty and that of Europe; the figure we are like to make abroad and the increase of knowledge, industry, and sense at home will render united Britain the principal seat of arts." (*Second Characters*, 19–20.)

He looks forward to a time when the people will develop a taste in the arts and when the demand for works of beauty will bring about a new standard of achievement. He advises the noblemen and landed-gentry, who are building country mansions with such prodigality, that they are not building for their own pleasure alone, but that their projects will be judged by their countrymen. They will "find little quarter from the public" if their houses, "of such a grandeur and magnificence as to become national ornaments," are erected merely to satisfy the whims of personal fancy. Shaftesbury anticipates a similar revival in music and painting. The Italian Opera, he tells us, had developed in Englishmen "an ear and judgment not inferior to the best now in the world"; while if a taste in painting was only now beginning, "in very few years, we shall make equal progress in this other science". To encourage these developments, Shaftesbury wished to see a Royal Academy that would foster a love of the arts. He envisaged, not direct State intervention, but a body that would achieve for the arts what the Royal Society had already done for the sciences. At the time this must have seemed rather a visionary scheme, but in 1754 it was realized in fact and there was founded the Royal Society of Arts.

Shaftesbury's taste in architecture and interior decoration tended, as in literature, to be orthodox and, at times, even conservative. Like most of those with a classical taste, he was suspicious of the new and fashionable enthusiasm for Oriental art. "The Indian figures, the Japan work, the enamel . . . the luscious colours and glossy paint", he tells the readers of *Advice to An Author*, will only debase a real taste. They may give pleasure at first sight, but only a meretricious and superficial one. He realized, and correctly, that the new naturalistic designs in tapestries, chintzes and furniture, which were based upon the free and asymmetrical patterns of the East, would destroy the classical canons of taste. The cult of the Oriental, which grew up as the century advanced, would have appalled him, and we may be sure that had he lived to see it, he would have waxed ironical at the great pagoda erected by Sir William Chambers at Kew in the 1780's, and other monuments to Chinese taste.

Even Wren's churches, which formed an impressive feature of the new London, provoked his censure. The campaign waged against Wren at this time was undoubtedly the outcome of political spite as much as of artistic principles; yet it was not simply Whiggish prejudice that animated Shaftesbury's attack upon the architect of St. Paul's. His *Letter Concerning Design* is a most interesting document which not only throws light upon the change in taste that preferred the Palladian to Wren's architecture, but helps us to understand something of the nature of Shaftesbury's classicism. It was not that he considered Wren's buildings extravagant and florid; he does, indeed, call them 'Gothic', but his main point is that he felt they would stand condemned by 'national taste'. It was not that they were extravagant, but that they were exact, mathematical and conformable to *a priori* laws which had been prescribed by the scientists. Shaftesbury felt that architecture should be the reflection of men's feelings and sense, the expression of a balanced and sane outlook, not merely an exercise in solid geometry; a good building should display the same virtues as a good life—order, balance, and control, together with a grace and beauty that go beyond mere rules. All these can be regarded, of course, as classical virtues, but we should realize that they are not identical with scientific values. Some writers have seen in the neo-classicism of this period merely the reflection of the growing scientific regard for concise and formal accuracy. There may be good grounds for this suggestion, but with Shaftesbury it was not so. The classicism which manifests itself in his appreciation of architecture and the other arts presupposes a humanity, a warmth and a graciousness that form no part of scientific exactitude.

Shaftesbury's influence played an important part in popularizing the Palladian style of architecture.[1] The *Letter Concerning Design* saw a decline in popularity of the great leaders of architectural fashion, Wren and Vanbrugh. Moreover, it gave a purpose to the new Palladian group by suggesting to them "two of the noblest subjects in architecture", a Royal Palace and the Houses of Parliament, which it suggested should be built in a new style reflecting the improved public taste.

> "Our State, in this respect," he writes, "may prove more fortunate than our Church in having waited till a national taste was formed before these edifices were undertaken."
> (*Second Characters*, 21).

These two buildings, as Mr. Hussey informs us, were the ambition of the Palladian circle who cherished the revival of Inigo Jones's scheme for the reconstruction of the entire Whitehall area, within which there would be new Royal and Government buildings with a dignity of design suited to their purpose. Though the work on the

---

[1] For an interesting essay which confirms this point, see Mr. Christopher Hussey's *Introduction* to *The Work of William Kent* by Margaret Jourdain.

Houses of Parliament had to be abandoned and that on the Royal Palace was never started, we may still claim that we owe something to Shaftesbury's influence; for a good many of our present public buildings, including the Horse Guards and part of the Treasury, date from the Palladian period. These two buildings themselves were designed, indeed, by Shaftesbury's disciple, William Kent.

It is part of the paradox of Shaftesbury's position that, though his own taste in art was classical, his philosophy contained the seeds of romanticism. Just as in his ethical philosophy the suggestion that man was naturally good and needed no restraint led to a sentimental morality, so in aesthetics his insistence on taste led to a greater cultivation of individual sensibility. Both of these developments would have been repugnant to him, but both were the result of the deep ambiguity which runs through his philosophy; an ambiguity which derives from the attempt to hold the reason and the feelings in balance. Apart from this, however, there is another important respect in which his thought can be seen as one of the well-springs of romanticism; this is his doctrine of nature.

The appeal to authority, to the examples and precepts of classical antiquity, had given way at the end of the seventeenth century to the appeal to nature.

"First follow Nature, and your judgment frame
By her just standard, which is still the same,"

had been the advice of Pope in his *Essay on Criticism*. The trouble was that nature could mean different things to different men. The appeal might be still the same, but nature itself in Shaftesbury's day was capable of a variety of interpretations. In fact it was the ambiguity of the concept of nature that allowed a revolution in thought to take place without anyone being conscious of the change. Broadly speaking, there were two meanings that were assigned to the concept at this time: the first of these was the mathematical and mechanical order given to nature by physical science; the other was the harmonious order with which contemporary Platonism endowed nature. The two were often confused, for both interpretations stressed what seemed to be the same things and, superficially, they were in agreement. But fundamentally they were quite different. The one conceived the order to be precise, mechanical and immutable; the other regarded it as evolving and organic, and a revelation of the divine order to which it only approximated. The one, if you like, tended to neo-classicism; the other to romanticism; but there, if you press the point, you find yourself at a loss, for the two terms are hopelessly inadequate when writing of the literature, and still more when writing of the men, of this period. They are untrustworthy signposts in what is a difficult countryside. The truth is that many men of this age, including Shaftesbury himself, were both romantic and classical at one and the same time; and it was the ambiguity of the word 'Nature' that allowed them to be so.

What has come to be known as the romantic movement may be seen as starting with the revolt of eighteenth-century Platonism against the scientific view of nature; and paradoxically the revolt was initiated by men who are often regarded as die-hard classicists. It is significant that Platonism, which was a formative influence in the early growth of romanticism should flourish once again at its hey-day; nor is it an accident that the romantic revolt started not in literature, but in gardening. It is in the naturalistic landscape-garden of the early eighteenth century that we see the first evidence of a reaction to the precision and formalism of neo-classicism. Here again, however, it is not the wholesale sweeping away of everything classical, for in gardens such as Stowe, Longleat, Rousham and Badminton, which were all designed on the new principles, we find Doric temples and classical pavilions; and many of the great houses which they encompass are pure Palladian in architecture.

Shaftesbury's praise of the apparent irregularities of nature, and the high value he assigned to the sublime were important factors in bringing about a change of taste in gardening. In *The Moralists* he had himself indicated the implications of his philosophy for the art of gardening:

"I shall no longer resist the passion growing in me for things of a natural kind, where neither art nor the caprice of man has spoilt the genuine order by breaking in upon that primitive state. Even the rude rocks, the mossy caverns, the irregular unwrought grottos and the broken falls of water, with all the horrid graces of the wilderness itself, as representing Nature more, will be the more engaging, and appear with a magnificence beyond the formal mockery of princely gardens." (*Characteristics*, II, 125.)

Addison, as always, was quick to seize the point. In his well-known essay, *Spectator* 414, which appeared only a couple of years later, he writes:

"The beauties of the most stately garden or palace lie in a narrow compass, the imagination immediately runs them over, and requires something else to gratify her; but, in the wide fields of nature, the sight wanders up and down without confinement, and is fed with an infinite variety of images, without any certain stint or number. For this reason we always find the poet in love with a country life. . . ."

Addison also made fun of the formal *parterre* and the topiary work which preferred trees "cut and trimmed into a mathematical figure". Unlike Shaftesbury he even welcomed the naturalistic designs of the fashionable chinoiserie, for, he tells us, the natives of China, preferring the concealed art that imitates nature, "laugh at the plantations of our Europeans, which are lain out by the rule and line".

Pope, in an equally famous passage of his *Epistle of the Use of Riches*, which he addressed to the Earl of Burlington, the patron of the Palladian group, satirizes the *nouveaux riches*, who spend their wealth on tasteless and extravagant estates. Their gardens instead of conforming to the new principles, are too often an ostentatious exhibition of the now discredited love of formality.

> "His gardens next your admiration call,
> On ev'ry side you look, behold the Wall!
> No pleasing Intricacies intervene,
> No artful wildness to perplex the scene;
> Grove nods at grove, each Alley has a brother,
> And half the platform just reflects the other.
> The suff'ring eye inverted Nature sees,
> Trees cut to Statues, Statues thick as trees;
> With here a Fountain, never to be play'd;
> And there a Summer-house, that knows no shade."
>
> (ll. 113-122.)

The reference to the wall is an interesting example of how the concept of sublimity was given practical effect. Pope's line means, of course, that the luckless man of wealth had not yet learned of the *ha-ha*, the dry-ditch used in place of the wall, so as not to restrict the view as one sauntered along the walks of the new landscape-gardens. Pope also contributed essays to *The Guardian*, which satirized the formal garden with its trimmed hedges and trees. Indeed, the new fashion grew apace, aided by many men of letters who all asked in their various ways the same rhetorical question as Batty Langley in the *New Principles of Gardening* (1728): "Is there anything more shocking than a stiff regular garden?"

There can be no doubt that the Age of Anne saw a great change in the art of gardening. Marvell could say of the garden at Appleton House,

> ". . . Nature here hath been so free
> As if she said leave this to me,
> Art would more neatly have defaced
> What she had laid so sweetly waste;"

but such a sentiment was unusual in the seventeenth century, for then formality had been the fashion. Simple gardens did exist, but the importation of Continental ideas had made them the exception rather than the rule. In Elizabethan days the formal garden of the Italian Renaissance had been popular in England, but by the time of the Restoration the elaborate designs which Charles II brought back from France, and which influenced the lay-out of Hampton Court, had caused it to disappear. The accession of William and Mary had introduced a Dutch influence, which, though more modest in intention than the French, again emphasized neatness and symmetry. With the early eighteenth century, however, there began the characteristically English fashion of landscape-gardening; a fashion that originated in the reaction, which we have associated with Shaftesbury, to the scientific view of nature. If uncultivated nature, with all its irregularities, is an expression of the first original and perfect beauty of the Godhead, then the obvious task in laying out a garden is to make it as much like nature as possible. This, the very first principle of landscape-gardening, cuts right across the attempt to reduce the garden to a mathematical pattern. William Mason, Cambridge don and friend of Gray, describes the history of the English garden in execrable verse, but shows some insight into the basic issues when he writes:

> ". . . As Nature then
> Avoids, disdains, abhors all equal lines,
> So Mechanism pursues, admires, adores.
> Hence is their enmity; and sooner hope
> With hawk and dove to draw the Cyprian car
> Than reconcile these jarring principles."
> (*The English Garden*, 1772, Bk. I.)

By Mason's time the two views of nature to which we have referred were drawing apart, and the earlier confusion between them had ceased to exist; it is significant that by nature he should mean something diametrically opposed to mechanism.

One of the first to practise the new art of landscape-gardening was William Kent, protégé of Burlington, friend of Pope, and disciple of Shaftesbury. Kent was an architect, painter and furniture designer, as well as being a landscape-gardener, but he is known to us chiefly as one who stands at the beginning of the tradition of which the most famous exponent was perhaps Lancelot ("Capability") Brown. He was one of the very first who, in Horace Walpole's phrase, "leaped the fence, and saw that all nature was a garden". The basis of the new art he popularized was that gardens should be designed, and parks laid out, on the principles of landscape painting. Gardens should merge into parks and parks into the surrounding landscape, so that the entire scene should be a unity to the beholder's eye. Walks were to be planned so as to give distant views; trees were to be planted so as to balance the colours and formation of the surrounding countryside; streams and lakes so disposed as to conform with the natural contours. The object was not to superimpose a garden upon the countryside, but to blend it with the landscape. To destroy natural features, says William Mason, would be like tearing out part of the canvases of Poussin and Claude Lorraine, the painters whose work was to be taken as a model by the landscape-gardener.

"O great Poussin! O Nature's darling, Claude!
What if some rash and sacrilegious hand
Tore from your canvass those umbrageous pines
That frown in front and give each azure hill
The charm of contrast!" (*ibid.*, Bk. I.)

It might be objected that all this is not the acceptance of nature, wild and untamed as she is, but the disciplining of nature; a softening of the outlines, and something as artificial in its way as the most formal garden. Is not a natural garden really a contradiction in terms? Are there not, on the one side, nature, and on the other, gardens, which are an artificial creation? Are not nature and art terms which are necessarily opposed? Such questions really misunderstand the philosophical presuppositions of the art of landscape-gardening. To be sure, landscape-gardening is an art, but its end is not to render nature artificial. Its purpose is to realize the ideal beauty which we only glimpse in nature as she actually is. To leap over the garden-wall does not bring us into another, but perfect, garden. It only introduces us to a world, which, while still possessing evidence of its original form, is but a shadow of that first garden, from which our ancestors were driven by an angel bearing a sword of flame. Like the painter, the landscape-gardener is trying to realize an ideal; an ideal which is not a mathematically precise order, but is revealed in the crags and torrents, the stern places of nature as well as the smooth. The landscape-gardener is an artist; to him more than any other is given the opportunity to co-operate with the plastic spirit of nature. Not only his imagination but his materials are creative. Shaftesbury would have endorsed cordially Mason's injunction:

"Take thy plastic spade,
It is thy pencil; take thy seeds, thy plants,
They are thy colours; and by these repay
With interest every charm she lent thy art." (*ibid.*, Bk. I.)

For landscape-gardening was a striking example of what he had striven for; an art that was based upon a Platonic philosophy.

Landscape-gardening marked the beginning of a new taste in the arts. Painting, architecture, furniture, interior decoration and even the design of fabrics were all to reflect the change. Pictures that showed wild and mountain scenery were to become increasingly popular; buildings, which had been erected according to a classical pattern, were now to give place to more ornate and even Chinese and Gothic structures, especially on the estates of those who regarded themselves as the vanguard of artistic development. Furniture and fabrics were to show a greater freedom of design, reflecting in their lines the new regard for naturalistic curves and asymmetrical patterns. Literature, too, embraced a liking for the emotional and sentimental, the Gothic and romantic: though here we must not oversimplify the situation, for against the cult of the graveyard, and the revival of ballad and chivalry, must be set the determined attempts made in the middle of the century to hold to classical standards. Moreover, the growth of a philosophy which suggested that all knowledge derives from sensation necessarily restricted the scope of poetry and weakened any notion that it could be either prophecy or vision. We have already seen good reasons for thinking that Shaftesbury would probably have been on the side of those who wished to maintain classical standards; yet we cannot be sure, for his philosophy was directed against scientific method and empiricism. Because classicism tended more and more to become identified with empiricism, we must rank him as a romantic as well as a neo-classicist.

III

Shaftesbury's influence in the field of philosophy was not as great as in the arts. However, in ethics he remained a considerable figure. Bishop Butler, in the Preface to the 1729 edition of *Fifteen Sermons*, acknowledged his agreement with Shaftesbury's plea for the autonomy of ethics, while reserving his judgment upon other points; and Shaftesbury can rightly be regarded as the founder of the moral-sense school of the eighteenth century. In aesthetics, too, his influence was an enduring force. We have seen something of this already in the case of the more important writers, but a further indication is given by the constant appearance of lesser known books, such as James Harris's *Three Treatises on Art*, which was dedicated to him and is an exposition of his critical theory. Yet in spite of all this, there is no doubt that Shaftesbury's philosophy was overshadowed by the growth of empiricism. In particular the figure of his old tutor, Locke, dominated the century and dwarfed all other philosophers. Only those, such as Berkeley and Hume, who carried Locke's own thought a stage farther, were able to hold a candle to the steady but powerful radiance of the *Essay Concerning Human Understanding*. All other luminaries paled into insignificance. Moreover, the empirical philosophy gathered strength as the century wore on. That is why we find the high reputation Shaftesbury's works enjoyed at the beginning of the century suffering an eclipse towards the end. Lord Monboddo, for example, writing in the 1770s, says of him,

> ". . . in my younger days, that is about fifty years ago, all his writings and particularly his Rhapsody [*The Moralists*], were much esteemed. But I do not know how it has happened, none of his writings at present appear to be in any estimation."
> (*Origin and Progress of Language.*)

To Monboddo and his contemporaries the reason may not have been apparent, but to us it is quite clear. The times were out of joint for Shaftesbury's philosophy, and his influence was really no more than an underground movement in territory that had become occupied by the forces of a rival philosophy. Skirmishes there might be, but the main battle was over for almost a century.

The struggle with Hobbes had been a long and severe one, and even in Shaftesbury's day the *Leviathan* was still a powerful force against a view of life that believed in the supernatural and valued the poetic imagination. Furthermore, Hobbes had been counted an atheist, while his antagonists, the Cambridge Platonists, as well as being philosophers, were on the side of the angels. With Locke it was a different story. Locke was a Christian, whereas his pupil's orthodoxy was in some doubt. Here it was a straightforward issue between two philosophies and there is no doubt that as a philosopher, Shaftesbury was no match for Locke. Shaftesbury was not interested in such questions as how the mind can be said to have knowledge; he regarded such a subject as a minor irrelevance to the main philosophical issues. In this he made a cardinal error, since the main issues were being fought out within the framework of the theory of knowledge and not to see this was really to have lost the fight from the outset. What Shaftesbury needed was a philosophy that would defend the claims of the poetic imagination from the suggestion that science had superseded metaphysics and that all knowledge which does not come from sensory observation is illusory. There are elements in Shaftesbury's writings which might have been developed into such a philosophy, but they do not amount to a coherent system. Many, like Pope, were to reject what they felt instinctively would give their poetic genius validity, simply because they could not defend such a philosophy against the more solid claims of Locke.

What this meant for poetry must be left for our final chapter. All that remains to be said here is a word about Shaftesbury's reputation abroad. It would be beyond the scope of this study to trace in detail his influence on Continental writers and a mere mention must be sufficient. In France, Le Clerc and Voltaire knew his writings and Diderot, especially, was influenced by him, and in 1769 a French translation of his collected works was published in Geneva. It was in Germany, however, that Shaftesbury became an important figure and exerted a great influence on aesthetic thinking. Lessing, Mendelssohn, Wieland, Herder, Kant and Schiller all knew, and were stimulated by, his writings. Both Diderot and Lessing were indebted to Shaftesbury for the suggestion that painting and poetry could fruitfully be compared as alternative means for the expression of thought in an artistic medium. Such a comparison suggested that the artist is one whose thinking cannot be comprehended conceptually, and so prepared the way for that rehabilitation of the artistic imagination which was made by Kant. In Germany, Shaftesbury was regarded as a romantic figure. Herder, in particular, in his

Adrastea used almost extravagant language when speaking of the *Characteristics*, and, while insisting on the Hellenic quality of Shaftesbury's thought, conceived this Hellenism in romantic and not classical terms. In the same way, Shaftesbury was interpreted in Scandinavia as one who exalted a life of emotion rather than reason, and his influence upon the eighteenth-century Danish writer, Ludwig Holberg and the Swedish critic, Thomas Thorild, was such that it can only be described as making for romanticism.[1]

These Continental writers all seized on the more liberal aspects of Shaftesbury's doctrines, and in this way he became an important figure in the development of the romantic movement. This was possible on the Continent, where his thought did not have to contend with a vigorous and developing empirical tradition of philosophy as it did in England, and it is this fact, too, that explains why his reputation increased abroad, while at home it declined. So great, indeed, was this decline that it brought about the supreme irony whereby later writers amongst his own countrymen, such as Coleridge, appeared to know nothing of his work and yet were only too ready to welcome his ideas in the more sophisticated form given them by German philosophy.

---

[1] I am indebted for this information concerning Shaftesbury's Scandinavian influence to Dr. Henrik Neiiendam of Copenhagen.

CHAPTER X

THE CRISIS OF REASON

Art is purposeful adaptation of Appearance to Reality. Now "purposeful adaptation" implies an end, to be obtained with more or less success. This end, which is the purpose of art, is twofold—namely Truth and Beauty. The perfection of art has only one end, which is Truthful Beauty. But some measure of success has been reached, when either Truth or Beauty is gained. In the absence of Truth, Beauty is on a lower level, with a defect of massiveness. In the absence of Beauty, Truth sinks to triviality. Truth matters because of Beauty. (A. N. Whitehead, *Adventures of Ideas*.)

I

THE advance of scientific method, together with the growth of a philosophy which put its main emphasis upon the analysis of sense experience, made a tremendous impact upon the poetry and the poets of the eighteenth century. Science, for its part, had for some time haunted men's imaginations with the spectre of a dead and silent universe, totally unlike what the poet had conceived it to be. Many now felt that what the poet pictured must simply be something he had read into the structure of the universe; a poetic gloss upon reality, something unconvincing and chimerical. What was real was matter and mechanical forces. Philosophy, too, seemed to suggest the same conclusion, for it held that any statement that could not be tested by sense experience must be regarded either as the expression of an emotional state, or simply as meaningless. A true statement, it maintained, was one that could be verified empirically, and poetry was ruled out, not so much as something that was untrue, but rather as something that had no relation to the truth. Even when concerned with empirical knowledge, it was felt that poetry could only express very hazily what statements of fact could put more exactly. In the main the function of poetry was considered to be either to express the wishes and hopes of the poet himself, or to soothe and please the reader. Both these are legitimate aims, of course, but they give a very limited scope to poetry. Put at its crudest, they imply that poetry can be either wish-fulfilment or entertainment, but nothing else.

It is not surprising that the poets of the Augustan period often felt themselves at odds with contemporary thought; that the gifts which science brought, if not actually feared, were not universally acceptable. Pope and Swift were only the most prominent of a large number who regarded science as a dangerous, if not a destructive, force. The trouble was that they and others with them had nothing to offer in answer to the positivistic spirit which had manifested itself: their attitude was largely a negative one. The only answer that seemed possible was in terms of an older philosophy which saw the universe as the expression of a world of spirit in visible and material form. Shaftesbury's writings were a brave attempt to carry this philosophy forward, but were not really competent to deal with an empiricism that grew in strength as the century advanced. Platonism 'alone and palely loitering' never became an effective force until rescued by those who could give an answer to the more radical of the empiricists. It dwindled to little more than a habit of mind, a nostalgic looking over the shoulder to a poetic view of reality that science had destroyed. In England this was even truer than in Germany and English aesthetics in the eighteenth century exhibits little trace of Platonic influence.

The truth is that Shaftesbury's answer to empiricism was inadequate. It was no good advancing an interpretation of the universe in Platonic terms, without the necessary philosophical backing to substantiate it. There are, indeed, parts of Shaftesbury's philosophy which, if they had been developed, would have led to a theory of knowledge that could meet the claims of empiricism. The pity is that he never developed them. Such was his impatience with disciplined metaphysical thinking that he never took these elements farther than the formulation given them by the Cambridge Platonists. It is easy enough to blame him for this now, but if we put ourselves in his situation we can see how he may be justified. His task, as he regarded it, was not to strengthen the philosophical position of the Cambridge group, but to extend their thinking to other spheres and to bring it home to the hearts of men. Such was his disposition, and such he deemed were the demands of the times in which he lived. Shaftesbury has not been the only one to consider so-called practical issues more important than academic philosophy, and moreover there are certain considerations which vindicate his decision, if such a word can be used to describe what was probably not a self-conscious act. Before it could be philosophically refuted, there had to be built up a realization that empiricism was unsatisfactory because it failed to give an adequate account, amongst other things, of men's artistic experience. Philosophies are not constructed as a matter of pure thought; they have to take account of human experience, and men had yet to experience the full disillusionment brought about by the prevailing philosophy before a new system of thought could be constructed. A discussion of this would be out of place here nor, indeed, have I the competence to undertake it, but there would seem to be good reason for thinking that the idealist reaction to empiricism started in many cases in the field of aesthetics. The reaction in the first place seems to have been a revolt of artistic sensibility. It may be, then, that Shaftesbury was right to make his task the creation and encouragement of such sensibility rather than plunging into the deep waters of metaphysics.

The result of his decision, however, was that many poets who wished to embrace what may loosely be called a Platonic viewpoint were attracted, in spite of themselves, by the fascination of the new philosophy. The older picture of the universe appealed more to their poetic sensibility, but the new philosophy made demands that their reason could not resist. Their poetic inspiration constructed a world that was undoubtedly beautiful, but there still remained the question whether such a construction were true. The result was that against all their instincts they were forced into a dualism that made beauty the object of poetry, while truth remained the concern of science. Their dilemma is well illustrated by the lines Akenside addressed to his friend Caleb Hardinge.

> "Lead thou where'er my labour lies,
> And English fancy's eager flame
> To Grecian purity chastize;
> While hand in hand at Wisdom's shrine,
> Beauty with Truth I strive to join,
> And grave assent with glad applause;
> To paint the story of the soul,
> And Plato's visions to control
> By Verulamian Laws."
> (*Ode to Caleb Hardinge, M.D.*)

To Akenside and others like him, the cogency of Locke's thought proved irresistible, and they found it difficult to justify their own poetic aspirations with philosophical argument. This was true throughout the eighteenth century, and poetry had to struggle on without the support of philosophy. Where a poet felt himself at odds with the prevailing philosophy his dissatisfaction rarely became more than a matter of sensibility. Even Blake (for whom the three persons of the unholy Trinity were Bacon, Locke, and Newton), although he saw more clearly than most what the empirical tradition had done to poetry, was unable to formulate any rival system of thought. In *There is no Natural Religion* Blake retorts to empiricism, or the philosophy of the Five Senses, as he calls it:

"Man's perceptions are not bounded by organs of perception; he perceives more than sense (tho' ever so acute) can discover."

He realized that some power of the mind not derived from sense-experience is necessary if even the perception and ordering of that sense-experience were to be possible; that there must be an imaginative power of the mind which is free of sense-knowledge, for otherwise there could be no advance even in scientific and philosophical thinking. Without such a power the mind would simply reflect and record events as the dials on an engine reflect and record the movement of the parts.

"If it were not for the Poetic or Prophetic character, the Philosophic and Experimental would soon be at the ratio of all things, and stand still, unable to do other than repeat the same dull round over again." (*ibid.*)

Newton, who stood for scientific method, and Locke, who represented a philosophy bounded by sense-perception, were the arch-villains of the piece for Blake. His remarks on Sir Joshua Reynolds's *Discourses* and on Burke's *Treatise on the Sublime and Beautiful* show what he considered the tradition of Locke and Newton had done for poetry; it had robbed art of any vitalizing aesthetic. It is impossible to do justice to a man as complex as Blake in a brief reference of this kind, and yet it is true to say that, in spite of his profundity of insight, his dissatisfaction with the empirical philosophy was not in itself an adequate answer. Blake was an artist and a mystic rather than a philosopher. Though many of his statements imply certain philosophical presuppositions, his task was not to make philosophically explicit his disagreement with the prevailing thought, but to mythologize and allegorize the intuitive awareness of the artist. This is not to criticize Blake adversely, for as the second excerpt from *There is no Natural Religion*, which was quoted above, itself contends, the job of the artist is to stimulate and challenge the philosopher by pressing upon his attention the products of an imaginative awareness which belongs primarily to the artist. Blake's dissatisfaction, though not enough in itself, was perhaps a necessary prelude to the philosophical change which it heralded.

For any sort of philosophical answer England had to wait for Coleridge. Coleridge, to his own cost, was both a poet and a philosopher. Like Blake, he felt ill at ease as a poet in the face of a system of thought which did less than justice to the artistic imagination. Coleridge's reaction from Hartley and empiricism was initially the revolt of poetic sensibility, an attempt to hold on to an interpretation of reality which accorded with what his poetic awareness told him must be true. But he realized that this was not enough. To cling to the sort of thinking which was pre-scientific, and which did nothing to meet the attacks of the new psychological explanation of the poetic imagination, was merely to indulge in sentimental reverie. The attacks had to be met, and an answer made in terms which comprehended and did not evade the prevailing philosophy. A century of experience had taught him what Shaftesbury had no means of learning, that what poetry needed was a deeper and more penetrating philosophy. Yet it is significant that in formulating his answer, Coleridge should have returned to the same starting point as Shaftesbury and should have found in seventeenth-century Platonism the inspiration for his theory of imagination. Only by returning to the cross-roads where Shaftesbury stood could poetry and philosophy meet again. Without going back, neither poetry nor philosophy could again become travelling companions, fortifying and ministering to each other in their common journey.

II

Does this mean, as is sometimes foolishly asserted, that the eighteenth century was unable to produce poetry? Does the absence of a sympathetic philosophy mean that poets, in the words of W. B. Yeats, "must bid the Muse go pack,"

> "Until imagination, ear and eye,
> Can be content with argument and deal
> In abstract things; or be derided by
> A sort of battered kettle at the heel"?[1]

Some have suggested this and held that eighteenth-century poetry was not poetry at all. A. E. Housman, for instance, in his Leslie

[1] W. B. Yeats, *The Tower, Collected Poems*, Macmillan & Co.

Stephen Lecture, *The Name and Nature of Poetry*, given in Cambridge in 1933, writes as follows:

> "There is also such a thing as sham poetry, a counterfeit deliberately manufactured and offered as a substitute. In English the great historical example is certain verse produced abundantly and applauded by high and low in what for literary purposes is loosely called the eighteenth century."

It is significant that in the same context Housman should mention Matthew Arnold, for it is probably Arnold more than any one other person who has been responsible for the growth of this attitude towards the eighteenth century.

Wordsworth and Coleridge, though critical, were more discriminating. For them the fault of eighteenth-century poetry was its creation of a special diction remote from the language of prose, and they regarded the poetry of Gray as the outstanding example of this fault. For Arnold, on the other hand, eighteenth-century verse was bad because it was too prosaic and Gray the one example of a real poet in what otherwise would have been a poetic wilderness.

> "Gray, a born poet," he writes, "fell upon an age of prose. He fell upon an age whose task was such as to call forth in general men's powers of understanding, wit and cleverness, rather than their deepest powers of mind and soul. As regards literary production, the task of the eighteenth century in England was not the poetic interpretation of the world, its task was to create a plain, clear, straightforward, efficient prose. Poetry obeyed the bent of mind requisite for the due fulfilment of this task of the century. It was intellectual, argumentative, ingenious; not seeing things in their truth and beauty, not interpretative. Gray, with the qualities of mind and soul of a genuine poet, was isolated in his century." (*Essays in Criticism*, Second Series, III.)

Now, it may be asked, is not Arnold's argument precisely the argument that might be advanced after a consideration of the facts we have been studying? Is not his description of eighteenth-century poetry just what we might expect from the influence on literature of Locke's philosophy? Certainly there is a germ of truth in Arnold's judgment; the eighteenth century was an age in which prose became clearer and more workmanlike and in which poetry stood nearer to prose than at some other times. The mistake he makes is in claiming too much; of allowing one truth to fill his mind to the exclusion of more important truths. Every age, in assessing the immediately preceding one, is bound to be biased in its own favour and to react too strongly against what has gone before, and this is particularly true of the Victorian attitude to the eighteenth century. Even today a Victorian habit of mind persists and obscures the truth about the eighteenth century: the critical dogmas of Matthew Arnold still hang heavy upon us.

The philosophical temper of an age certainly makes its mark upon the sort of poetry that is written, but this does not mean that good poetry was impossible in the eighteenth century. In the first place, Locke's was not the only tradition of philosophy, and in the second, even if we allow the dominance of empiricism, its effect was felt mainly as a certain restriction of the scope of poetry. The boundaries of the sort of experience which Pope deals with in the *Rape of the Lock* are not very extensive. But can anyone doubt that here is a poem which displays real imaginative power? It may not be great poetry, if by that we mean poetry which deals with great themes, but it shows a complete mastery of the form adopted by the poet and an ability that cannot be described simply as wit. One is irresistibly reminded of Dr. Johnson's question in his *Life of Pope*.

"If Pope be not a poet, where is poetry to be found?"

The same question might be asked, with regard to other Augustan poets, of those who have made too hasty judgments of their poetry. Later critics often failed to understand Augustan poetry because they failed to realize that the poets of the eighteenth century did not share a common purpose with the poets of their own day. Pope's poetry was inspired chiefly by literary forces and he was not attempting the same thing as Wordsworth, who was regarded by the nineteenth century as the great examplar of what a poet should be. Pope was not endeavouring to assess the influence of natural objects upon the human mind, nor was he trying primarily to describe nature at all. We shall fail to understand even such poems as *Windsor Forest*, where there is a more evident intention of description and where Pope's love of the Thames valley is unmistakable, if we think of them as Wordsworthian. To appreciate *Windsor Forest* we have to realize that it is written within a pastoral convention; it is not merely what Johnson called 'local poetry'. The shepherds and their flocks do not belong to any Berkshire known to us; the nymphs and fairies are never far away, and in the distance we can hear the horns of elfland faintly blowing.

Even so, it is too sweeping to say, as Arnold does,

> "The poetic language of our eighteenth century in general is the language of men composing *without their eye on the object.*" (*ibid.* The italics are Arnold's.)

If this is true of anyone, it is true of Gray. In the case of Pope it fails to realize the purpose of his writing, and it is equally untrue of the many eighteenth-century poets whose aim really was to describe natural scenery. For men who composed with their eye on the object we need go no farther than Cowper or Crabbe. In their poetry we get an accurate picture of the countryside; there is not only detailed description, but an emotional tone which captures the atmosphere of the Home Counties and the landscape of the Suffolk Marshes.

Their poetry can rightly be called 'Nature-poetry', for it is really descriptive, whereas Romantic poetry more often treats nature as a religious principle than as landscape. It was part of what might be called the Romantic heresy to turn the natural order into God Himself. The transcendence of God became so unimportant to the Romantics, and the natural order so valuable in itself, that God was little more, in their view, than an immanent principle investing the world of nature. Quite different was the sentiment expressed in Addison's splendid hymn,

> "The spacious firmament on high,
> With all the blue ethereal sky,
> And spangled Heavens, a shining frame,
> Their great Original proclaim."

It was always the temptation of Romanticism to turn itself into a form of Pantheism; to distort the belief of seventeenth-century Platonism that nature was a revelation of God into the belief that nature was God.

Sir Herbert Grierson in his *Classical and Romantic*, declares that it is an

> "undeniable fact that it is to Plato the greatest Romantics have always turned to find philosophical expression for their mood— Spenser, Wordworth, Shelley, the German romantic philosophers

Schelling and Fichte,—Plato's romantic conception of an ideal world concealed behind the visible, his 'city laid up in heaven', his daring deduction of all being and knowledge from the Idea of the Good. It was Plato who, despite his condemnation of the poets, effected that interrelation of philosophy and poetry which has characterised every great romantic movement."[1]

Perhaps it would be more exact to speak of Platonism rather than Plato, but the main point is undoubtedly right. Nevertheless, we should bear in mind that the Platonism of nineteenth-century romanticism was not identical with the Platonism of earlier times; it was a lop-sided affair. Platonism, as we meet it at the Renaissance and in the seventeenth century, was balanced between the Greek ideal of reason and the appeal of the senses and emotions; a balance that could be easily disturbed. With Milton the balance was hardly in doubt; but Plato's charioteer has never found his steeds easy to manage, and the sensuous and emotional qualities of Spenser's poetry, for instance, were held in check by the reason perhaps more often than they were reconciled to it. Similarly, in the seventeenth century the balance could be upset and an undue regard for the irrational element in man could produce the veneration for magical and pseudo-mystical writing that occurs from time to time in the history of neo-Platonism; or it could easily become the exaggerated regard for emotion untempered by rational control, which we meet in the strange outbursts of some seventeenth-century religious sects.

Shaftesbury's ideal was the Greek conception of reason as the sovereign power in the kingdom of the mind, but we have already seen how difficult he and, even more, subsequent thinkers, found it to hold fast to this ideal. We have already perceived something of the way in which reason and emotion became two elements in an irresoluble dualism for the eighteenth century. It is strange that the eighteenth century should be called the Age of Reason in literature, when so many of its great writers walked the borderland between sanity and madness: when Dean Swift declined into a doddering and crippling imbecility; when William Cowper twice attempted his own life in fits of madness and ended his days in a depression that bordered on insanity; when Collins became mad, and when Gray was haunted all his life by that deep melancholy which settled on his mind like a cloud; when even Johnson, who is so frequently and so wrongly represented as merely animated by common sense, was obsessed with a fear of madness and had what we can only call a

[1] *The Leslie Stephen Lecture* for 1923, Cambridge, at the University Press.

morbid terror of death. It would be equally untrue to suggest that the eighteenth century was devoid of the larger manifestations of feeling which can make themselves felt throughout society. We should remember, for instance, that this was the century which saw the rise of the Wesleyan movement; a movement that could not be described as unemotional, either in its forms of worship, or in the imagery and language of its hymns.

How is it then that this conception of the eighteenth century has come to be so widely held? The description of the period as an Age of Reason is true not because the century lacked emotion, but rather in the sense that it recognized the dangers which unbridled emotion could bring. The Augustans were suspicious of emotion, not because they were unaware of it, but because they knew it all too well and were rather frightened of the extravagant and excessive forms that emotion could take. The century started with unhappy memories of what unrestricted passion could lead to in the political sphere and had in mind the struggles of the Civil War and the intrigues and insurrections of the Restoration. Indeed, collectively as well as individually, the Augustans were conscious of the misery and terror that could ensue when reason's reign was overthrown by passion.

The trouble for the eighteenth century was that reason and emotion had become antithetical; two parts of a dualism which could not be resolved. By restricting the scope of the reason and by making it a faculty which could not go beyond the bounds of empirical verification, eighteenth-century philosophy threw men's larger hopes and aspirations to the winds of pure emotionalism. By failing to see that a good deal that lies beyond the limits of the understanding might be validated by a reason of a wider kind, the empiricists abrogated instead of establishing the sovereignty of reason. As the empirical philosophy developed the situation became worse; as the century wore on the appeal of the emotions grew greater while the authority of reason became even smaller. It is true that one tradition of romanticism recognized that the dualism must be resolved, that the scope of reason must be extended, but the influence of other forms of romanticism simply brought about an assertion of the feelings at the expense of reason. Though neither, perhaps, existed in the simple form often ascribed to it, we can still say that extreme romanticism and extreme neo-classicism made the same mistake. Both accepted the dualism of the reason and the emotions; the only difference being that ultra-romanticism asserted one element of the dualism, while strict neo-classicism

P

asserted the other. It was thus that neo-classicism and romanticism came to be antithetical terms, while basically they were united in error.

III

To identify romanticism with the feelings and neo-classicism with the reason, however, is too crude and facile an account of the matter. What we have been considering can be more accurately expressed by saying that while romanticism at first recognized that the eighteenth century had confused a dualism between the understanding and the reason with a dualism between the reason and the emotions, the extremer and later forms of romanticism turned the reason into something not very different from mere emotionalism and thus fell back into error again. Romanticism, in many of its nineteenth-century manifestations, believed that what did not fall within the categories of scientific explanation could be validated only by the personal intuition of the artist. In this way all man's supernatural aspirations and insights were left with little more substantiation than the artist's intensity of feeling. Many in the eighteenth century had been ready to use Shaftesbury's own weapon of ridicule to call in question a faith in the supernatural; it was a sceptical age when, in the words of the contemporary historian, William Robertson, men would no longer "hurry with precipitation to the Holy Land", or believe "that Christ would quickly appear to judge the world." But instead of arguing the case, many of the Romantics accepted the indefensibility of anything beyond the boundaries of physical nature, save on the grounds of their own feeling.

Coleridge, of course, was an exception to this. He saw clearly that the reason and the understanding were not the same thing, and he never equated reason with the emotions. He belonged to what might be called, without paradox, the classical tradition of romanticism, a tradition which included Spenser, Vaughan, Shaftesbury and Wordsworth, and which never allowed an abrogation of reason, let alone a cult of emotionalism. He believed that "reason in her most exalted mood" was the loftiest faculty in man and could go beyond sensory knowledge. It was a great loss to English aesthetics and to English thought in the nineteenth century that Coleridge never developed his philosophy with the systematic thoroughness it demanded and deserved. Yet even Coleridge seems never to have realized the importance of relating the reason and the understanding, of working out the connection between our empirical knowledge and the rest of our knowledge. The eighteenth-century problem, though it became more philosophically precise in his hands, still persisted, in the dualism between the reason and the understanding.

It is, indeed, a dualism which still shapes and influences criticism today. Contemporary philosophy professes a greater interest in the nature of language than in metaphysical inquiry, yet even in this preoccupation with language the dualism between reason and understanding shows itself. In fact, the theory of language propounded by certain of the logical positivists seems to have reverted once again to a crude dichotomy between reason and emotion. Language, according to this theory, is either cognitive or emotive. Cognitive statements are either the tautologous propositions of mathematics and logic, or synthetic propositions which can be verified empirically. Emotive statements merely express or arouse emotion; they may spur one to action, but they are not meaningful as are cognitive statements. Metaphysics, ethics and aesthetics are all examples of emotive language, according to these writers, and poetry, of course, is a clear case of its use. This has been accepted by some critics who welcome the suggestion that knowledge is a matter for the scientist, and that poetry is concerned only with the feelings.

At the other extreme, however, are those who believe that poetry has its own access to the truth and that it can be independent of empirical knowledge. These, too, do not base their conviction on any clear conception of the rôle of reason, for if they speak of reason at all, it is of something quite divorced from the understanding. More often their notion of poetic awareness implies a naïve acceptance of irrationalism, a belief that the impulses of the human mind which lie below the levels of consciousness, somehow carry their own guarantee of truth. Contemporary criticism, in fact, seems to be split into opposite extremes, both of which are rooted in irrationalism and both of which are the outcome of the distinction, which ought never to have been made, between classicism and romanticism.

The foremost of modern critics who have adopted a strictly empirical philosophy has been Mr. I. A. Richards. Though I believe that Mr. Richards's opinions have since changed, at the time when he exerted most influence, the keystone of his critical theory was the distinction noted above between cognitive and emotive language. This is brought out quite clearly in *Science and Poetry* (1926), where, in the chapter entitled *Poetry and Beliefs*, he writes:

"It will be admitted—by those who distinguish between scientific statement, where truth is ultimately a matter of verification as this is understood in the laboratory, and emotive utterance, where 'truth' is primarily acceptability *by* some attitude, and more remotely is the acceptability *of* this attitude itself—that it is *not* the poet's business to make true statements."[1]

Mr. Richards argued in his *Principles of Literary Criticism*, that the value of poetry consists in its satisfaction of what he called 'appetencies'. Value, he contended, increases in proportion to the number of such appetencies satisfied; a theory which reduced poetry to the level of pushpin. Poetry is valuable, according to Mr. Richards, simply because of its therapeutic properties; it can give us psychological poise and can resolve our emotional conflicts, but is not concerned with the truth.

Now it may be that Mr. Richards himself has discarded this theory, it may be that the position he took up has been abandoned by many of his followers; yet the critical apparatus which was erected on the foundations he laid is still with us. The study of literature is still invaded by positivistic techniques, which turn literature into an object of analytical inquiry and which either ignore the realm of values, or try to explain it away on psychological grounds. Some of these techniques are no doubt useful and have perhaps led to more careful textual study in the field of literary studies, but even where they are legitimate they have tended to obscure the central concern of literary criticism, which is surely aesthetic value.

The other important point to grasp in considering the sort of modern criticism which has been inspired by Mr. Richards, is its irrationalism. This may seem surprising when we reflect that such criticism prides itself upon good sense and clear ideas. Yet how many modern critics who are anxious to assure us that poetry cannot go beyond empirical knowledge are the very ones to insist that poetry is not really poetry if it confines itself to such knowledge. Those critics who welcome with raptures the philosophical principles of Mr. Richards's sort of empiricism are most often the ones who dismiss contemptuously the poetry of the eighteenth century which, after all, grew up in the shadow of empiricism. Poetry, on their view, cannot be concerned with the truth, whether of an empirical or a non-empirical kind. It is mere whimsy, a flight of the fancy which has no importance. The only satisfaction they give to the man who

[1] I. A. Richards, *Science and Poetry*, Kegan Paul, Trench, Trubner & Co. Ltd.

attaches some meaning to the poetry he reads, is that religion and ethics are assigned to the same fate. These, too, are irrational pursuits, which signify only a psychological craving which can be given no logical justification.

By claiming so little for poetry these critics really ally themselves with those who claim too much, with those who not only think that art is concerned with the truth, but speak as though truth were in some way the special prerogative of art. Both parties are united in a joint pursuit of irrationalism. This is borne out in a striking manner by the statements made about poetry by two critics so opposed in their views as Mr. Richards and W. B. Yeats. Mr. Richards ridiculed W. B. Yeats for trying to believe in faeries and leprechauns, yet he himself could say with the iconoclastic bravado of the nineteen-twenties:

> "It is very probable that the Hindenburg Line to which the defence of our traditions retired as a result of the onslaughts of the last century will be blown up in the near future. If this should happen a mental chaos such as man has never experienced may be expected. We shall then be thrown back, as Matthew Arnold foresaw, upon poetry. It is capable of saving us; it is a perfectly possible means of overcoming chaos." (*Science and Poetry*, pp. 82–3.)

The question that at once comes to mind is: Are Mr. Richards's views, as expressed here, so different from W. B. Yeats's and is there so much to choose between a psychological and an Irish mythology?

The attacks on the validity of reason which have become popular in more recent currents of thought display the same reconciliation between a narrowly empiricist tradition of philosophy and a belief in mystical insight, fraught with emotion. Many of the writers, especially on the literary wing of the movement called existentialism, are anxious to emphasize the severe limitations of our knowledge, and yet, almost in the same breath, speak of the 'leap into transcendence', which they believe it is possible to make in various kinds of religious and artistic experiences. It is not possible to know reality, according to these writers, either in the case of the outer world or in the case of our own inner core of self-existence. All that the artist can do, they would argue, is to express a reality which he cannot know; he is no more than a sort of medium through which reality manifests itself. This sounds a very modest claim to make and reflects that side of existentialism which seeks to question the scope of human achievements; it is one of the limitations existentialism would impose upon the value of the empirical sciences, systematic theology, and ethics, as well as upon art. Yet this modesty is matched with an equal intellectual presumption; for though the artist may not *know* reality, the claim is sometimes made that art confronts us with reality itself, and somehow in a way that is supposed to be superior to the ordinary person's experience of it. The ordinary man, the argument proceeds, is forced to organize his experience towards practical ends, while the philosophers, scientists and other systematic thinkers organize experience in conceptual and rational patterns. The artist is free of all this: his experience is reality unfettered by the need to view things from either a practical or a theoretical perspective. It will be seen at once that this line of thought is an open invitation to the artist to indulge his most irrational fancies and instinctive urges, to set a higher value on feeling than on thought, to believe that his sub-conscious dreams are the stuff of reality.

It would be a mistake, however, to regard existentialism simply as irrationalist. It originated, it is true, as a reaction to the Hegelian desire to comprehend everything in terms of pure rationality. Nevertheless, like strict empiricism and logical positivism, it has also been motivated by the desire to find certitude, even at the cost of releasing certain areas of experience from the scope of rational inquiry; the desire to say, here at least we can be sure that we have knowledge, even if outside these boundaries there is confusion and ignorance. The trouble has been that by withdrawing to such prepared positions as logical positivism and existentialism have made for reason, the whole defence system of man's intellectual enterprise seems to have been jeopardized. What was to have been an orderly retreat on the part of reason has turned into a rout at the hands of emotionalism.

All this may seem rather a far cry from the subject of Shaftesbury and eighteenth-century criticism, yet it is not so. The history of thought since the Enlightenment has been mirrored in the attempts to define the nature and scope of reason. Once the supremacy of reason was questioned, it became inevitable that thought should oscillate uneasily between the claims of the reason and the emotions. Shaftesbury's philosophy was an attempt to give due satisfaction to man's emotional needs while acknowledging the sovereignty of reason. As a philosophy it may not meet all our intellectual objections, and his type of Platonism is perhaps too genial to withstand the chilling winds that blow across the intellectual scene today. Yet Shaftesbury has a contemporary significance that we should ponder, for it is the temper of his approach as well as his actual thought that merits our attention. Shaftesbury had the vision of a society in which artistic enterprise and political endeavour would encourage and strengthen each other in devotion to a common purpose; in which 'manners' and 'taste' would be more than conventional shibboleths, or personal prejudices, and would issue from a love of beauty and goodness. He believed that emotion could live in fruitful and happy marriage with the reason. These things might once have been set aside as unworthy of the name of vision; they once perhaps seemed pale and insignificant beside the dreams and hopes that caught men's minds. To us, today, when the dreams have turned into nightmares and the hopes receded as mere will-o'-the-wisps, Shaftesbury's thought may once again be welcomed for its sanity and moderation.

APPENDIX

THE following is a complete list of Shaftesbury's published works.

Select Sermons of Benjamin Whichcote, ed. with Preface by Shaftesbury, 1698.

Characteristics of Men, Manners, Opinions, Times. Three vols., 1711, 1714 (revised text), 1723, 1727, 1732, 1733, 1737, etc.; ed. W. M. Hatch, 1870; ed. J. M. Robertson, two vols., 1900. The *Characteristics* includes the following treatises with date of first publication:
> *Letter Concerning Enthusiasm*, 1708.
> *Sensus Communis; an essay on the Freedom of Wit and Humour*, 1709.
> *The Moralists*, 1709.
> *Soliloquy, or Advice to an Author*, 1710.
> *An Inquiry concerning Virtue*, printed in 1699 without Shaftesbury's permission.
> *Miscellaneous Reflections on the preceding Treatises, and other Critical Subjects.* First published in the *Characteristics* (1711).
> *Historical Draught or Tablature of the Judgment of Hercules*, 1713. Included in the 1714 edition of the *Characteristics*.
> *Letter Concerning Design.* Published for first time in the 1732 edition of the *Characteristics*.
>
> The last two essays were not intended by Shaftesbury to form part of the *Characteristics*. They are not included in Robertson's edition but have been reprinted in *Second Characters*, ed. Rand.

Several Letters, written by a Noble Lord to a Young Man at the University, 1716.

Letters from the late Earl of Shaftesbury to R. Molesworth Esq., 1721.

The Original Letters of Locke, Sidney and Shaftesbury, ed. T. Forster, 1830.

The Life, Unpublished Letters and Philosophical Regimen of Anthony, Earl of Shaftesbury, ed. B. Rand, London and New York, 1900.

Second Characters, or the Language of Forms, ed. B. Rand, Cambridge, 1914.

INDEX

A

Absalom and Achitophel, 35, 96
Addison, Joseph, 56, 61, 86, 93, 97, 116–18, 120, 134, 135, 138–40, 146, 150–2, 154–6, 160–3, 165, 180, 184, 195, 200, 201, 215
Addison, Kant and Wordsworth, 154 n.
Adrastea, 207
Advancement and Reformation of Modern Poetry, The, 73, 123
Advancement of Learning, The, 87
Adventures of Ideas, 208
Aesthetic Theory of Thomas Hobbes, The, 29 n.
Ainsworth, Michael, 47–8, 57, 79, 84
Akenside, Mark, 116, 117, 118, 120, 123, 140, 159–61, 163, 170–1, 183, 187, 188, 193, 210
Albion and Albanius, 36
Alciphron, or the Minute Philosopher, 169–70
Answer to Davenant, 29
Apology for Heroic Poetry, An, 91, 123
Aristotle, 87, 88, 95, 96, 101, 103, 123, 127, 168, 177, 182
Arnold, Matthew, 213, 214, 215
Art of Poetry, The, 184
Art of Sinking in Poetry, The, 145
Art Poétique, 89, 91
Ascham, Roger, 16
Ashley, Maurice, 46, 49
Augustan Age in England, The, 186
Augustine, Saint, 73, 101
Aurelius, Marcus, 59, 73

B

Babbitt, Irving, 143
Bacon, Francis, 87, 151, 211
——Thomas Sclater, 38

Bart'lemy Fair, 166
Bathurst, Earl (Allen Bathurst), 193
Battle of the Books, The, 86, 87, 179
Bayle, Pierre, 41
Bee, The, 186
Bellori, Giovanni, 101, 102
Bentley, Richard, 86, 87, 88
Bergson, Henri, 25, 173
Berkeley, Bishop George, 169–70, 172, 205
Berwick, Duke of (James Fitz-James), 51
Bibliothèque Choisie, 36, 166
Biographia Britannica, 59
Biographia Literaria, 110, 111–12, 114
Birch, Thomas, 39 n., 42 n., 57, 88
Blackwell, Thomas, 125
Blair, Hugh, 133, 193
Blake, William, 116, 211–12
Blount, Sir Thomas Pope, 93
Boehme, Jacob, 110
Boileau-Despréaux, Nicolas, 72, 89–92, 93, 145
Bolingbroke, Lord (Henry St. John), 191–2, 193, 195, 195 n.
Bosanquet, Bernard, 73, 145
Boswell, James, 193
Bouhours, Dominique, 94, 128
Brown, John, 168 n., 171
——Lancelot ('Capability'), 203
Browne, Sir Thomas, 13, 26
Buckingham, Duke of (George Villiers), 96
Bunyan, John, 27
Burke, Edmund, 139, 148, 150, 153, 160 n., 161–3
Burlington, Earl of (Richard Boyle), 195, 201, 203
Burnet, Bishop Gilbert, 16, 47–8
Bush, Professor D., 14, 118 n.
Butler, Bishop Joseph, 205
Butt, Professor John, 177
Butterfield, Professor H., 33

225

C

Caleb Hardinge, *Ode to*, 210
Cambridge Platonists, Ch. I *passim*, 48, 55, 56, 61, 62, 65, 85, 114, 146, 195, 206, 209
Caracci, The, 52
Carritt, Mr. E. F., 154
Catalogue of Royal and Noble Authors, 39 n., 63
Chambers, Sir William, 197
Chesterfield, Lord (Philip Dormer Stanhope), 174
Chevy Chase, *Spectator* Papers on, 93
Cibber, Colley, 177
Classical and Romantic, 215
Closterman, John, 52, 53, 60
Coleridge, S. T., 22, 69, 105, 108–18, 163–4, 207, 212, 213, 218
Collier, Jeremy, 93, 180
Collingwood, R. G., 62
Collins, Anthony, 80, 169
——William, 216
Comus, 24 n.
Conjectura Cabbalistica, 18
Cooper, John Gilbert, 135, 187
Corneille, Pierre, 91, 93, 95
Coste, Pierre, 54
Covent Garden Journal, The, 185
Cowley, Abraham, 22, 88
Cowper, William, 215, 216
Crabbe, George, 215
Crashaw, Richard, 21
Crelle, 53
Critique of Judgment, The, 113, 153–5
Critique of Pure Reason, The, 147
Cropley, Sir John, 38, 49, 50, 52, 54, 57
Cross, Mr. W. L., 182 n.
Crousaz, Jean-Pierre de, 192
Cudworth, Ralph, 15, 16, 25, 26, 28, 30, 64, 85, 146, 188, 194, 195 n.

D

Davenant, Sir William, 31, 92
Davideis, 22
Dejection, An Ode, 69

De la Comedie Angloise, 89
Dennis, John, 31, 73, 92, 99, 101, 102, 123, 125, 126, 128, 145, 148, 156, 180
Denoue (or Denoune), Daniel, 38
De Origine Mali, 191
De Quincey, Thomas, 56
Descartes, René, 14, 15, 24, 25
Des Maizeaux, Pierre, 54
Destiny of Nations, The, 109
Dictionnaire Universelle, 41
Diderot, Denis, 206
Discourse concerning Ridicule, 169
Discourse of Human Nature, 169
Discourse upon Comedy, A, 126, 127
Dissertation upon the Epistles of Phalaris, 86
Divine Hymn on the Creation, A, 21, 26
Divine Legation of Moses, The, 170
Dryden, John, 29, 31, 33, 34, 35, 36, 72, 88, 91, 92, 93, 94, 95–8, 99, 101, 102, 123, 125, 134, 174, 175, 177
Du Grand et du Sublime, 145
Duke, Richard, 36
Dunciad, The, 63, 191, 192, 195

E

East Coker, 108
Eighteenth Century Background, The, 143 n.
Elements of Criticism, 135
Eliot, Mr. T. S., 108
Eloge Historique de feu M. Locke, 36
Enchiridion Ethicum, 47
English Ballad on the Taking of Namur, 92
English Emblem Books, 27
English Garden, The, 202, 203, 204
Englishman and his History, The, 33
Enquiry into the Life and Writings of Homer, 125
Enthusiast, The, 186
Entretiens d'Ariste et d'Eugène, 128
Epictetus, 59
Epistle of the Use of Riches, 201
Epistles of Phalaris, The, 86

Essay Concerning Human Understanding, 83, 115, 186, 187, 190, 205
Essay of Dramatic Poesy, 72, 91, 93
Essay on Criticism, 73, 91, 125, 128, 145, 175, 176, 199
Essay on Gibing, 184
Essay on Man, 72, 76, 176, 190–195
Essay on the Genius and Writings of Pope, 115 n., 125, 191
Essays in Criticism, 213
Essays on Men and Manners, 135
Essays on the Characteristics, 168 n., 171
Essay upon the Ancient and Modern Learning, 86–7
Essay upon Unnatural Flights in Poetry, 94
Eternal and Immutable Morality, 195 n.
Evans, A. W., 191 n.
Evelyn, John, 88
Ewer, Jane, v. Lady Shaftesbury
——Thomas, 48
Examen de l'Essai de M. Pope sur l'Homme, 192
Excursion, The, (Mallett's), 152
Excursion, The, (Wordsworth's), 141

F

Farquhar, George, 31, 125, 126, 127, 128
Faust, 173–4
Fichte, Johanns, 216
Fielding, Henry, 182–3, 185
Fifteen Sermons, 205
Forrester, James, 136
Forster, Thomas, 57
Fowler, Thomas, xi, 42 n., 57, 191
Fragments or Minutes of Essays, 195 n.
Freeman, Miss Rosemary, 27, 121
Frost at Midnight, 109
Furley, Benjamin, 39, 40, 44, 48, 57

G

General Dictionary, The, 39 n., 42 n., 57, 59, 88
Genesis of Romantic Theory, The, 151

Gift of Poetry, The, 115
Gildon, Charles, 31, 87, 93, 94, 125, 128
Godolphin, Earl of (Sidney Godolphin), 40
Godwin, William, 160
Goethe, Johann W. von, 119, 173–4
Goldsmith, Oliver, 184, 186
Granville, George, v. Lansdowne
Gray, Thomas, 56, 202, 213, 215, 216
Gribelin, Simon, 53, 60
Grierson, Sir Herbert, 215
Grounds of Criticism in Poetry, The, 148
Guardian, The, 201
Gulliver's Travels, 179

H

Halifax, Earl of (Charles Montagu), 39 n., 49
Harris, James, 187, 205
Hartley, David, 110, 212
Heinsius, Daniel, 175
Herbert, George, 21
Herder, Johann, 206
Hervey, Lord (John Hervey), 177
Hibernicus' Letters, 168–9
Historical Account of the English Poets, An, 181
History of Aesthetic, 73, 88, 145
History of English Poetry, Warton's, 125
History of Henry Fielding, The, 182 n.
History of his Own Time, Burnet's, 16, 17
Hoadly, Bishop Benjamin, 170
Hobbes, Thomas, Ch. I *passim*, 46, 55, 60, 61, 62, 77, 78, 82–3, 84, 95, 97, 98, 100, 101, 103, 104, 124, 143, 146–7, 151, 159, 168–9, 183, 205, 206
Hogarth, William, 178, 184
Holberg, Ludvig, 207
Horace, 59, 72, 91, 96, 123, 174, 176
Housman, A. E., 212
Hume, David, 135, 139, 205
Hurd, Richard, 93, 192
Hussey, Mr. Christopher, 198 n.

Hutcheson, Francis, 116, 132, 134, 135, 139, 168–9, 170
Hymn of Heavenly Beautie, A, 20
Hymns to Love and Beauty, 21

I

Idea of Nature, The, 62
Imitations of Horace, v. under *Satires and Epistles*.
Inquiry into our Ideas of Beauty and Virtue, 132
Inspiration of Pope's Poetry, The, 177 n.
Italian Landscape in Eighteenth-Century England, 52

J

Jacob, Giles, 181
Johnson, Samuel, 22, 102, 145, 148, 170, 193, 214, 216
Jones, Inigo, 136, 198
Joseph Andrews, 182–3
Jourdain, Miss Margaret, 198 n.
Julian and Maddalo, 119
Juvenal, 91, 174

K

Kames, Lord (Henry Home), 135
Kant, Immanuel, 112–14, 118, 120, 136–41, 142, 147, 150, 152, 153–5, 162–4, 206
Kent, William, 195, 199, 203
King, Archbishop William, 191, 195
Kippis, Andrew, 59

L

La Bruyère, Jean, 94
Lamb, Charles, 56
Langbaine, Gerard, 93
Langley, Batty, 201
Lansdowne, Lord (George Granville), 94
Large Account of the Taste in Poetry, 126, 180
Law, William, 110

Le Bossu, René, 93
Le Clerc, Jean, 35, 36, 37, 41, 54, 166, 206
Lectures on Rhetoric, 133
Leibnitz, Gottfried W. von, 54, 63, 166, 191
Leland, John, 171
Lessing, Gotthold, 206
Letters Concerning Taste, 135
Letters of a Late Eminent Prelate, 192
Letters on Chivalry and Romance, 93
Lettres sur les Anglais, 190
Leviathan, 28, 30, 97, 147, 206
Lewis, Mr. C. S., 24, 173
Life of Cowley, 22
Life of Pope, 214
Locke, John, 34, 35–8, 41, 48, 53, 55, 57, 60, 61, 79–80, 83–5, 104, 115, 143, 147, 153, 160, 163, 164, 186, 189, 190, 193, 205–206, 210, 211, 213–14
London Journal, The, 170
Longinus, Dionysius, 72, 145, 149, 150
Lorraine, Claude, 203
Lyrical Ballads, The, 156

M

Mallet, David, 152, 160
Mandeville, Bernard, 182
Manière de bien penser, La, 94
Manwaring, Mrs. Elizabeth, 52
Marlborough, Duke of (John Churchill) 40, 43, 52
Marvell, Andrew, 22, 202
Mason, William, 202, 203, 204
Mattheis, Paolo de, 53, 190
Meditations of Marcus Aurelius, 73
Melmoth, William, 59
Memorabilia, 53, 66, 190
Mendelssohn, Moses, 206
Méré, Chevalier de, 94
Micklethwayte, Thomas, 54
Mill, John Stuart, 110
Milton, John, 21, 22–4, 31, 86, 100, 114, 146, 173, 216
Miscellanies in Verse and Prose, 156
Modern Poets Against the Ancients, 87

Molesworth, Robert (Viscount Molesworth), 48, 49, 51, 57
Monboddo, Lord (James Burnett), 205
Monk, Mr. S. H., 160 n.
Montagu, Charles, v. Halifax.
——Lady Mary Wortley, 177
Moore, Mr. C. A., 187
More, Henry, 16, 18, 21, 23, 24, 25, 47, 110
Muratori, Ludovico, 151
Mythology and the Romantic Tradition, 118 n.

N

Name and Nature of Poetry, The, 213
Needler, Henry, 187
Neiiendam, Dr. Henrik, 207 n.
New Principles of Gardening, 201
Newton, Sir Isaac, 34, 105, 143, 160, 193, 194, 211
Nicolson, Miss Marjorie Hope, 24
Norris, John, 21, 26, 28, 85

O

Observations on the Faerie Queene, 125
Ode to the Royal Society, 22
Of Active and Retired Life, 59
Of the Sublime and Beautiful, v. *Philosophical Inquiry*.
On Mr. Milton's Paradise Lost, 22
On the Sublime, 72, 145
Orford, Earl of (Edward Russell), 49
Original and Progress of Satire, The, 91, 175
Origin and Progress of Language, The, 205

P

Paradise Lost, 23, 24, 31, 146, 156, 174, 176
Paradise Lost, Spectator Papers on, 93
Paradise Regained, 24
Parallel of Poetry and Painting, A, 102
Parnell, Thomas, 115
Pepys, Samuel, 88

Perfetta Poesia, 151
Peterborough, Earl of (Charles Mordaunt), 45
Philips, Ambrose, 179
Phillips, Edward, 125 n.
Philo, Judaeus, 18
Philosophical Inquiry into ... the Sublime and Beautiful, 148, 153, 162–3
Pilgrim's Progress, The, 27
Plato, 20, 22, 47, 60, 99, 101, 147, 170, 215–16
Pleasures of the Imagination, The (Akenside's), 117, 123, 140–1, 160–1, 170, 183, 188
Pleasures of the Imagination, The, (Spectator Papers on), 116, 134, 150–2
Plotinus, 110
Polite Philosopher, The, 136
Poole, Thomas, 105
Pope, Alexander, 63, 72, 73, 76, 86, 91, 97, 125, 128, 145, 170 175–8, 182, 184, 190–5, 199, 201, 203, 206, 209, 214, 215
Poussin, Nicolas, 52, 101, 203
Preface to Annus Mirabilis, 29
Preface to Divine Dialogues, 25
Preface to Don Sebastian, 96
Preface to Gondibert, 92
Preface to Paradise Lost, 24 n., 173
Prelude, The, 100
Prior, Matthew, 92
Proclus, Diadochus, 101, 110
Prometheus, 68, 104, 106, 109, 118–19
Prometheus (Goethe's), 119
Psychozoia, or the Life of the Soul, 21

R

Rand, Benjamin, ix, 42 n.
Rape of the Lock, The, 176, 214
Rapin, René, 72, 89–90, 91, 93, 145, 179
Rasselas, 102, 145
Reflections upon a Letter concerning Enthusiasm, 166
Reflections upon Ancient and Modern Learning, 88
Réflexions sur la Poétique, 72, 89–90, 93, 179

INDEX

Réflexions sur Longin, 145
Rehearsal, The, 96
Religio Medici, 13, 26
Remarks on Prince Arthur, 92, 102, 126
Remarks on Several Parts of Italy, 156
Remarks upon a Letter ... concerning Enthusiasm, 166
Reni, Guido, 52
Republic, The, 101
Review, The, 36
Reynolds, Sir Joshua, 116
Rhetoric (Aristotle's), 168
Richards, Mr. I. A., 219–21
Robertson, Professor J. G., 151
—— J. M., ix
—— William, 218
Roderick Random, 46
Rosa, Salvator, 52, 53, 158
Rousseau, Jean-Baptiste, 14
Rousseau and Romanticism, 143 n.
Royal Society, The, 22, 34, 88, 95, 97, 197
Russell, Lady, 50
Rutland, Earl of (John Manners), 37
Rymer, Thomas, 93, 99, 101

S

Saint-Évremond, Charles, 89, 94
Samson Agonistes, 24 n.
Satires and Epistles of Horace Imitated, 176, 178
Schelling, Friedrich W. J. von, 216
Schiller, Johann C. F. von, 206
Science and Poetry, 219–20, 221
Seasons, The, 33, 159–60, 189–90
Seventeenth Century Background, The, 20
Shaftesbury, First Earl of (Anthony Ashley Cooper), 34, 35–8
—— Second Earl of (Anthony Ashley Cooper), 35–8, 42
—— Third Earl of (Anthony Ashley Cooper), Letters, v. Note at end of Ch. II; Life of, Ch. II; Writings, 55–6, Appendix
—— Fourth Earl of (Anthony Ashley Cooper), 33 n., 42 n., 46, 51, 54, 57

Shaftesbury, Lady, wife to the third Earl, 48, 50, 51, 57
Shaftesbury and Hutcheson, xi, 57, 191
Shaftesbury and the Ethical Poets in England, 187 n.
Shakespeare, William, 100, 161
Shelley, Percy Bysshe, 119, 215
Shenstone, William, 135, 190
Short View of ... the English Stage, 180
Soame, Sir William, 91
Socrates, 60
Somers, Lord (John Somers), 42, 43, 45, 49, 55, 196
Spectator, The, 55, 56, 61, 86, 116, 134, 150–2, 161, 165, 168, 180, 184, 200
Spenser, Edmund, 20, 215, 216, 218
Spinoza, Benedict, 59
Sprat, Thomas, 88
Stanhope, Earl of (James Stanhope), 54, 83, 84
Statesman's Manual, The, 108, 109
Sublime, The, 160 n.
Sunderland, Earl of (Charles Spencer), 49
Swift, Jonathan, 86, 87, 179, 181, 182, 184, 209, 216
System of Logic, A, 110

T

Tale of a Tub, The, 181
Tatler, The, 55, 185
Temple, Sir William, 31, 86, 87, 92, 94, 97, 124, 125, 128
Theatrum Poetarum, 125 n.
Theobald, Lewis, 177
Theodicée (Leibnitz's), 63, 191
There is no Natural Religion, 211
Thomson, James, 33, 159–60, 163, 187, 188–90, 193
Thorild, Thomas, 207
Thorpe, Mr. C., 29 n.
Thoughts concerning Education, 37
Thoughts on Laughter, 168–70
Three Treatises on Art, 205
Tindall, Matthew, 46
Toland, John, 42, 45, 48, 49, 55, 57
Tom Jones, 182

Tower, The, 212
Traherne, Thomas, 21
Traité du Poème Épique, 93
Treatise of Human Nature, A, 135
Trenchard, Sir John, 38
True Intellectual System, The, 15, 17, 146

V

Vanbrugh, Sir John, 195, 198
Van Limborch, Phillipe, 41, 48
Vaughan, Henry, 21, 218
View of the Principal Deistical Writers, A, 171
Voltaire, François, 190, 206

W

Waller, Edmund, 161
Walpole, Horace, 39 n., 63, 203
Wanley, Humfrey, 88
Warburton, Bishop William, 170, 192, 193, 195
Warburton and the Warburtonians, 191 n.
Warton, Joseph, 115 n., 125, 170, 186, 191
Warton, Thomas, 125
Wharton, Marquis of (Thomas Wharton), 49
Wheelock, Bryan, 53
——John, 44
Whichcote, Benjamin, 16, 48, 55, 82
Whitehead, A. N., 14, 208
Wieland, Christoph, 206
Wilkins, John, 16
Wilkinson, Henry, 45, 58
Willey, Professor Basil, 14, 20, 142–3
Windsor Forest, 214
Works and Wonders of Almighty Power, The, 160
Wordsworth, William, 100, 107, 141, 142, 160, 213, 214, 215, 218
Worthington, John, 16
Wotton, William, 88, 94, 124, 166
Wren, Sir Christopher, 34, 197, 198

X

Xenophon, 53, 59, 60, 66, 190

Y

Yeats, W. B., 212, 221

For Product Safety Concerns and Information please contact our EU representative GPSR@taylorandfrancis.com
Taylor & Francis Verlag GmbH, Kaufingerstraße 24, 80331 München, Germany

www.ingramcontent.com/pod-product-compliance
Lightning Source LLC
Chambersburg PA
CBHW071835300426
44116CB00009B/1549